THE
HIDING PLACE

by Corrie ten Boom
With
John and Elizabeth
Sherrill

BANTAM BOOKS
NEW YORK • TORONTO • LONDON • SYDNEY • AUCKLAND

*This edition contains the complete text
of the original hardcover edition.*
NOT ONE WORD HAS BEEN OMITTED.

RL 6, IL age 13 and up

THE HIDING PLACE

*A Bantam Book / published by arrangement with
Fleming H. Revell Company*

PUBLISHING HISTORY

*Chosen Books published November 1971
Bantam edition / October 1974*

ISBN 0-553-25669-6

Published simultaneously in the United States and Canada

Bantam Books are published by Bantam Books, a division of Bantam Doubleday Dell
Publishing Group, Inc. Its trademark, consisting of the words "Bantam Books" and the
portrayal of a rooster, is Registered in U.S. Patent and Trademark Office and in other
countries. Marca Registrada. Bantam Books, 1540 Broadway, New York, New York 10036.

PRINTED IN THE UNITED STATES OF AMERICA

OPM   74

THE
HIDING PLACE

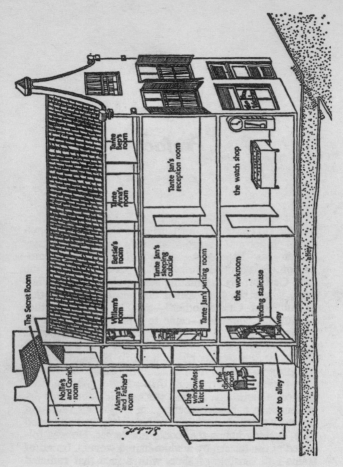

The Secret Room

Tante Bep's room

Tante Anna's room

Betsie's room

Willem's room

Tante Jan's reception room

Tante Jan's sleeping cubicle

Tante Jan's sitting room

the watch shop

the workroom

winding staircase

way

Nollie's and Corrie's room

Mama's and Father's room

the windowless kitchen

the dining room

door to alley

alley

THE BEJE (pronounced bay-yay).
Schematic drawing of the tilting, centuries-old house still
to be found in the center of Haarlem, Holland.

Preface

When we were doing the research for *God's Smuggler*, a name kept cropping up: Corrie ten Boom. This Dutch lady—in her mid-seventies when we first began to hear of her—was Brother Andrew's favorite traveling companion. Brother Andrew is a missionary behind the Iron Curtain; his fascinating stories about her in Vietnam, where she had earned that most honorable title "Double-old Grandmother"—and in a dozen other Communist countries—came to mind so often that we finally had to hold up our hands to stop his flow of reminiscence. "We could never fit her into the book," we said. "She sounds like a book in herself." It's the sort of thing you say. Not meaning anything.

It was in May, 1968, that we attended a church service in Germany. A man was speaking about his experiences in a Nazi concentration camp. His face told the story more eloquently than his words: pain-haunted eyes, shaking hands that could not forget. He was followed at the lectern by a white-haired woman, broad of frame and sensible of shoe, with a face that radiated love, peace, joy. But—the story that these two people were relating was the same! She too had been in a concentration camp, seen the same savagery, suffered the same losses. His response was easy to understand. But hers?

We stayed behind to talk with her. And as we did, we realized that we were meeting Andrew's Corrie.

Cornelia ten Boom's world-wide ministry of comfort and counsel had begun there in the concentration camp where she had found, as the prophet Isaiah promised, "a hiding place from the wind, a covert from the tempest . . . the shadow of a great rock in a weary land."

On subsequent visits we got to know this amazing woman well. Together we visited the crooked little Dutch house—one room wide—where till her fifties she lived the uneventful life of a spinster watchmaker, little dreaming as she cared for her older sister and their elderly father that a world of high adventure lay just around the corner. We went to the garden in south Holland where young Corrie gave her heart away forever. To the big brick house in Haarlem where Pickwick served real coffee in the middle of the war. . . .

And all the while we had the extraordinary feeling that we were not looking into the past but into the future. As though these people and places were speaking to us not about things that had already happened but about the world that lay ahead of us in the 1970s. Already we found ourselves actually putting into practice how-to's we learned from her about:

- handling separation
- getting along with less
- security in the midst of insecurity
- forgiveness
- how God can use weakness
- facing death
- dealing with difficult people
- how to love your enemies
- what to do when evil wins

We commented to her about the practicalness of everything she recalled, how her memories seemed to throw a spotlight on problems and decisions we faced here and now. "But," she said, "this is what the past is for! Every experience God gives us, every person He puts in our lives is the perfect preparation for the future that only He can see."

Every experience, every person. . . . Father, who did the finest watch repairs in Holland and then forgot to send the bill. Mama, whose body became a prison, but whose spirit soared free. Betsie, who could make a party out of three potatoes and some twice-used tea leaves. As we looked into the twinkling blue eyes of this undefeatable woman, we wished that these people were part of our own lives.

And then, of course, we realized that they could be. . . .

John and *Elizabeth Sherrill*

July, 1971
Chappaqua, New York

1

The One Hundredth Birthday Party

I jumped out of bed that morning with one question in my mind—sun or fog? Usually it was fog in January in Holland, dank, chill, and gray. But occasionally—on a rare and magic day—a white winter sun broke through. I leaned as far as I could from the single window in my bedroom; it was always hard to see the sky from the Beje. Blank brick walls looked back at me, the backs of other ancient buildings in this crowded center of old Haarlem. But up there where my neck craned to see, above the crazy roofs and crooked chimneys, was a square of pale pearl sky. It was going to be a sunny day for the party!

I attempted a little waltz as I took my new dress from the tipsy old wardrobe against the wall. Father's bedroom was directly under mine but at seventy-seven he slept soundly. That was one advantage to growing old, I thought, as I worked my arms into the sleeves and surveyed the effect in the mirror on the wardrobe door. Although some Dutch women in 1937 were wearing their skirts knee-length, mine was still a cautious three inches above my shoes.

You're not growing younger yourself, I reminded my reflection. Maybe it was the new dress that made me look more critically at myself than usual: forty-five years old, unmarried, waistline long since vanished.

My sister Betsie, though seven years older than I, still had that slender grace that made people turn and look after her in the street. Heaven knows it wasn't her clothes; our little watch shop had never made much money. But when Betsie put on a dress something wonderful happened to it.

On me—until Betsie caught up with them—hems sagged, stockings tore, and collars twisted. But today, I thought, standing back from the mirror as far as I could in the small room, the effect of dark maroon was very smart.

Far below me down on the street, the doorbell rang. Callers? Before 7:00 in the morning? I opened my bedroom door and plunged down the steep twisting stairway. These stairs were an afterthought in this curious old house. Actually it was two houses. The one in front was a typical tiny old-Haarlem structure, three stories high, two rooms deep, and only one room wide. At some unknown point in its long history its rear wall had been knocked through to join it with the even thinner, steeper house in back of it—which had only three rooms, one on top of the other—and this narrow corkscrew staircase squeezed between the two.

Quick as I was, Betsie was at the door ahead of me. An enormous spray of flowers filled the doorway. As Betsie took them, a small delivery boy appeared. "Nice day for the party, Miss," he said, trying to peer past the flowers as though coffee and cake might already be set out. He would be coming to the party later, as indeed, it seemed, would all of Haarlem.

Betsie and I searched the bouquet for the card. "Pickwick!" we shouted together.

Pickwick was an enormously wealthy customer who not only bought the very finest watches but often came upstairs to the family part of the house above the shop. His real name was Herman Sluring; Pickwick was the name Betsie and I used between ourselves because he looked so incredibly like the illustrator's drawing in our copy of Dickens. Herman Sluring was without doubt the ugliest man in Haarlem. Short, immensely fat, head bald as a Holland cheese, he was so wall-eyed that you were never quite sure whether he was looking at you or someone else—and as kind and generous as he was fearsome to look at.

The flowers had come to the side door, the door the family used, opening onto a tiny alleyway, and Betsie and I carried them from the little hall into the shop. First was the workroom where watches and clocks were repaired. There was the high bench over which Father had bent for so many years, doing the delicate, painstaking work that was known as the finest in Holland. And there in the center of the room was my bench, and next to mine Hans the apprentice's, and against the wall old Christoffels'.

Beyond the workroom was the customers' part of the shop with its glass case full of watches. All the wall clocks were striking 7:00 as Betsie and I carried the flowers in and looked for the most artistic spot to put them. Ever since childhood I had loved to step into this room where a hundred ticking voices welcomed me. It was still dark inside because the shutters had not been drawn back from the windows on the street. I unlocked the street door and stepped out into the Barteljorisstraat. The other shops up and down the narrow street were shuttered and silent: the optician's next door, the dress shop, the baker's, Weil's Furriers across the street.

I folded back our shutters and stood for a minute admiring the window display that Betsie and I had at last agreed upon. This window was always a great source of debate between us, I wanting to display as much of our stock as could be squeezed onto the shelf, and Betsie maintaining that two or three beautiful watches, with perhaps a piece of silk or satin swirled beneath, was more elegant and more inviting. But this time the window satisfied us both: it held a collection of clocks and pocketwatches all at least a hundred years old, borrowed for the occasion from friends and antique dealers all over the city. For today was the shop's one hundredth birthday. It was on this day in January 1837 that Father's father had placed in this window a sign: TEN BOOM. WATCHES.

For the last ten minutes, with a heavenly disregard for the precisions of passing time, the church bells of Haarlem had been pealing out 7:00 o'clock, and now half a block away in the town square, the great bell of St. Bavo's solemnly donged seven times. I lingered in the street to count them, though it was cold in the January dawn. Of course everyone in Haarlem had radios now, but I could remember when the life of the city had run on St. Bavo time, and only trainmen and others who needed to know the exact hour had come here to read the "astronomical clock." Father would take the train to Amsterdam each week to bring back the time from the Naval Observatory and it was a source of pride to him that the astronomical clock was never more than two seconds off in the seven days. There it stood now, as I stepped back into the shop, still tall and gleaming on its concrete block, but shorn now of eminence.

The doorbell on the alley was ringing again; more flowers. So it went for an hour, large bouquets and small ones, elaborate set pieces and home-grown plants in clay pots. For although the party was for the shop, the affection of a city was for Father. "Haarlem's Grand Old Man" they called him and they were setting about to prove it. When the shop and the workroom would not hold another bouquet, Betsie and I started carrying them upstairs to the two rooms above the shop. Though it was twenty years since her death, these were still "Tante Jans's rooms." Tante Jans was Mother's older sister and her presence lingered in the massive dark furniture she had left behind her. Betsie set down a pot of greenhouse-grown tulips and stepped back with a little cry of pleasure.

"Corrie, just look how much brighter!"

Poor Betsie. The Beje was so closed in by the houses around that the window plants she started each spring never grew tall enough to bloom.

At 7:45 Hans, the apprentice, arrived and at 8:00 Toos, our saleslady-bookkeeper. Toos was a sour-faced, scowling individual whose ill-temper had made it impossible for her to keep a job until—ten years ago—she had come to work for Father. Father's gentle courtesy had disarmed and mellowed her and, though she would have died sooner than admit it, she loved him as fiercely as she disliked the rest of the world. We left Hans and Toos to answer the doorbell and went upstairs to get breakfast.

Only three places at the table, I thought, as I set out the plates. The dining room was in the house at the rear, five steps higher than the shop but lower than Tante Jans's rooms. To me this room with its single window looking into the alley was the heart of the home. This table, with a blanket thrown over it, had made me a tent or a pirate's cove when I was small. I'd done my homework here as a schoolchild. Here Mama read aloud from Dickens on winter evenings while the coal whistled in the brick hearth and cast a red glow over the tile proclaiming, "Jesus is Victor."

We used only a corner of the table now, Father, Betsie and I, but to me the rest of the family was always there. There was Mama's chair, and the three aunts' places over there (not only Tante Jans but Mama's other two sisters had also lived with us). Next to me had sat my other sister, Nollie, and Willem, the only boy in the family, there beside Father.

Nollie and Willem had had homes of their own many years now, and Mama and the aunts were dead, but still I seemed to see them here. Of course their chairs hadn't stayed empty long. Father could never bear a house without children and whenever he heard of a child in need of a home a new face would appear at the table. Somehow, out of his watch shop that never made money he fed and dressed and cared for eleven more children after his own four were grown. But now these, too, had grown up and married or gone off to work, and so I laid three plates on the table.

Betsie brought the coffee in from the tiny kitchen, which was little more than a closet off the dining room, and took bread from the drawer in the sideboard. She was setting them on the table when we heard Father's step coming down the staircase. He went a little slowly now on the winding stairs; but still as punctual as one of his own watches, he entered the dining room, as he had every morning since I could remember, at 8:10.

"Father!" I said kissing him and savoring the aroma of cigars that always clung to his long beard, "a sunny day for the party!"

Father's hair and beard were now as white as the best tablecloth Betsie had laid for this special day. But his blue eyes behind the thick round spectacles were as mild and merry as ever, and he gazed from one of us to the other with frank delight.

"Corrie, dear! My dear Betsie! How gay and lovely you both look!"

He bowed his head as he sat down, said the blessing over bread, and then went on eagerly, "Your mother—how she would have loved these new styles and seeing you both looking so pretty!"

Betsie and I looked hard into our coffee to keep from laughing. These "new styles" were the despair of our young nieces, who were always trying to get us into brighter colors, shorter skirts, and lower necklines. But conservative though we were, it was true that Mama had never had anything even as bright as my deep maroon dress or Betsie's dark blue one. In Mama's day married women—and unmarried ones "of a certain age"—wore black from the chin to the ground. I had never seen Mama and the aunts in any other color.

"How Mama would have loved everything about today!" Betsie said. "Remember how she loved 'occasions'?"

Mama could have coffee on the stove and a cake in the oven as fast as most people could say, "best wishes." And since she knew almost everyone in Haarlem, especially the poor, sick and neglected, there was almost no day in the year that was not for somebody, as she would say with eyes shining, "a very special occasion!"

And so we sat over our coffee, as one should on anniversaries, and looked back—back to the time when Mama was alive, and beyond. Back to the time when Father was a small boy growing up in this same house. "I was born right in this room," he said, as though he had not told us a hundred times. "Only of course it wasn't the dining room then, but a bedroom. And the bed was in a kind of cupboard set into the wall with no windows and no light or air of any kind. I was the first baby who lived. I don't know how many there were before me, but they all died. Mother had tuberculosis you see, and they didn't know about contaminated air or keeping babies away from sick people."

It was a day for memories. A day for calling up the past. How could we have guessed as we sat there —two middle-aged spinsters and an old man—that in place of memories we were about to be given adventure such as we had never dreamed of? Adventure and anguish, horror and heaven were just around the corner, and we did not know.

Oh Father! Betsie! If I had known would I have gone ahead? Could I have done the things I did?

But how could I know? How could I imagine this white-haired man, called Opa—Grandfather—by all the children of Haarlem, how could I imagine this man thrown by strangers into a grave without a name?

And Betsie, with her high lace collar and her gift for making beauty all around her, how could I picture this dearest person on earth to me standing naked before a roomful of men? In that room on that day, such thoughts were not even thinkable.

Father stood up and took the big brass-hinged Bible from its shelf as Toos and Hans rapped on the door and came in. Scripture reading at 8:30 each morning for all who were in the house was another of the fixed points around which life in the Beje revolved. Father opened the big volume and Betsie and I held our breaths. Surely, today of all days, when there was still so much to do, it would not be a whole chapter! But he was turning to the Gospel of Luke where we'd left off yesterday—such long chapters in Luke too. With his finger at the place, Father looked up.

"Where is Christoffels?" he said.

Christoffels was the third and only other employe in the shop, a bent, wizened little man who looked older than Father though actually he was ten years younger. I remembered the day six or seven years earlier when he had first come into the shop, so ragged and woebegone that I'd assumed that he was one of the beggars who had the Beje marked as a sure meal. I was about to send him up to the kitchen where Betsie kept a pot of soup simmering when he announced with great dignity that he was considering permanent employment and was offering his services first to us.

It turned out that Christoffels belonged to an almost vanished trade, the itinerant clockmender who trudged on foot throughout the land, regulating and repairing the tall pendulum clocks that were the pride of every Dutch farmhouse. But if I was surprised at the grand manner of this shabby little man I was even more astonished when Father hired him on the spot.

"They're the finest clockmen anywhere," he told me later, "these wandering clocksmiths. There's not a repair job they haven't handled with just the tools in their sack."

And so it had proved through the years as people from all over Haarlem brought their clocks to him. What he did with his wages we never knew; he had remained as tattered and threadbare as ever. Father hinted as much as he dared—for next to his shabbiness Christoffels' most notable quality was his pride—and then gave it up.

And now, for the first time ever, Christoffels was late.

Father polished his glasses with his napkin and started to read, his deep voice lingering lovingly over the words. He had reached the bottom of the page when we heard Christoffels' shuffling steps on the stairs. The door opened and all of us gasped. Christoffels was resplendent in a new black suit, new checkered vest, a snowy white shirt, flowered tie, and stiff starched collar. I tore my eyes from the spectacle as swiftly as I could, for Christoffels' expression forbade us to notice anything out of the ordinary.

"Christoffels, my dear associate," Father murmured in his formal, old-fashioned way, "what joy to see you on this—er—auspicious day." And hastily he resumed his Bible reading.

Before he reached the end of the chapter the doorbells were ringing, both the shop bell on the street and the family bell in the alley. Betsie ran to make more coffee and put her taartjes in the oven while Toos and I hurried to the doors. It seemed that everyone in

Haarlem wanted to be first to shake Father's hand. Before long a steady stream of guests was winding up the narrow staircase to Tante Jans's rooms where he sat almost lost in a thicket of flowers. I was helping one of the older guests up the steep stairs when Betsie seized my arm.

"Corrie! We're going to need Nollie's cups right away! How can we——?"

"I'll go get them!"

Our sister Nollie and her husband were coming that afternoon as soon as their six children got home from school. I dashed down the stairs, took my coat and my bicycle from inside the alley door, and was wheeling it over the threshold when Betsie's voice reached me, soft but firm.

"Corrie, your new dress!"

And so I whirled back up the stairs to my room, changed into my oldest skirt and set out over the bumpy brick streets. I always loved to bike to Nollie's house. She and her husband lived about a mile and a half from the Beje, outside the cramped old center of the city. The streets there were broader and straighter; even the sky seemed bigger. Across the town square I pedaled, over the canal on the Grote Hout bridge and along the Wagenweg, reveling in the thin winter sunshine. Nollie lived on Bos en Hoven Straat, a block of identical attached houses with white curtains and potted plants in the windows.

How could I foresee as I zipped around the corner, that one summer day, when the hyacinths in the commercial bulb flats nearby were ripe and brown, I would brake my bicycle here and stand with my heart thudding in my throat, daring to go no closer for fear of what was taking place behind Nollie's starched curtains?

Today I careened onto the sidewalk and burst through the door with never a knock. "Nollie, the Beje's jammed already! You ought to see! We need the cups right now!"

Nollie came out of the kitchen, her round pretty face flushed with baking. "They're all packed by the door. Oh I wish I could go back with you—but I've got batches of cookies still to bake and I promised Flip and the children I'd wait for them."

"You're—*all* coming, aren't you?"

"Yes, Corrie, Peter will be there." Nollie was loading the cups into the bicycle bags. As a dutiful aunt I tried to love all my nieces and nephews equally. But Peter . . . well, was Peter. At thirteen he was a musical prodigy and a rascal and the pride of my life.

"He's even written a special song in honor of the day," Nollie said. "Here now, you'll have to carry this bagful in your hand, so be careful."

The Beje was more crowded than ever when I got back, the alley so jammed with bicycles I had to leave mine at the corner. The mayor of Haarlem was there in his tailcoat and gold watch chain. And the postman and the trolley motorman and half a dozen policemen from the Haarlem Police Headquarters just around the corner.

After lunch the children started coming and, as children always did, they went straight to Father. The older ones sat on the floor around him, the smallest ones climbed into his lap. For in addition to his twinkling eyes and long cigar-sweet beard, Father ticked. Watches lying on a shelf run differently from watches carried about, and so Father always wore the ones he was regulating. His suit jackets had four huge inside pockets, each fitted with hooks for a dozen watches, so that wherever he went the hum of hundreds of little wheels went gaily with him. Now with a child on each knee and ten more crowded close, he drew from another pocket his heavy cross-shaped winding key, each of the four ends shaped for a different size clock. With a flick of his finger he made it spin, gleaming, glinting. . . .

Betsie stopped in the doorway with a tray of cakes. "He doesn't know there's anyone else in the room," she said.

I was carrying a stack of soiled plates down the stairs when a little shriek below told me that Pickwick had arrived. We used to forget, we who loved him, what a shock the first sight of him could be to a stranger. I hurried down to the door, introduced him hastily to the wife of an Amsterdam wholesaler, and got him upstairs. He sank his ponderous bulk into a chair beside Father, fixed one eye on me, the other on the ceiling, and said, "Five lumps, please."

Poor Pickwick! He loved children as much as Father did, but while children took to Father on sight, Pickwick had to win them. He had one trick, though, that never failed. I brought him his cup of coffee, thick with sugar, and watched him look around in mock consternation. "But my dear Cornelia!" he cried. "There's no table to set it on!" He glanced out of one wide-set eye to make sure the children were watching. "Well, it's a lucky thing I brought my own!" And with that he set cup and saucer on his own protruding paunch. I had never known a child who could resist it; soon a respectful circle had gathered round him.

A little later Nollie and her family arrived. "Tante Corrie!" Peter greeted me innocently. "You don't *look* one hundred years old!" And before I could swat him he was sitting at Tante Jans's upright piano filling the old house with melody. People called out requests—popular songs, selections from Bach chorales, hymns—and soon the whole room was joining in the choruses.

How many of us were there, that happy afternoon, who were soon to meet under very different circumstances! Peter, the policemen, dear ugly Pickwick, all of us were there except my brother Willem and his family. I wondered why they should be so late. Willem and his wife and children lived in the town of Hilversum, thirty miles away: still, they should have been here by now.

Suddenly the music stopped and Peter from his perch on the piano bench hissed across the room, "Opa! Here's the competition!"

I glanced out the window. Turning into the alley were Mr. and Mrs. Kan, owners of the other watch shop on the street. By Haarlem standards they were newcomers, having opened their store only in 1910 and so been on the Barteljorisstraat a mere twenty-seven years. But since they sold a good many more watches than we did, I considered Peter's comment factual enough.

Father, however, was distressed. "Not competitors, Peter!" he said reprovingly. "Colleagues!" And lifting children quickly off his knees, he got up and hurried to the head of the stairs to greet the Kans.

Father treated Mr. Kan's frequent visits to the shop below as social calls from a cherished friend. "Can't you see what he's doing?" I would rage after Mr. Kan had gone. "He's finding out how much we're charging so he can undersell us!" Mr. Kan's display window always featured in bold figures prices exactly five guilders below our own.

And Father's face would light up with a kind of pleased surprise as it always did on those rare occasions when he thought about the business side of watchmaking. "But Corrie, people will save money when they buy from him!" And then he would always add, "I wonder how he does it."

Father was as innocent of business know-how as his father had been before him. He would work for days on a difficult repair problem and then forget to send a bill. The more rare and expensive a watch, the less he was able to think of it in terms of money. "A man should pay for the privilege of working on such a watch!" he would say.

As for merchandising methods, for the first eighty years of the shop's history the shutters on the streets had been closed each evening promptly at 6:00. It was not until I myself had come into the business twenty years ago that I had noticed the throngs of strollers crowding the narrow sidewalks each evening and had seen how the other stores kept their windows lighted and open. When I pointed this out to Father he was as delighted as though I had made a profound discovery. "And if people see the watches it might make them want to buy one! Corrie, my dear, how very clever you are!"

Mr. Kan was making his way toward me now, full of cake and compliments. Guilty for the jealous thoughts I harbored I took advantage of the crowd and made my escape downstairs. The workroom and shop were even more crowded with well-wishers than the upstairs rooms. Hans was passing cakes in the back room, as was Toos in the front, wearing the nearest thing to a smile that her perpetually downdrawn lips would permit. As for Christoffels, he had simply and astonishingly expanded. It was impossible to recognize that stooped and shabby little man in the glorious figure at the door, greeting newcomers with a formal welcome followed by a relentless tour of the shop. Quite obviously it was the greatest day of his life.

All through the short winter afternoon they kept coming, the people who counted themselves Father's friends. Young and old, poor and rich, scholarly gentlemen and illiterate servant girls—only to Father did it seem that they were all alike. That was Father's secret: not that he overlooked the differences in people; that he didn't know they were there.

And still Willem was not here. I said goodbye to some guests at the door and stood for a moment gazing up and down the Barteljorisstraat. Although it was only 4:00 in the afternoon the lights in the shops were coming on against the January dusk. I still had a great deal of little-sister worship for this big brother, five years older than I, an ordained minister and the only ten Boom who had ever been to college. Willem saw things, I felt. He knew what was going on in the world.

Oftentimes, indeed, I wished that Willem did not see quite so well, for much that he saw was frightening. A full ten years ago, way back in 1927, Willem had written in his doctoral thesis, done in Germany, that a terrible evil was taking root in that land. Right at the university, he said, seeds were being planted of a contempt for human life such as the world had never seen. The few who had read his paper had laughed.

Now of course, well, people weren't laughing about Germany. Most of the good clocks came from there, and recently several firms with whom we had dealt for years were simply and mysteriously "out of business." Willem believed it was part of a deliberate and large-scale move against Jews; every one of the closed businesses was Jewish. As head of the Dutch Reformed Church's program to reach Jews, Willem kept in touch with these things.

Dear Willem, I thought, as I stepped back inside

and closed the door, he was about as good a salesman of the church as Father was of watches. If he'd converted a single Jew in twenty years I hadn't heard about it. Willem didn't try to change people, just to serve them. He had scrimped and saved enough money to build a home for elderly Jews in Hilversum—for the elderly of all faiths, in fact, for Willem was against any system of segregation. But in the last few months the home had been deluged with younger arrivals— all Jews and all from Germany. Willem and his family had given up their own living quarters and were sleeping in a corridor. And still the frightened, homeless people kept coming, and with them tales of a mounting madness.

I went up to the kitchen where Nollie had just brewed a fresh pot of coffee, picked it up, and continued with it upstairs to Tante Jans's rooms. "What does he want?" I asked a group of men gathered around the cake table as I set down the pot. "This man in Germany, does he want war?" I knew it was poor talk for a party, but somehow thoughts of Willem always set my mind on hard subjects.

A chill of silence fell over the table and spread swiftly around the room.

"What does it matter?" a voice broke into it. "Let the big countries fight it out. It won't affect us."

"That's right!" from a watch salesman. "The Germans let us alone in the Great War. It's to their advantage to keep us neutral."

"Easy for you to talk," cried a man from whom we bought clock parts. "Your stock comes from Switzerland. What about us? What do I do if Germany goes to war? A war could put me out of business!"

And at that moment Willem entered the room. Behind him came Tine, his wife, and their four children. But every eye in the room had settled on the figure whose arm Willem held in his. It was a Jew in his early thirties in the typical broad-brimmed black hat and long black coat. What glued every eye to this man was his face. It had been burned. In front of his right ear dangled a gray and frizzled ringlet, like the hair of a very old man. The rest of his beard was gone, leaving only a raw and gaping wound.

"This is Herr Gutlieber," Willem announced in German. "He just arrived in Hilversum this morning. Herr Gutlieber, my father."

"He got out of Germany on a milk truck," Willem told us rapidly in Dutch. "They stopped him on a streetcorner—teen-aged boys in Munich—set fire to his beard."

Father had risen from his chair and was eagerly shaking the newcomer's hand. I brought him a cup of coffee and a plate of Nollie's cookies. How grateful I was now for Father's insistence that his children speak German and English almost as soon as Dutch.

Herr Gutlieber sat down stiffly on the edge of a chair and fixed his eyes on the cup in his lap. I pulled up a chair beside him and talked some nonsense about the unusual January weather. And around us conversation began again, a hum of party talk rising and falling.

"Hoodlums!" I heard the watch salesman say. "Young hooligans! It's the same in every country. The police'll catch up with 'em—you'll see. Germany's a civilized country."

And so the shadow fell across us that winter afternoon in 1937, but it rested lightly. Nobody dreamed that this tiny cloud would grow until it blocked out the sky. And nobody dreamed that in this darkness each of us would be called to play a role: Father and Betsie and Mr. Kan and Willem—even the funny old Beje with its unmatching floor levels and ancient angles.

In the evening after the last guest had gone I climbed the stairs to my room thinking only of the past. On my bed lay the new maroon dress; I had forgotten to put it back on. "I never did care about clothes," I thought. "Even when I was young. . . ."

Childhood scenes rushed back at me out of the night, strangely close and urgent. Today I know that such memories are the key not to the past, but to the future. I know that the experiences of our lives, when we let God use them, become the mysterious and perfect preparation for the work He will give us to do.

I didn't know it then—nor, indeed, that there was any new future to prepare for in a life as humdrum and predictable as mine. I only knew as I lay in my bed at the top of the house that certain moments from long ago stood out in focus against the blur of years. Oddly sharp and near they were, as though they were not yet finished, as though they had something more to say. . . .

2

Full Table

It was 1898 and I was six years old. Betsie stood me in front of the wardrobe mirror and gave me a lecture.

"Just look at your shoes! You've missed every other button. And those old torn stockings your very first day at school? See how nice Nollie looks!"

Nollie and I shared this bedroom at the top of the Beje. I looked at my eight-year-old sister: sure enough, her high-buttoned shoes were neatly fastened. Reluctantly I pulled off mine while Betsie rummaged in the wardrobe.

At thirteen, Betsie seemed almost an adult to me. Of course Betsie had always seemed older because she couldn't run and roughhouse the way other children did. Betsie had been born with pernicious anemia. And so while the rest of us played tag or bowl-the-hoop or had skate races down frozen canals in winter, Betsie sat and did dull grown-up things like embroidery. But Nollie played as hard as anyone and wasn't much older than I and it didn't seem fair that she should always do everything right.

"Betsie," she was saying earnestly, "I'm *not* going to wear that great ugly hat to school just because Tante Jans paid for it. Last year it was that ugly gray one— and this year's is even worse!"

Betsie looked at her sympathetically. "Well, but . . . you can't go to school without a hat. And you know we can't afford another one."

"We don't have to!"

With an anxious glance at the door, Nollie dropped to her knees, reached beneath the single bed which was all our tiny room would hold, and drew out a little round hat box. Inside nestled the smallest hat I had ever seen. It was of fur, with a blue satin ribbon for under the chin.

"Oh, the darling thing!" Betsie lifted it reverently from the box and held it up to the patch of light that struggled into the room over the surrounding rooftops. "Where did you ever——"

"Mrs. van Dyver gave it to me." The van Dyvers owned the millinery shop two doors down. "She saw me looking at it and later she brought it here, after Tante Jans picked out . . . *that.*"

Nollie pointed to the top of the wardrobe. A deep-rimmed brown bonnet with a cluster of lavender velvet roses proclaimed in every line the personage who had picked it out. Tante Jans, Mama's older sister, had moved in with us when her husband died to spend, as she put it, "what few days remain to me," though she was still only in her early forties.

Her coming had greatly complicated life in the old house—already crowded by the earlier arrivals of Mama's other two sisters, Tante Bep and Tante Anna—since along with Tante Jans had come quantities of furniture, all of it too large for the little rooms at the Beje.

For her own use Tante Jans took the two second-story rooms of the front house, directly over the watch shop and workroom. In the first room she wrote the flaming Christian tracts for which she was known all over Holland, and in the second received the well-to-do ladies who supported this work. Tante Jans believed that our welfare in the hereafter depended on how much we could accomplish here on earth. For sleep she partitioned off a cubicle from her writing room just large enough to hold a bed. Death, she often said, was waiting to snatch her from her work, and so she kept her hours of repose as brief and businesslike as possible.

I could not remember life in the Beje before Tante

Jans's arrival, nor whose these two rooms had been before. Above them was a narrow attic beneath the steep, sloping roof of the first house. For as long as I could recall, this space had been divided into four truly miniature rooms. The first one, looking out over the Barteljorisstraat—and the only one with a real window—was Tante Bep's. Behind it, strung like railroad compartments off a narrow aisle, were Tante Anna's, Betsie's, and our brother Willem's. Five steps up from these rooms, in the second house behind, was Nollie's and my small room, beneath ours Mama's and Father's room, and beneath theirs the dining room with the kitchen tacked like an afterthought to the side of it.

If Tante Jans's share in this crowded house was remarkably large, it never seemed so to any of us living there. The world just naturally made place for Tante Jans. All day long the horse-drawn trolley clopped and clanged past our house to stop at the Grote Markt, the central town square half a block away. At least that was where it stopped for other people. When Tante Jans wished to go somewhere she stationed herself on the sidewalk directly in front of the watchshop door and as the horses thundered close, held up a single gloved finger. It looked to me more possible to stop the sun in the sky than to halt the charge of that trolley before its appointed place. But it stopped for Tante Jans, brakes squealing, horses nearly falling over one another, and the driver tipped his tall hat as she swept aboard.

And this was the commanding eye past which Nollie had to get the little fur hat. Tante Jans had bought most of the clothing for us three girls since coming to live with us, but her gifts had a price. To Tante Jans, the clothes in fashion when she was young represented God's final say on human apparel; all change since then came from the style-book of the devil. Indeed, one of her best-known pamphlets exposed him as the inventor of the mutton sleeve and the bicycle skirt.

"I know!" I said now as the buttonhook in Betsie's swift fingers sped up my shoes, "you could fit the fur hat right inside the bonnet! Then when you get outside, take the bonnet off!"

"Corrie!" Nollie was genuinely shocked. "That wouldn't be honest!" And with a baleful glance at the big brown hat she picked up the little fur one and started after Betsie round the stairs down to breakfast.

I picked up my own hat—the despised gray one from last year—and trailed after them, one hand clinging to the center post. Let Tante Jans see the silly hat then. I didn't care. I never could understand all the fuss over clothes.

What I did understand, what was awful and alarming, was that this was the day I was to start school. To leave this old house above the watch shop, leave Mama and Father and the aunts, in fact leave behind everything that was certain and well-loved. I gripped the post so tight that my palm squeaked as I circled around. The elementary school was only a block and a half away, it was true, and Nollie had gone there two years without difficulty. But Nollie was different from me; she was pretty and well-behaved and always had her handkerchief.

And then, as I rounded the final curve, the solution came to me, so clear and simple that I laughed out loud. I just wouldn't go to school! I'd stay here and help Tante Anna with the cooking and Mama would teach me to read and I'd never go into that strange ugly building at all. Relief and comfort flooded me and I took the last three steps in a bound.

"Shhh!" Betsie and Nollie were waiting for me outside the dining room door. "For heaven's sake, Corrie, don't do anything to get Tante Jans started wrong," Betsie said. "I'm sure," she added doubtfully, "that Father and Mama and Tante Anna will like Nollie's hat."

"Tante Bep won't," I said.

"She never likes anything," Nollie said, "so she doesn't count."

Tante Bep, with her perpetual, disapproving scowl, was the oldest of the aunts and the one we children liked least. For thirty years she had worked as a governess in wealthy families and she continually compared our behavior with that of the young ladies and gentlemen she was used to.

Betsie pointed to the Frisian clock on the stair-wall, and with a finger on her lips silently opened the dining room door. It was 8:12: breakfast had already begun.

"Two minutes late!" cried Willem triumphantly.

"The Waller children were never late," said Tante Bep.

"But they're here!" said Father. "And the room is brighter!"

The three of us hardly heard: Tante Jans's chair was empty.

"Is Tante Jans staying in bed today?" asked Betsie hopefully as we hung our hats on their pegs.

"She's making herself a tonic in the kitchen," said Mama. She leaned forward to pour our coffee and lowered her voice. "We must all be specially considerate of dear Jans today. This is the day her husband's sister died some years ago—or was it his cousin?"

"I thought it was his aunt," said Tante Anna.

"It was a cousin and it was a mercy," said Tante Bep.

"At any rate," Mama hurried on, "you know how these anniversaries upset dear Jans, so we must all try to make it up to her."

Betsie cut three slices from the round loaf of bread while I looked around the table trying to decide which adult would be most enthusiastic about my decision to stay at home. Father, I knew, put an almost religious importance on education. He himself had had to stop school early to go to work in the watch shop, and though he had gone on to teach himself history, theology, and literature in five languages, he always regretted the missed schooling. He would want me to go —and whatever Father wanted, Mama wanted too.

Tante Anna then? She'd often told me she couldn't manage without me to run errands up and down the steep stairs. Since Mama was not strong, Tante Anna did most of the heavy housework for our family of nine. She was the youngest of the four sisters, with a spirit as generous as Mama's own. There was a

myth in our family, firmly believed in by all, that
Tante Anna received wages for this work—and indeed every Saturday Father faithfully paid her one
guilder. But by Wednesday when the greengrocer came
he often had to ask for it back, and she always had it,
unspent and waiting. Yes, she would be my ally in this
business.

"Tante Anna," I began, "I've been thinking
about you working so hard all day when I'm in school
and——"

A deep dramatic intake of breath made us all
look up. Tante Jans was standing in the kitchen doorway, a tumbler of thick brown liquid in her hand.
When she had filled her chest with air she closed her
eyes, lifted the glass to her lips and drained it down.
Then with a sigh she let out the breath, set the glass
on the sideboard and sat down.

"And yet," she said, as though we had been discussing the subject, "what do doctors know? Dr. Blinker prescribed this tonic—but what can medicine really do? What good does anything do when one's Day
arrives?"

I glanced round the table; no one was smiling.
Tante Jans's preoccupation with death might have been
funny, but it wasn't. Young as I was I knew that fear
is never funny.

"And yet, Jans," Father remonstrated gently,
"medicine has prolonged many a life."

"It didn't help Zusje! And she had the finest
doctors in Rotterdam. It was this very day when she
was taken—and she was no older than I am now, and
got up and dressed for breakfast that day, just as I
have."

She was launching into a minute-by-minute account of Zusje's final day when her eyes lit on the
peg from which dangled Nollie's new hat.

"A fur muff?" she demanded, each word bris-
tling with suspicion. "At this time of year!"

"It isn't a muff, Tante Jans," said Nollie in a
small voice.

"And is it possible to learn what it is?"

"It's a hat, Tante Jans," Betsie answered for her,

"a surprise from Mrs. van Dyver. Wasn't it nice of——"

"Oh no. Nollie's hat has a brim, as a well-brought-up girl's should. I know. I bought—and paid —for it myself."

There were flames in Tante Jans's eyes, tears in Nollie's when Mama came to the rescue. "I'm not at *all* sure this cheese is fresh!" She sniffed at the big pot of yellow cheese in the center of the table and pushed it across to Father. "What do you think, Casper?"

Father, who was incapable of practicing deceit or even recognizing it, took a long and earnest sniff. "I'm sure it's perfectly fine, my dear! Fresh as the day it came. Mr. Steerwijk's cheese is always——" Catching Mama's look he stared from her to Jans in confusion. "Oh—er—ah, Jans—ah, what do you think?"

Tante Jans seized the pot and glared into it with righteous zeal. If there was one subject which engaged her energies even more completely than modern clothing it was spoiled food. At last, almost reluctantly it seemed to me, she approved the cheese, but the hat was forgotten. She had plunged into the sad story of an acquaintance "my very age" who had died after eating a questionable fish, when the shop people arrived and Father took down the heavy Bible from its shelf.

There were only two employes in the watch shop in 1898, the clock man and Father's young apprentice-errand boy. When Mama had poured their coffee, Father put on his rimless spectacles and began to read:

"Thy word is a lamp unto my feet, and a light unto my path. . . . Thou art my hiding place and my shield: I hope in thy word . . . ."

What kind of hiding place, I wondered idly as I watched Father's brown beard rise and fall with the words. What was there to hide from?

It was a long, long psalm; beside me Nollie began to squirm. When at last Father closed the big volume, she, Willem, and Betsie were on their feet in an instant and snatching up their hats. Next minute they had raced down the last five stairs and out the alley door.

More slowly the two shopworkers got up and followed them down the stairs to the shop's rear entrance. Only then did the five adults notice me still seated at the table.

"Corrie!" cried Mama. "Have you forgotten you're a big girl now? Today you go to school too! Hurry, or you must cross the street alone!"

"I'm not going."

There was a short, startled silence, broken by everybody at once.

"When I was a girl——" Tante Jans began.

"Mrs. Waller's children——" from Tante Bep.

But Father's deep voice drowned them out. "Of course she's not going alone! Nollie was excited today and forgot to wait, that's all. Corrie is going with me."

And with that he took my hat from its peg, wrapped my hand in his and led me from the room. My hand in Father's! That meant the windmill on the Spaarne, or swans on the canal. But this time he was taking me where I didn't want to go! There was a railing along the bottom five steps: I grabbed it with my free hand and held on. Skilled watchmaker's fingers closed over mine and gently unwound them. Howling and struggling I was led away from the world I knew into a bigger, stranger, harder one. . . .

Mondays, Father took the train to Amsterdam to get the time from the Naval Observatory. Now that I had started school it was only in the summer that I could go with him. I would race downstairs to the shop, scrubbed, buttoned, and pronounced passable by Betsie. Father would be giving last-minute instructions to the apprentice. "Mrs. Staal will be in this morning to pick up her watch. This clock goes to the Bakker's in Bloemendaal."

And then we would be off to the station, hand in hand, I lengthening my strides and he shortening his to keep in step. The train trip to Amsterdam took only half an hour, but it was a wonderful ride. First the close-wedged buildings of old Haarlem gave way to separate houses with little plots of land around them. The spaces between houses grew wider. And then we were in the country, the flat Dutch farmland stretching to the horizon, ruler-straight canals sweeping past the window. At last, Amsterdam, even bigger than Haarlem, with its bewilderment of strange streets and canals.

Father always arrived a couple of hours before the time signal in order to visit the wholesalers who supplied him with watches and parts. Many of these were Jews, and these were the visits we both liked best. After the briefest possible discussion of business, Father would draw a small Bible from his traveling case; the wholesaler, whose beard would be even longer and fuller than Father's, would snatch a book or a scroll out of a drawer, clap a prayer cap onto his head; and the two of them would be off, arguing, comparing, interrupting, contradicting—reveling in each other's company.

And then, just when I had decided that this time I had really been forgotten, the wholesaler would look up, catch sight of me as though for the first time, and strike his forehead with the heel of his hand.

"A guest! A guest in my gates and I have offered her no refreshment!" And springing up he would rummage under shelves and into cupboards and before long I would be holding on my lap a plate of the most delicious treats in the world—honey cakes and date cakes and a kind of confection of nuts, fruits, and sugar. Desserts were rare in the Beje, sticky delights like these unknown.

By five minutes before noon we were always back at the train station, standing at a point on the platform from which we had a good view of the tower of the Naval Observatory. On the top of the tower where it could be seen by all the ships in the harbor was a tall shaft with two movable arms. At the stroke of 12:00 noon each day the arms dropped. Father would stand at his vantage point on the platform almost on tiptoe with the joy of precision, holding his pocket watch and a pad and pencil. There! Four seconds fast. Within an hour the "astronomical clock" in the shop in Haarlem would be accurate to the second.

On the train trip home we no longer gazed out the window. Instead we talked—about different things as the years passed. Betsie's graduation from secondary school in spite of the months missed with illness. Whether Willem, when he graduated, would get the scholarship that would let him go on to the university. Betsie starting work as Father's bookkeeper in the shop.

Oftentimes I would use the trip home to bring up things that were troubling me, since anything I asked at home was promptly answered by the aunts. Once —I must have been ten or eleven—I asked Father about a poem we had read at school the winter before. One line had described "a young man whose face was not shadowed by sexsin." I had been far too shy to ask the teacher what it meant, and Mama had blushed scarlet when I consulted her. In those days just after the turn of the century sex was never discussed, even at home.

So the line had stuck in my head. "Sex," I was pretty sure, meant whether you were a boy or a girl, and "sin" made Tante Jans very angry, but what the two together meant I could not imagine. And so, seated next to Father in the train compartment, I suddenly asked, "Father, what is sexsin?"

He turned to look at me, as he always did when answering a question, but to my surprise he said nothing. At last he stood up, lifted his traveling case from the rack over our heads, and set it on the floor.

"Will you carry it off the train, Corrie?" he said.

I stood up and tugged at it. It was crammed with the watches and spare parts he had purchased that morning.

"It's too heavy," I said.

"Yes," he said. "And it would be a pretty poor father who would ask his little girl to carry such a load. It's the same way, Corrie, with knowledge. Some knowledge is too heavy for children. When you are older and stronger you can bear it. For now you must trust me to carry it for you."

And I was satisfied. More than satisfied—wonderfully at peace. There were answers to this and all my hard questions—for now I was content to leave them in my father's keeping.

Evenings at the Beje there was always company and music. Guests would bring their flutes or violins and, as each member of the family sang or played an instrument, we made quite an orchestra gathered around the upright piano in Tante Jans's front room.

The only evenings when we did not make our own music was when there was a concert in town. We could not afford tickets but there was a stage door at the side of the concert hall through which sounds came clearly. There in the alley outside this door we and scores of other Haarlem music lovers followed every note. Mama and Betsie were not strong enough to stand so many hours, but some of us from the Beje would be there, in rain and snow and frost, and while from inside we would hear coughs and stirrings, there was never a rustle in the listeners at the door.

Best of all was when there were concerts at the cathedral, because a relative was sexton there. Just inside his small private entrance a wooden bench ran along the wall. Here we sat, our backs chilled by the ancient stone, our ears and hearts warmed by the music.

The great golden organ was one that Mozart had played, and some of its notes seemed to come from heaven itself. Indeed, I was sure that heaven was like St. Bavo's, and probably about the same size. Hell, I knew, was a hot place, so heaven must be like this cold, dank, holy building, where smoke rose like incense from the footwarmers of the paying customers. In heaven, I fervently believed, everybody had footwarmers. Even in the summer the chill never left the marble grave slabs on the floor. But when the organist touched the keys we scarcely noticed—and when he played Bach, not at all.

I was following Mama and Nollie up a dark, straight flight of stairs where cobwebs clutched at our hair and mice scuttled away ahead of us. The building was less than a block from the Beje, and probably a century newer, but here was no Tante Anna to wax and scrub.

We were going to see one of the many poor families in the neighborhood whom Mama had adopted. It never occurred to any of us children that we ourselves were poor; "the poor" were people you took baskets to. Mama was always cooking up nourishing broths and porridges for forgotten old men and pale young mothers—on days, that is, when she herself was strong enough to stand at the stove.

The night before, a baby had died, and with a basket of her own fresh bread Mama was making the prescribed call on the family. She toiled painfully up the railless stairs, stopping often for breath. At the top a door opened into a single room that was obviously cooking, eating, and sleeping quarters all at once. There were already many visitors, most of them standing for lack of chairs. Mama went at once to the young mother, but I stood frozen on the threshold. Just to the right of the door, so still in the homemade crib, was the baby.

It was strange that a society which hid the facts of sex from children made no effort to shield them from death. I stood staring at the tiny unmoving form with my heart thudding strangely against my ribs. Nollie, always braver than I, stretched out her hand and touched the ivory-white cheek. I longed to do it too, but hung back, afraid. For a while curiosity and terror struggled in me. At last I put one finger on the small curled hand.

It was cold.

Cold as we walked back to the Beje, cold as I washed for supper, cold even in the snug gas-lit dining room. Between me and each familiar face around the table crept those small icy fingers. For all Tante Jans's talk about it, death had been only a word. Now I knew that it could really happen—if to the baby, then to Mama, to Father, to Betsie!

Still shivering with that cold, I followed Nollie up to our room and crept into bed beside her. At last we heard Father's footsteps winding up the stairs. It was the best moment in every day, when he came up to tuck us in. We never fell asleep until he had arranged the blankets in his special way and laid his hand for a moment on each head. Then we tried not to move even a toe.

But that night as he stepped through the door I burst into tears. "I need you!" I sobbed. "You can't die! You can't!"

Beside me on the bed Nollie sat up. "We went to see Mrs. Hoog," she explained. "Corrie didn't eat her supper or anything."

Father sat down on the edge of the narrow bed. "Corrie," he began gently, "when you and I go to Amsterdam—when do I give you your ticket?"

I sniffed a few times, considering this.

"Why, just before we get on the train."

"Exactly. And our wise Father in heaven knows when we're going to need things, too. Don't run out ahead of Him, Corrie. When the time comes that some of us will have to die, you will look into your heart and find the strength you need—just in time."

3

Karel

I first met Karel at one of the "occasions" for which Mama was famous. Afterward I never could remember whether it was a birthday, a wedding anniversary, a new baby—Mama could make a party out of anything. Willem introduced him as a friend from Leiden and he shook hands with us one by one. I took that long strong hand, looked up into those deep brown eyes and fell irretrievably in love.

As soon as everyone had coffee I sat down just to gaze at him. He seemed quite unaware of me, but that was only natural. I was a child of fourteen, while he and Willem were already university men, sprouting straggly beards and breathing out cigar smoke with their conversation.

It was enough, I felt, to be in the same room with Karel. As for being unnoticed, I was thoroughly used to that. Nollie was the one boys noticed, though like so many pretty girls, she seemed not to care. When a boy asked for a lock of her hair—the standard method in those days of declaring passion—she would pull a few strands from the ancient gray carpet in our bedroom, tie them with a sentimental blue ribbon, and make me the messenger. The carpet was quite threadbare by now, the school full of broken hearts.

I, on the other hand, fell in love with each boy in my class in turn, in a kind of hopeless, regular rhythm. But since I was not pretty, and far too bash-

30

ful to express my feelings, a whole generation of boys was growing up unaware of the girl in seat thirty-two.

Karel, though, I thought as I watched him spooning sugar into his cup, was different. I was going to love Karel forever.

It was two years before I saw Karel again. That was the winter, 1908, that Nollie and I made a trip to the university at Leiden to pay Willem a visit. Willem's sparsely furnished room was on the fourth floor of a private home. He gathered both Nollie and me into a bear-hug and then ran to the window.

"Here," he said, taking in from the sill a cream bun he had been keeping cold there. "I bought this for you. You'd better eat it quick before my starving friends arrive."

We sat on the edge of Willem's bed gulping down the precious bun; I suspected that to buy it Willem had had to go without lunch. A second later the door slammed open and in burst four of his friends—tall, deep-voiced young men in coats with twice-turned collars and threadbare cuffs. Among them was Karel.

I swallowed the last bite of cream bun, wiped my hands on the back of my skirt and stood up. Willem introduced Nollie and me around. But when he came to Karel, Karel interrupted.

"We know each other already." He bowed ever so slightly. "Do you remember? We met at a party at your home." I glanced from Karel to Nollie—but no, he was looking straight at me. My heart poured out a rapturous reply, but my mouth was still filled with the sticky remains of bun and it never reached my lips. Soon the young men were seated at our feet on the floor, all talking eagerly and at once.

Perched beside me on the bed, Nollie joined in as naturally as though visiting a university was an everyday event for us. For one thing, she looked the part: at eighteen she was already in long skirts, while I was acutely conscious of the six inches of thick black school-girl stockings between the hem of my dress and the top of my shoes.

Also, Nollie had things to talk about: the year before she had started Normal School. She didn't really want to be a teacher, but in those days universities did not offer scholarships to girls and Normal Schools were inexpensive. And so she chatted easily and knowledgeably about things of interest to students—this new theory of relativity by a man called Einstein, and whether Admiral Peary would really reach the North Pole.

"And you, Corrie. Will you go on to be a teacher, too?"

Sitting on the floor at my feet, Karel was smiling at me. I felt a blush rise beneath my high collar.

"Next year, I mean," he persisted. "This is your final year in secondary school, isn't it?"

"Yes. I mean—no. I'll stay home with Mama and Tante Anna."

It came out so short and flat. Why did I say so little when I wanted to say so very much? . . .

That spring I finished school and took over the work of the household. It had always been planned that I would do this, but now there was an added reason. Tante Bep had tuberculosis.

The disease was regarded as incurable: the only known treatment was rest at a sanatorium and that was only for the rich. And so for many months Tante Bep lay in her little closet of a room, coughing away her life.

To keep down the risk of infection, only Tante Anna went in or out. Around the clock she nursed her older sister, many nights getting no sleep at all, and so the cooking and washing and cleaning for the family fell to me. I loved the work, and except for Tante Bep would have been completely happy. But over everything lay her shadow: not only the illness, but her whole disgruntled and disappointed life.

Often I would catch a glimpse inside when I handed in a tray or Tante Anna passed one out. There were the few pathetic mementos of thirty years in other people's homes. Perfume bottles—empty many years—because well-bred families always gave the governess perfume for Christmas. Some faded Daguerrotypes of children who by now must have children and grandchildren of their own. Then the door would shut. But I would linger in that narrow passage under the eaves, yearning to say something, to heal something. Wanting to love her better.

I spoke once about my feelings to Mama. She too was more and more often in bed. Always before when pain from the gallstones had got too bad she'd had an operation. But a small stroke after the last one made further surgery impossible, and many days, making up a tray for Tante Bep, I carried one upstairs to Mama also.

This time when I brought in her lunch she was writing letters. When Mama wasn't supplying the neighborhood with caps and baby dresses from her flying needles, she was composing cheery messages for shut-ins all over Haarlem. The fact that she herself had been shut-in much of her life never seemed to occur to her. "Here's a poor man, Corrie," she cried as I came in, "who's been cooped up in a single room for three years. Just think, shut away from the sky!"

I glanced out Mama's single window at the brick wall three feet away. "Mama," I said as I set the tray on the bed and sat down beside it, "can't we do something for Tante Bep? I mean, isn't it sad that she has to spend her last days here where she hates it, instead of where she was so happy? The Wallers' or someplace?"

Mama laid down her pen and looked at me. "Corrie," she said at last, "Bep has been just as happy here with us—no more and no less—than she was anywhere else."

I stared at her, not understanding.

"Do you know when she started praising the Wallers so highly?" Mama went on. "The day she left them. As long as she was there, she had nothing but complaints. The Wallers couldn't compare with the van Hooks where she'd been before. But at the van Hooks she'd actually been miserable. Happiness isn't something that depends on our surroundings, Corrie. It's something we make inside ourselves."

Tante Bep's death affected her sisters in characteristic fashion. Mama and Tante Anna redoubled their cooking and sewing for the needy in the neighborhood, as though realizing how brief was anyone's lifetime of service. As for Tante Jans, her own particular specter moved very close. "My own sister," she would exclaim at odd moments of the day. "Why, it might as well have been me!"

A year or so after Tante Bep's death, a new doctor took over Dr. Blinker's house calls. The new man's name was Jan van Veen and with him came his young sister and nurse, Tine van Veen. With him also came a new gadget for taking blood pressure. We had no idea what this meant but everyone in the household submitted to having the strip of cloth wrapped around his arm and air pumped into it.

Tante Jans, who loved medical paraphernalia of every kind, took a tremendous fancy to the new doctor and from then on consulted him as often as her finances would permit. And so it was Dr. van Veen, a couple of years later, who first discovered that Tante Jans had diabetes.

In those days this was a death sentence as surely as tuberculosis had been. For days the household was numb with the shock of it. After all these years of fearing even the idea, here was the dread thing itself. Tante Jans went straight to bed on hearing the news.

But inaction went poorly with her vigorous personality and one morning to everyone's surprise she appeared for breakfast in the dining room precisely at 8:10, with the announcement that doctors were often wrong. "All these tests and tubes," said Tante Jans, who believed in them implicitly, "what do they really prove?"

And from then on she threw herself more forcefully than ever into writing, speaking, forming clubs, and launching projects. Holland in 1914, like the rest of Europe, was mobilizing for war, and the streets of Haarlem were suddenly filled with young men in uniform. From her windows overlooking the Barteljorisstraat, Tante Jans watched them idling by, gazing aimlessly into the shop windows, most of them young, penniless, and lonesome. And she conceived the idea of a soldiers' center.

It was a novel idea for its day and Tante Jans

threw all the passion of her nature into it. The horse-drawn trolley on the Barteljorisstraat had recently been replaced with a big new electric one. But it still squealed to a stop, spitting sparks from rails and wire, when Tante Jans stood imperiously before the Beje. She would sweep aboard, her long black skirts in one hand, in the other a list of the well-to-do ladies who were about to become patronesses of the new venture. Only those of us who knew her best were aware, beneath all the activity, of the monstrous fear which drove her on.

And meanwhile her disease posed financial problems. Each week a fresh test had to be made to determine the sugar-content of her blood, and this was a complicated and expensive process requiring either Dr. van Veen or his sister to come to the house.

At last Tine van Veen taught me to run the weekly test myself. There were several steps involved, the most crucial being to heat the final compound to exactly the right temeprature. It was hard to make the old coal-burning range in our dark kitchen do anything very precisely, but I finally learned how and from then on each Friday mixed the chemicals and conducted the test myself. If the mixture remained clear when heated, all was well. It was only if it turned black that I was to notify Dr. van Veen.

It was that spring that Willem came home for his final holiday before ordination. He had graduated from the university two years before and was now in his last months of theological school. One warm evening during his visit we were all sitting around the dining room table. Father with thirty watches spread out before him was marking in a little notebook in his precise, beautiful script: "two seconds lost," "five seconds gained," while Willem read aloud from a history of the Dutch Reformation.

All at once the bell in the alley rang. Outside the dining room window a mirror faced the alley door so that we could see who was there before going down to open it. I glanced into it and sprang up from the table.

"Corrie!" said Betsie reprovingly. "Your skirt!"

I could never remember that I was wearing long skirts now, and Betsie spent many evenings mending the rips I put in them when I moved too fast. Now I took all five steps in a bound. For at the door, a bouquet of daffodils in her hands, was Tine van Veen. Whether it was the soft spring night that put it in my mind, or Willem's dramatic, pulpit-trained voice, I suddenly knew that the meeting of these two people had to be a very special moment.

"For your mother, Corrie," Tine said, holding out the flowers as I opened the door. "I hope she's——"

"No, no, you carry the flowers! You look beautiful with them!" And without even taking her coat I pushed the startled girl up the stairs ahead of me.

I prodded her through the dining room door, almost treading on her heels to see Willem's reaction. I knew exactly how it would be. My life was lived just then in romantic novels; I borrowed them from the library in English, Dutch, and German, often reading ones I liked in all three languages, and I had played this scene where hero meets heroine a thousand times.

Willem rose slowly to his feet, his eyes never leaving Tine's. Father stood up too. "Miss van Veen," Father said in his old-fashioned manner, "allow me to present to you our son, Willem. Willem, this is the young lady of whose talent and kindness you have heard us speak."

I doubt if either one heard the introduction. They were staring at each other as though there were not another soul in the room or in the world.

Willem and Tine were married two months after his ordination. During all the weeks of getting ready, one thought stood out in my mind: Karel will be there. The wedding day dawned cool and sparkling. My eyes picked Karel immediately from the crowd in front of the church, dressed in top hat and tails as were all the male guests, but incomparably the handsomest there.

As for me, I felt that a transformation had taken place since he had seen me last. The difference between my twenty-one years and his twenty-six was not, after all, as big as it had once been.

But more than that, I felt—no, not beautiful. Even on such a romantic day as this I could not persuade myself of that. I knew that my jaw was too square, my legs too long, my hands too large. But I earnestly believed—and all the books agreed—that I would look beautiful to the man who loved me.

Betsie had done my hair that morning, laboring for an hour with the curling iron until it was piled high on my head—and so far, for a wonder, it had stayed. She'd made my silk dress too, as she'd made one for each of the women in the family, working by lamplight in the evenings because the shop was open six days a week and she would not sew on Sundays.

Now looking around me I decided that our home-made outfits were as stylish as any there. Nobody would guess, I thought as the gentle press toward the door began, that Father had given up his cigars and Tante Jans the coal fire in her rooms in order to buy the silk that swished so elegantly with us now.

"Corrie?"

In front of me stood Karel, tall black hat in his hands, his eyes searching my face as though he were not quite sure.

"Yes, it's me!" I said, laughing up at him. It's me, Karel, and it's you, and it's the moment I've been dreaming of!

"But you're so—so grown up. Forgive me, Corrie, of course you are! It's just that I've always thought of you as the little girl with the enormous blue eyes." He stared at me a little longer and then added softly, "And now the little girl is a lady, and a lovely one."

Suddenly the organ music swelling from the open door was for us, the arm he offered me was the moon, and my gloved hand resting upon it was the only thing that kept me from soaring right over the peaked roof-tops of Haarlem.

It was a windy, rainy Friday morning in January when my eyes told me what at first my brain refused to grasp. The liquid in the glass beaker on the kitchen stove was a muddy, sullen black.

I leaned against the old wooden sink and shut my eyes. "Please God, let me have made a mistake!" I went over in my mind the different steps, looked at the vials of chemicals, the measuring spoons. No. All just the same as I'd always done.

It was this wretched room then—it was always dark in this little cupboard of a kitchen. With a pot holder I snatched up the beaker and ran to the window in the dining room.

Black. Black as fear itself.

Still clutching the beaker I pounded down the five steps and through the rear door of the shop. Father, his jeweler's glass in his eye, was bent over the shoulder of the newest apprentice, deftly selecting an infinitesimal part from the array before them on the workbench.

I looked through the glass in the door to the shop, but Betsie, behind her little cashier's desk, was talking to a customer. Not a customer, I corrected myself, a nuisance—I knew the woman. She came here for advice on watches and then bought them at that new place, Kan's, across the street. Neither Father nor Betsie seemed to care that this was happening more and more.

As the woman left I burst through the door with the telltale beaker.

"Betsie!" I cried. "Oh Betsie, it's black! How are we going to tell her? What are we going to do?"

Betsie came swiftly from behind the desk and put her arms around me. Behind me Father came into the shop. His eyes traveled from the beaker to Betsie to me.

"And you did it exactly right, Corrie? In every detail?"

"I'm afraid so, Father."

"And I am sure of it, my dear. But we must have the doctor's verdict too."

"I'll take it at once," I said.

And so I poured the ugly liquid into a small bottle and ran with it over the slippery, rain-washed streets of Haarlem.

There was a new nurse at Dr. van Veen's and I spent a miserable, silent half-hour in the waiting room. At last his patient left and Dr. van Veen took the bottle into his small laboratory.

"There is no mistake, Corrie," he said as he emerged. "Your aunt has three weeks at the very most."

We held a family conference in the watch shop

when I got back: Mama, Tante Anna, Father, Betsie, and me (Nollie did not get home from her teaching job until evening). We agreed that Tante Jans must know at once.

"We will tell her together," Father decided, "though I will speak the necessary words. And perhaps," he said, his face brightening, "perhaps she will take heart from all she has accomplished. She puts great store on accomplishment, Jans does, and who knows but that she is right!"

And so the little procession filed up the steps to Tante Jans's room. "Come in," she called to Father's knock, and added as she always did, "and close the door before I catch my death of drafts."

She was sitting at her round mahogany table, working on yet another appeal for her soldiers' center. As she saw the number of people entering the room, she laid down her pen. She looked from one face to another, until she came to mine and gave a little gasp of comprehension. This was Friday morning, and I had not yet come up with the results of the test.

"My dear sister-in-law," Father began gently, "there is a joyous journey which each of God's children sooner or later sets out on. And, Jans, some must go to their Father empty-handed, but you will run to Him with hands full!"

"All your clubs . . . ," Tante Anna ventured.

"Your writings . . . ," Mama added.

"The funds you've raised . . . ," said Betsie.

"Your talks . . . ," I began.

But our well-meant words were useless. In front of us the proud face crumpled; Tante Jans put her hands over her eyes and began to cry. "Empty, empty!" she choked at last through her tears. "How can we bring anything to God? What does He care for our little tricks and trinkets?"

And then as we listened in disbelief she lowered her hands and with tears still coursing down her face whispered, "Dear Jesus, I thank You that we must come with empty hands. I thank You that You have done all—all—on the Cross, and that all we need in life or death is to be sure of this."

Mama threw her arms around her and they clung together. But I stood rooted to the spot, knowing that I had seen a mystery.

It was Father's train ticket, given at the moment itself.

With a flourish of her handkerchief and a forceful clearing of her nose, Tante Jans let us know that the moment for sentiment had passed.

"If I had a moment's privacy," she said, "I might get some work accomplished."

She glanced at Father, and into those stern eyes crept the nearest thing to a twinkle I had ever seen. "Not that the work matters, Casper. Not that it matters at all. But," she dismissed us crisply, "I'm not going to leave an untidy desk behind for someone else to clean up."

It was four months after Tante Jans' funeral that the long-awaited invitation came to Willem's First Sermon. After less than a year as assistant to a minister in Uithuizen, he had been given a church of his own in Brabant, the beautiful rural southern part of Holland. And in the Dutch Reformed Church, a minister's first sermon in his first church was the most solemn, joyous, emotional occasion that an unemotional people could conceive. Family and friends would come from great distances and stay for days.

From his own assistant pastorate, Karel wrote that he would be there and looked forward to seeing us all again. I endowed that word "all" with special meaning and pressed dresses and packed trunks in a delirium of anticipation.

It was one of Mama's bad times. She huddled in the corner of our train compartment, the hand that gripped Father's whitening at the knuckles each time the train lurched or swayed. But while the rest of us gazed out at long rows of poplars in their bright June green, Mama's eyes never left the sky. What to us was a trip through the country, to her was a feast of clouds and light and infinite blue distances.

Both the village of Made and the congregation of Willem's church had declined in recent years. But the church building itself, dating back to better days, was large, and so was Willem and Tine's house across the street. Indeed by Beje standards it was enormous; for the first few nights the ceiling seemed so far overhead that I could not sleep. Uncles and cousins and friends arrived each day, but no matter how many people moved in, the rooms always looked to me half empty.

Three days after we got there I answered the front door knocker and there stood Karel, coal dust from the train trip still speckling his shoulders. He tossed his brown carpetbag past me into the hall, seized my hand, and drew me out into the June sunshine. "It's a lovely day in the country, Corrie!" he cried. "Come walking!"

From then on it seemed taken for granted that Karel and I would go walking each day. Each time we wandered a little farther down the country lanes that wound in every direction away from the village, the dirt beneath our feet so different from the brick streets of Haarlem. It was hard to believe, at such moments, that the rest of Europe was locked in the bloodiest war in history. Even across the ocean the madness seemed to be spreading: the papers said America would enter.

Here in neutral Holland one sunlit June day followed another. Only a few people—like Willem—insisted that the war was Holland's tragedy too. His first sermon was on this theme. Europe and the world were changing, he said: no matter which side won, a way of life was gone forever. I looked around at his congregation of sturdy villagers and farmers and saw that they did not care for such ideas.

After the sermon, friends and more distant family started home. But Karel lingered on. Our walks lasted longer. Often we talked about Karel's future, and suddenly we were speaking not about what Karel was going to do, but about what *we* were going to do. We imagined that we had a huge old manse like this one to decorate, and rejoiced to discover that we had the same ideas about furniture, flowers, even the same favorite colors. Only about children did we disagree: Karel wanted four, while I held out stubbornly for six.

And all this while the word "marriage" was never spoken.

One day when Karel was in the village, Willem came out of the kitchen with two cups of coffee in his hands. Tine with a cup of her own was just behind him.

"Corrie," Willem said, handing me the coffee and speaking as though with effort, "has Karel led you to believe that he is——"

"Serious?" Tine finished his sentence for him.

The hateful blush that I could never control set my cheeks burning. "I ... no ... we ... why?"

Willem's face reddened too. "Because, Corrie, this is something that can never be. You don't know Karel's family. They've wanted one thing since he was a small child. They've sacrificed for it, planned for it, built their whole lives around it. Karel is to ... 'marry well' is the way I think they put it."

The big barren parlor seemed suddenly emptier still. "But—what about what Karel wants? He's not a small child now!"

Willem fixed his sober, deep-set eyes on mine. "He will do it, Corrie. I don't say he wants it. To him it's just a fact of life like any other. When we'd talk about girls we liked—at the university—he'd always say at the end, 'Of course I could never marry her. It would kill my mother.' "

The hot coffee scalded my mouth but I gulped it down and made my escape to the garden. I hated that gloomy old house and sometimes I almost hated Willem for always seeing the dark, hard side of things. Here in the garden it was different. There wasn't a bush, hardly a flower, that Karel and I hadn't looked at together, that didn't have a bit of our feeling for each other still clinging to it. Willem might know more than I did about theology and war and politics—but when it came to romance! Things like money, social prestige, family expectations, why, in the books they vanished like rainclouds, every time....

Karel left Made a week or so later, and his last words made my heart soar. Only months afterward did I remember how strangely he spoke them; the urgency, almost desperation in his voice. We were standing in the driveway of the manse waiting for the horse and cart which Made still regarded as the only dependable conveyance when there was a train to be caught. We had said goodbye after breakfast and if part of me was disappointed that he still had not proposed, another part of me was content just to be beside him. Now suddenly in the driveway he seized both my hands.

"Corrie, write to me!" he said, but not gaily. Pleadingly. "Write me about the Beje! I want to know everything. I want every detail of that ugly, beautiful, crumbling old house! Write about your father, Corrie! Write how he forgets to send the bills. Oh Corrie, it's the happiest home in Holland!"

And so it was, indeed, when Father, Mama, Betsie, Nollie, Tante Anna, and I returned. It had always been a happy place, but now each little event seemed to glow because I could share it with Karel. Every meal I cooked was an offering to him, each shining pot a poem, every sweep of the broom an act of love.

His letters did not come as often as mine went singing to him, but I put this down to his work. The minister he was assisting, he wrote, had turned the parish calling over to him: it was a wealthy congregation and large contributors expected frequent and unhurried visits from the clergy.

As time went by his letters came more seldom. I made up for it with mine and went humming my way through the summer and fall. One glorious, nippy November day when all of Holland was singing with me, the doorbell rang. I was washing the lunch dishes in the kitchen, but I ran through the dining room and down the steps before the rest of the family could stir.

I flung open the alley door and there was Karel.

Beside him was a young woman.

She stood smiling at me. I took in the hat with its sweeping feather, the ermine collar, the white-gloved hand resting on his arm. Then a blur seemed to move over the scene, for Karel was saying, "Corrie, I want you to meet my fiancée."

I must have said something. I must have led them up to Tante Jans's front room that we used now as a parlor. I only recall how my family came to the rescue, talking, shaking hands, taking coats, finding chairs, so that I would not have to do or say anything. Mama broke even her own record for making coffee. Tante Anna passed cakes. Betsie engaged the young woman in a discussion of winter fashions and Father pinned Karel in a corner with questions of the most international and impersonal nature. What did he make of the news that President Wilson was sending American troops to France?

Somehow the half-hour passed. Somehow I managed to shake her hand, then Karel's hand, and to wish them every happiness. Betsie took them down to the door. Before it clicked shut I was fleeing up the stairs to my own room at the top of the house where the tears could come.

How long I lay on my bed sobbing for the one love of my life I do not know. Later, I heard Father's footsteps coming up the stairs. For a moment I was a little girl again waiting for him to tuck the blankets tight. But this was a hurt that no blanket could shut out, and suddenly I was afraid of what Father would say. Afraid he would say, "There'll be someone else soon," and that forever afterward this untruth would lie between us. For in some deep part of me I knew already that there would not—soon or ever—be anyone else.

The sweet cigar-smell came into the room with Father. And of course he did not say the false, idle words.

"Corrie," he began instead, "do you know what hurts so very much? It's love. Love is the strongest force in the world, and when it is blocked that means pain.

"There are two things we can do when this happens. We can kill the love so that it stops hurting. But then of course part of us dies, too. Or, Corrie, we can ask God to open up another route for that love to travel.

"God loves Karel—even more than you do—and if you ask Him, He will give you His love for this man, a love nothing can prevent, nothing destroy.

Whenever we cannot love in the old, human way, Corrie, God can give us the perfect way."

I did not know, as I listened to Father's footsteps winding back down the stairs, that he had given me more than the key to this hard moment. I did not know that he had put into my hands the secret that would open far darker rooms than this—places where there was not, on a human level, anything to love at all.

I was still in kindergarten in these matters of love. My task just then was to give up my feeling for Karel without giving up the joy and wonder that had grown with it. And so, that very hour, lying there on my bed, I whispered the enormous prayer:

"Lord, I give to You the way I feel about Karel, my thoughts about our future—oh, You know! Everything! Give me Your way of seeing Karel instead. Help me to love him that way. That much."

And even as I said the words I fell asleep.

4

The Watch Shop

I was standing on a chair washing the big window in the dining room, waving now and then to passersby in the alley, while in the kitchen Mama peeled potatoes for lunch. It was 1918; the dreadful war was finally over: even in the way people walked you could sense a new hope in the air.

It wasn't like Mama, I thought, to let the water keep running that way; she never wasted anything.

"Corrie."

Her voice was low, almost a whisper.

"Yes, Mama?"

"Corrie," she said again.

And then I heard the water spilling out of the sink onto the floor. I jumped down from the chair and ran into the kitchen. Mama stood with her hand on the faucet, staring strangely at me while the water splashed from the sink over her feet.

"What is it, Mama!" I cried, reaching for the faucet. I pried her fingers loose, shut off the water, and drew her away from the puddle on the floor.

"Corrie," she said again.

"Mama, you're ill! We've got to get you to bed!"

"Corrie."

I put an arm beneath her shoulder and guided her through the dining room and up the stairs. At my cry Tante Anna came running down them and caught Mama's other arm. Together we got her onto her bed

the prescribed half-hour. There could have been no one in all Holland less informed about marriage than Tante Anna, but this was ritual: the older woman counseling the younger one down through the centuries—one could no more have got married without it than one could have dispensed with the ring.

Nollie was radiant, the following day, in her long white dress. But it was Mama I could not take my eyes off. Dressed in black as always, she was nevertheless suddenly young and girlish, eyes sparkling with joy at this greatest Occasion the ten Booms had ever held. Betsie and I took her into the church early and I was sure that most of the van Woerden family and friends never dreamed that the gracious and smiling lady in the first pew could neither walk alone nor speak.

It was not until Nollie and Flip came down the aisle together that I thought for the very first time of my own dreams of such a moment with Karel. I glanced at Betsie, sitting so tall and lovely on the other side of Mama. Betsie had always known that, because of her health, she could not have children, and for that reason had decided long ago never to marry. Now I was twenty-seven, Betsie in her mid thirties, and I knew that this was the way it was going to be: Betsie and I the unmarried daughters living at home in the Beje.

It was a happy thought, not a sad one. And that was the moment when I knew for sure that God had accepted the faltering gift of my emotions made four years ago. For with the thought of Karel—all shining round with love as thoughts of him had been since I was fourteen—came not the slightest trace of hurt. "Bless Karel, Lord Jesus," I murmured under my breath. "And bless her. Keep them close to one another and to You." And that was a prayer, I knew for sure, that could not have sprung unaided from Corrie ten Boom.

But the great miracle of the day came later. To close the service we had chosen Mama's favorite hymn, "Fairest Lord Jesus." And now as I stood singing it I heard, behind me in the pew, Mama's voice singing too. Word after word, verse after verse, she joined in, Mama who could not speak four words, singing the beautiful lines without a stammer. Her voice which had been so high and clear was hoarse and cracked, but to me it was the voice of an angel.

All the way through she sang, while I stared straight ahead, not daring to turn around for fear of breaking the spell. When at last everyone sat down, Mama's eyes, Betsie's, and mine were brimming with tears.

At first we hoped it was the beginning of Mama's recovery. But the words she had sung she was not able to say, nor did she ever sing again. It had been an isolated moment, a gift to us from God, His own very special wedding present. Four weeks later, asleep with a smile on her lips, Mama slipped away from us forever.

It was in late November that year that a common cold made a big difference. Betsie began to sniff and sneeze and Father decided that she must not sit behind the cashier's table where the shop door let in the raw winter air.

But Christmas was coming, the shop's busiest time: with Betsie bundled up in bed, I took to running down to the shop as often as I could to wait on customers and wrap packages and save Father clambering up and down from his tall workbench a dozen times an hour.

Tante Anna insisted she could cook and look after Betsie. And so I settled in behind Betsie's table, writing down sales and repair charges, recording cash spent for parts and supplies, and leafing through past records in growing disbelief.

But—there was no system here anywhere! No way to tell whether a bill had been paid or not, whether the price we were asking was high or low, no way in fact to tell if we were making money or losing it.

I hurried down the street to the bookseller one wintry afternoon, bought a whole new set of ledgers, and started in to impose method on madness. Many nights after the door was locked and the shutters closed I sat on in the flickering gaslight, poring over old inventories and wholesalers' statements.

Or I would question Father. "How much did you charge Mr. Hoek for that repair work last month?"

Father would look at me blankly. "Why . . . ah . . . my dear . . . I can't really . . ."

"It was a Vacheron, Father, an old one. You had to send all the way to Switzerland for the parts and here's their bill and——"

His face lit up. "Of course I remember! A beautiful watch, Corrie! A joy to work on. Very old, only he'd let dust get into it. A fine watch must be kept clean, my dear!"

"But how much did you charge, Father?"

I developed a system of billing and, increasingly, my columns of figures began to correspond to actual transactions. And increasingly, I discovered that I loved it. I had always felt happy in this little shop with its tiny voices and shelves of small shining faces. But now I discovered that I liked the business side of it too, liked catalogues and stock listings, liked the whole busy, energetic world of trade.

Every now and then when I remembered that Betsie's cold had settled in her chest and threatened, as hers always did, to turn into pneumonia, I would reproach myself for being anything but distressed at the present arrangement. And at night when I would hear the hard, racking cough from her bedroom below I would pray with all my heart for her to be better at once.

And then one evening two days before Christmas, when I had closed up the shop for the night and was locking the hallway door, Betsie came bursting in from the alley with her arms full of flowers. Her eyes when she saw me there were like a guilty child's.

"For Christmas, Corrie!" she pleaded. "We have to have flowers for Christmas!"

"Betsie ten Boom!" I exploded. "How long has this been going on? No wonder you're not getting better!"

"I've stayed in bed most of the time, honestly——" she stopped while great coughs shook her. "I've only got up for really important things."

I put her to bed and then prowled the rooms with new-opened eyes, looking for Betsie's "important things." How little I had really noticed about the house! Betsie had wrought changes everywhere. I marched back up to her room and confronted her with the evidence. "Was it important, Betsie, to rearrange all the dishes in the corner cupboard?"

She looked up at me and her face went red. "Yes it was," she said defiantly. "You just put them in any old way."

"And the door to Tante Jans's room? Someone's been using paint remover on it, and sandpaper too—and that's hard work!"

"But there's beautiful wood underneath, I just know it! For years I've wanted to get that old varnish off and see. Oh Corrie," she said, her voice suddenly small and contrite, "I know it's horrid and selfish of me when you've had to be in the shop day after day. And I will take better care of myself so you won't have to do it much longer; but, oh, it's been so glorious being here all day, pretending I was in charge, you know, planning what I'd do. . . ."

And so it was out. We had divided the work backwards. It was astonishing, once we'd made the swap, how well everything went. The house had been clean under my care; under Betsie's it glowed. She saw beauty in wood, in pattern, in color, and helped us to see it too. The small food budget which had barely survived my visits to the butcher and disappeared altogether at the bakery, stretched under Betsie's management to include all kinds of delicious things that had never been on our table before. "Just wait till you see what's for dessert this noon!" she'd tell us at the breakfast table, and all morning in the shop the question would shimmer in the back of our minds.

The soup kettle and the coffee pot on the back of the stove, which I never seemed to find time for, were simmering again the first week Betsie took over, and soon a stream of postmen and police, derelict old men and shivering young errand boys were pausing inside our alley door to stamp their feet and cup their hands around hot mugs, just as they'd done when Mama was in charge.

And meanwhile, in the shop, I was finding a joy in work that I'd never dreamed of. I soon knew that I wanted to do more than wait on customers and keep the accounts. I wanted to learn watch repair itself.

Father eagerly took on the job of teaching me. I eventually learned the moving and stationary parts, the chemistry of oils and solutions, tool and grindwheel and magnifying techniques. But Father's patience, his almost mystic rapport with the harmonies of watchworks, these were not things that could be taught.

Wristwatches had become fashionable and I enrolled in a school which specialized in this kind of work. Three years after Mama's death I became the first licensed woman watchmaker in Holland.

And so was established the pattern our lives were to follow for over twenty years. When Father had put the Bible back on its shelf after breakfast he and I would go down the stairs to the shop while Betsie stirred the soup pot and plotted magic with three potatoes and a pound of mutton. With my eye on income-and-outlay the shop was doing better and soon we were able to hire a saleslady to preside over the front room while Father and I worked in back.

There was a constant procession through this little back room. Sometimes it was a customer; most often it was simply a visitor—from a laborer with wooden klompen on his feet to a fleet owner—all bringing their problems to Father. Quite unabashedly, in the sight of customers in the front room and the employees working with us, he would bow his head and pray for the answer.

He prayed over the work, too. There weren't many repair problems he hadn't encountered. But occasionally one would come along that baffled even him. And then I would hear him say: "Lord, You turn the wheels of the galaxies. You know what makes the planets spin and You know what makes this watch run...."

The specifics of the prayer were always different,

for Father—who loved science—was an avid reader of a dozen university journals. Through the years he took his stopped watches to "the One who set the atoms dancing," or "Who keeps the great currents circling through the sea." The answers to these prayers seemed often to come in the middle of the night: many mornings I would climb onto my stool to find the watch that we had left in a hundred despairing pieces fitted together and ticking merrily.

One thing in the shop I never learned to do as well as Betsie, and that was to care about each person who stepped through the door. Often when a customer entered I would slip out the rear door and up to Betsie in the kitchen. "Betsie! Who is the woman with the Alpina lapel-watch on a blue velvet band—stout, around fifty?"

"That's Mrs. van den Keukel. Her brother came back from Indonesia with malaria and she's been nursing him. Corrie," as I sped back down the stairs, "ask her how Mrs. Rinker's baby is!"

And Mrs. van den Keukel, leaving the shop a few minutes later would comment mistakenly to her husband, "That Corrie ten Boom is just like her sister!"

Even before Tante Anna's death in the late 1920's, the empty beds in the Beje were beginning to fill up with the succession of foster children who for over ten years kept the old walls ringing with laughter and Betsie busy letting down hems and pants cuffs.

And meanwhile Willem and Nollie were having families—Willem and Tine four children, Nollie and Flip six. Willem had long since left the parish ministry, where his habit of speaking the hard truth had made a succession of congregations unhappy, and had started his nursing home in Hilversum, thirty miles from Haarlem.

Nollie's family we saw more often, as their school —of which Flip was now principal—was right in Haarlem. It was a rare day when one or another of their six was not at the Beje to visit Opa at his workbench or peer into Tante Betsie's mixing bowl or race up and down the winding steps with the foster children.

Indeed it was at the Beje that we first discovered young Peter's musical gift. It happened around our radio. We had first heard this modern wonder at a friend's house. "A whole orchestra," we kept repeating to each other—somehow that seemed especially difficult to produce inside a box. We began to put pennies aside toward a radio of our own.

Long before the sum was raised Father came down with the hepatitis that almost cost his life: during the long stay in the hospital his beard turned snow white. The day he returned home—a week after his seventieth birthday—a little committee paid us a visit. They represented shopkeepers, street sweepers, a factory owner, a canal bargeman—all people who had realized during Father's illness what he meant to them. They had pooled their resources and bought him a radio.

It was a large table model with an ornate shell-shaped speaker and it brought us many years of joy. Every Sunday Betsie would scour the papers, British, French, and German as well as our own, since the radio brought in stations from all over Europe, and plan the week's program of concerts and recitals.

It was one Sunday afternoon when Nollie and her family were visiting that Peter suddenly spoke up in the middle of a Brahms concerto.

"It's funny they put a bad piano on the radio."

"Sshhh," said Nollie, but, "What do you mean, Peter?" asked Father.

"One of the notes is wrong."

The rest of us exchanged glances: what could an eight-year-old know? But Father led the boy to Tante Jans's old upright. "Which note, Peter?"

Peter struck the keys up the scale till he reached B above middle C. "This one," he said.

And then everyone in the room heard it too: the B on the concert grand was flat.

I spent the rest of the afternoon sitting beside Peter on the piano bench giving him simple musical quizzes, uncovering a phenomenal musical memory and perfect pitch. Peter became my music student until—in about six months—he had learned everything I knew and went on to more expert teachers.

The radio brought another change to our lives, one that Father at first resisted. Every hour, over the BBC, we could hear the striking hours of Big Ben. And with his stopwatch in his hand corrected to the astronomical clock in the shop, Father conceded that the first stroke of the English clock time after time coincided with the hour.

Father remained, however, mistrustful of this English time. He knew several Englishmen—and they were invariably late. As soon as he was strong enough to travel by train again, he resumed his weekly trips to Amsterdam to get Naval Observatory time.

But as the months passed and Big Ben and the Observatory continued in perfect agreement, he went less regularly, and finally not at all. The astronomical clock in any case was so jarred and jiggled by the constant rattle of automobile traffic in the narrow street outside that it was no longer the precision instrument it had been. The ultimate ignominy came the day Father set the astronomical clock by the radio.

In spite of this and other changes, life for the three of us—Father, Betsie, and me—stayed essentially the same. Our foster children grew up and went away to jobs or to marry, but they were often in the house for visits. The Hundredth Anniversary came and went; the following day Father and I were back at our workbenches as always.

Even the people we passed on our daily walks were perfectly predictable. Though it was years now since his illness, Father still walked unsteadily and I still went with him on his daily stroll through the downtown streets. We took our walk always at the same time, after the midday dinner and before the shop reopened at two, and always over the same route. And since other Haarlemers were just as regular in their habits, we knew exactly whom we would meet.

Many of those we nodded to were old friends or customers, others we knew only from this daily encounter—the woman sweeping her steps on Koning Straat, the man who read the *World Shipping News* at the trolley stop on the Grote Markt. And our favorite, the man we called The Bulldog. This was not only because we never saw him without two large bulldogs on the end of a leash but because, with his wrinkled, jowly face and short bowlegs he looked exactly like one of his own pets. His obvious affection for the animals was what touched us: as they went along he constantly muttered and fussed at them. Father and The Bulldog always tipped their hats to one another ceremoniously as we passed.

And while Haarlem and the rest of Holland strolled and bowed and swept its steps, the neighbor on our east geared for war. We knew what was happening—there was no way to keep from knowing. Often in the evening, turning the dial on the radio, we would pick up a voice from Germany. The voice did not talk, or even shout. It screamed. Oddly, it was even-tempered Betsie who reacted most strongly, hurtling from her chair and flinging herself at the radio to shut off the sound.

And yet, in the interludes, we forgot. Or, when Willem was visiting and would not let us forget, or when letters to Jewish suppliers in Germany came back marked "Address Unknown," we still managed to believe that it was primarily a German problem. "How long are they going to stand for it?" we said. "They won't put up with that man for long."

Only once did the changes taking place in Germany reach inside the little shop on the Barteljorisstraat, and that was in the person of a young German watchmaker. Germans frequently came to work under Father for a while, for his reputation reached even beyond Holland. So when this tall good-looking young man appeared with apprentice papers from a good firm in Berlin, Father hired him without hesitation. Otto told us proudly that he belonged to the Hitler Youth. Indeed it was a puzzle to us why he had come to Holland, for he found nothing but fault with Dutch people and products. "The world will see what Germans can do," he said often.

His first morning at work he came upstairs for coffee and Bible reading with the other employes; after that he sat alone down in the shop. When we asked him why, he said that though he had not understood the Dutch words, he had seen that Father was reading from the Old Testament which, he informed us, was the Jews' "Book of Lies."

I was shocked, but Father was only sorrowful. "He has been taught wrong," he told me. "By watching us, seeing that we love this Book and are truthful people, he will realize his error."

It was several weeks later that Betsie opened the door from the hallway and beckoned to Father and me. Upstairs on Tante Jans's tall mahogany chair sat the lady who ran the rooming house where Otto lived. Changing the bed sheets that morning, she said, she had found something under his pillow. And she drew from her market satchel a knife with a curving ten-inch blade.

Again, Father put the best interpretation on it. "The boy is probably only frightened, alone in a strange country. He probably bought it to protect himself."

It was true enough that Otto was alone. He spoke no Dutch, nor made any effort to learn, and besides Father, Betsie, and me, few people in this working-class part of the city spoke German. We repeated our invitation to join us upstairs in the evenings, but whether he did not care for our choice of radio programs, or because the evening ended as the morning began, with prayer and Bible reading, he seldom did.

In the end, Father did fire Otto—the first employe he had ever discharged in more than sixty years in business. And it was not the knife or the anti-Semitism that finally brought it about, but Otto's treatment of the old clock mender, Christoffels.

From the very first I had been baffled by his brusqueness with the old man. It wasn't anything he did—not in our presence anyway—but what he didn't do. No standing back to let the older man go first, no helping on with a coat, no picking up a dropped tool. It was hard to pin down. One Sunday when Father, Betsie, and I were having dinner at Hilversum I commented on what I had concluded was simple thoughtlessness.

Willem shook his head. "It's very deliberate," he

said. "It's because Christoffels is old. The old have no value to the State. They're also harder to train in the new ways of thinking. Germany is systematically teaching disrespect for old age."

We stared at him, trying to grasp such a concept. "Surely you are mistaken, Willem!" Father said. "Otto is extremely courteous to me—unusually so. And I'm a good deal older than Christoffels."

"You're different. You're the boss. That's another part of the system: respect for authority. It is the old and the weak who are to be eliminated."

We rode the train home in stunned silence—and we started watching Otto more closely. But how could we know, how in the Holland of 1939 could we have guessed, that it was not in the shop where we could observe him but in the streets and alleys outside that Otto was subjecting Christoffels to a very real, small persecution. "Accidental" collisions and trippings, a shove, a heel ground into a toe, were making the old clockman's journeys to and from work times of terror.

The erect and shabby little man was too proud to report any of this to us. It was not until the icy February morning that Christoffels stumbled into the dining room with a bleeding cheek and a torn coat that the truth came out. Even then, Christoffels said nothing. But running down to the street to pick up his hat, I encountered Otto surrounded by an indignant little cluster of people who had seen what happened. Rounding the corner into the alley, the young man had deliberately forced the older one into the side of the building and ground his face against the rough bricks.

Father tried to reason with Otto as he let him go, to show him why such behavior was wrong. Otto did not answer. In silence he collected the few tools he had brought with him and in silence left the shop. It was only at the door that he turned to look at us, a look of the most utter contempt I had ever seen.

5

Invasion

The slender hands of the clock on the stair wall pointed to 9:25 as we left the dining room that night. That in itself was unusual in our orderly lives. Father was eighty years old now, and promptly at 8:45 each evening—an hour sooner than formerly—he would open the Bible, the signal for prayers, read one chapter, ask God's blessing on us through the night, and by 9:15 be climbing the stairs to his bedroom. Tonight, however, the Prime Minister was to address the nation at 9:30. One question ached through all of Holland like a long-held breath: Would there be war?

We circled up the steps to Tante Jans's rooms and Father went to warm up the big table radio. We did not so often spend the evenings up here listening to music now. England, France, and Germany were at war; their stations carried mostly war reports or code messages and many frequencies were jammed. Even Dutch stations carried mostly war news, and that we could hear just as well on the small portable radio we kept now in the dining room, a gift from Pickwick the Christmas before.

This, though, was to be a major broadcast; somehow we all felt it merited the large old set with its elaborate speaker. We sat now, waiting for 9:30, tense and upright in the high-backed wooden chairs, avoiding as if by a kind of premonition the cushioned and comfortable seats.

Then the Prime Minister's voice was speaking to us, sonorous and soothing. There would be no war. He had had assurances from high sources on both sides. Holland's neutrality would be respected. It would be the Great War all over again. There was nothing to fear. Dutchmen were urged to remain calm and to——

The voice stopped. Betsie and I looked up, astonished. Father had snapped off the set and in his blue eyes was a fire we had never seen before.

"It is wrong to give people hope when there is no hope," he said. "It is wrong to base faith upon wishes. There will be war. The Germans will attack and we will fall."

He stamped out his cigar stub in the ashtray beside the radio and with it, it seemed, the anger too, for his voice grew gentle again. "Oh, my dears, I am sorry for all Dutchmen now who do not know the power of God. For we will be beaten. But He will not." He kissed us both goodnight and in a moment we heard the steps of an old man climbing the stairs to bed.

Betsie and I sat rooted to our chairs. Father, so skilled at finding good in every situation, so slow to believe evil. If Father saw war and defeat, then there was no other possibility at all.

I sat bolt upright in my bed. What was that? There! There it was again! A brilliant flash followed a second later by an explosion which shook the bed. I scrambled over the covers to the window and leaned out. The patch of sky above the chimney tops glowed orange-red.

I felt for my bathrobe and thrust my arms through the sleeves as I whirled down the stairs. At Father's room I pressed my ear against the door. Between bomb bursts I heard the regular rhythm of his breathing.

I dived down a few more steps and into Tante Jans's rooms. Betsie had long since moved into Tante Jans's little sleeping cubicle where she would be nearer the kitchen and the doorbell. She was sitting up in the bed. I groped toward her in the darkness and we threw our arms round each other.

Together we said it aloud:

"War."

It was five hours after the Prime Minister's speech. How long we clung together, listening, I do not know. The bombing seemed mostly to be coming from the direction of the airport. At last we tiptoed uncertainly out to Tante Jans's front room. The glowing sky lit the room with a strange brilliance. The chairs, the mahogany bookcase, the old upright piano, all pulsed with an eerie light.

Betsie and I knelt down by the piano bench. For what seemed hours we prayed for our country, for the dead and injured tonight, for the Queen. And then, incredibly, Betsie began to pray for the Germans, up there in the planes, caught in the fist of the giant evil loose in Germany. I looked at my sister kneeling beside me in the light of burning Holland. "Oh Lord," I whispered, "listen to Betsie, not me, because I cannot pray for those men at all."

And it was then that I had the dream. It couldn't have been a real dream because I was not asleep. But a scene was suddenly and unreasonably in my mind. I saw the Grote Markt, half a block away, as clearly as though I were standing there, saw the town hall and St. Bavo's and the fish mart with its stair-stepped façade.

Then as I watched, a kind of odd, old farm wagon —old fashioned and out of place in the middle of a city—came lumbering across the square pulled by four enormous black horses. To my surprise I saw that I myself was sitting in the wagon. And Father too! And Betsie! There were many others, some strangers, some friends. I recognized Pickwick and Toos, Willem and young Peter. All together we were slowly being drawn across the square behind those horses. We couldn't get off the wagon, that was the terrible thing. It was taking us away—far away, I felt—but we didn't want to go. . . .

"Betsie!" I cried, jumping up, pressing my hands to my eyes. "Betsie, I've had such an awful dream!"

I felt her arm around my shoulder. "We'll go down to the kitchen where the light won't show, and we'll make a pot of coffee."

The booming of the bombs was less frequent and farther away as Betsie put on the water. Closer by was the wail of fire alarms and the beep of the hose trucks. Over coffee, standing at the stove, I told Betsie what I had seen.

"Am I imagining things because I'm frightened? But it wasn't like that! It was real. Oh Betsie, was it a kind of vision?"

Betsie's finger traced a pattern on the wooden sink worn smooth by generations of ten Booms. "I don't know," she said softly. "But if God has shown us bad times ahead, it's enough for me that He knows about them. That's why He sometimes shows us things, you know—to tell us that this too is in His hands."

For five days Holland held out against the invader. We kept the shop open, not because anyone was interested in watches, but because people wanted to see Father. Some wanted him to pray for husbands and sons stationed at the borders of the country. Others, it seemed to me, came just to see him sitting there behind his workbench as he had for sixty years and to hear in the ticking clocks a world of order and reason.

I never opened my workbench at all but joined Betsie making coffee and carrying it down. We brought down the portable radio, too, and set it up on the display case. Radio was Haarlem's eyes and ears and very pulse-rate, for after that first night, although we often heard planes overhead, the bombing never came so close again.

The first morning over the radio came instructions that ground-floor windows must be taped. Up and down the Barteljorisstraat shopowners were out on the sidewalk; there was an unaccustomed neighborhood feel as advice, rolls of adhesive, and tales of the night's terror passed from door to door. One store owner, an outspoken anti-Semite, was helping Weil the Jewish furrier put up boards where a pane of glass had shaken loose. The optician next door to us, a silent, withdrawn individual, came over and taped the top of our display window where Betsie and I could not reach.

A few nights later the radio carried the news we

dreaded: the Queen had left. I had not cried the night of the invasion but I cried now, for our country was lost. In the morning the radio announced tanks advancing over the border.

And suddenly all of Haarlem was in the streets. Even Father, whose daily stroll was as predictable as his own clock chimes, broke his routine to go walking at the unheard-of hour of 10:00 A.M. It was as though we wanted to face what was coming together, the whole city united, as though each would draw strength from each other Hollander.

And so the three of us walked, jostled by the crowd, over the bridge on the Spaarne, all the way to the great wild cherry tree whose blossoms each spring formed such a white glory that it was called the Bride of Haarlem. A few faded petals clung now to the new-leafed branches, but most of the Bride's flowers had fallen, forming a wilted carpet beneath us.

A window down the street flew open.

"We've surrendered!"

The procession in the street stopped short. Each told his neighbor what we had all heard for ourselves. A boy of maybe fifteen turned to us with tears rolling down his cheeks. "I would have fought! I wouldn't ever have given up!" Father stooped down to pick up a small bruised petal from the brick pavement; tenderly he inserted it in his buttonhole.

"That is good, my son," he told the youngster. "For Holland's battle has just begun."

But during the first months of occupation, life was not so very unbearable. The hardest thing to get used to was the German uniform everywhere. German trucks and tanks in the street, German spoken in the shops. Soldiers frequently visited our store, for they were getting good wages and watches were among the first things they bought. Toward us they took a superior tone as though we were not-quite-bright children. But among themselves, as I listened to them excitedly discussing their purchases, they seemed like young men anywhere off on a holiday. Most of them selected women's watches for mothers and sweethearts back home.

Indeed, the shop never made so much money as during that first year of the war. With no new shipments coming in, people bought up everything we had in stock, even the *winkeldochters,* the "shop-daughters," merchandise that had lain around so long it seemed part of the furniture. We even sold the green marble mantel clock with the twin brass cupids.

The curfew too, at first, was no hardship for us, since it was originally set at 10:00 P.M., long after we were indoors in any case. What we did object to were the identity cards each citizen was issued. These small folders containing photograph and fingerprints had to be produced on demand. A soldier or a policeman—the Haarlem police were now under the direct control of the German Commandant—might stop a citizen at any time and ask to see his card; it had to be carried in a pouch about the neck. We were issued ration cards too, but at least that first year, the coupons represented food and merchandise actually available in the stores. Each week the newspapers announced what the current coupons could be exchanged for.

That was another thing it was hard to adjust to— newspapers that no longer carried news. Long glowing reports of the successes of the German army on its various fronts. Eulogies of German leaders, denunciations of traitors and saboteurs, appeals for the unity of the "Nordic peoples." But not news that we could trust.

And so we depended again on the radio. Early in the occupation, Haarlemers were ordered to turn in all private sets. Realizing it would look strange if our household produced none at all, we decided to turn in the portable and hide the larger, more powerful instrument in one of the many hollow spaces beneath the old twisting staircase.

Both suggestions were Peter's. He was sixteen at the time of the invasion and shared with other Dutch teenagers the restless energy of anger and impotence. Peter installed the table radio beneath a curve in the stairs just above Father's room and expertly replaced the old boards, while I carried the smaller one down to the big Vroom en Dreesman department store where the radio collection was being made. The army clerk looked at me across the counter.

"Is this the only radio you own?"

"Yes."

He consulted a list in front of him. "Ten Boom, Casper, Ten Boom, Elizabeth, at the same address. Do either of them own a radio?"

I had known from childhood that the earth opened up and the heavens rained fire upon liars, but I met his gaze.

"No."

Only as I walked out of the building did I begin to tremble. Not because for the first time in my life I had told a conscious lie. But because it had been so dreadfully easy.

But we had saved our radio. Every night Betsie or I would remove the stair tread and crouch over the radio, the volume barely audible, while the other one thumped the piano in Tante Jans's room as hard as she could, to hear the news from England. And at first the news over the radio and the news in our captive press was much the same. The German offensive was everywhere victorious. Month after month the Free Dutch broadcasts could only urge us to wait, to have courage, to believe in the counter-offensive which must surely some day be mounted.

The Germans had repaired the bomb damage to the airport and were using it now as a base for air raids against England. Night after night we lay in bed listening to the growl of engines heading west. Occasionally English planes retaliated and then the German fighters might intercept them right over Haarlem.

One night I tossed for an hour while dogfights raged overhead, streaking my patch of sky with fire. At last I heard Betsie stirring in the kitchen and ran down to join her.

She was making tea. She brought it into the dining room where we had covered the windows with heavy black paper and set out the best cups. Somewhere in the night there was an explosion; the dishes in the cupboard rattled. For an hour we sipped our tea and talked, until the sound of planes died away and the sky was silent. I said goodnight to Betsie at the door to Tante Jans's rooms and groped my way up the dark stairs to my own. The fiery light was gone from the sky. I felt for my bed: there was the pillow. Then in the darkness my hand closed over something hard. Sharp too! I felt blood trickle along a finger.

It was a jagged piece of metal, ten inches long.

"Betsie!"

I raced down the stairs with the shrapnel shard in my hand. We went back to the dining room and stared at it in the light while Betsie bandaged my hand. "On your pillow," she kept saying.

"Betsie, if I hadn't heard you in the kitchen——"

But Betsie put a finger on my mouth. "Don't say it, Corrie! There are no 'if's' in God's world. And no places that are safer than other places. The center of His will is our only safety—O Corrie, let us pray that we may always know it!"

The true horror of occupation came over us only slowly. During the first year of German rule there were only minor attacks on Jews in Holland. A rock through the window of a Jewish-owned store. An ugly word scrawled on the wall of a synagogue. It was as though they were trying us, testing the temper of the country. How many Dutchmen would go along with them?

And the answer, to our shame, was many. The National Socialist Bond, the quisling organization of Holland, grew larger and bolder with each month of occupation. Some joined the NSB simply for the benefits: more food, more clothing coupons, the best jobs and housing. But others became NSBers out of conviction. Nazism was a disease to which the Dutch too were susceptible, and those with an anti-Semitic bias fell sick of it first.

On our daily walk Father and I saw the symptoms spread. A sign in a shop window: JEWS WILL NOT BE SERVED. At the entrance to a public park: NO JEWS. On the door of the library. In front of restaurants, theaters, even the concert hall whose alley we knew so much better than its seats.

A synagogue burned down and the fire trucks came. But only to keep the flames from spreading to the buildings on either side.

One noon as Father and I followed our familiar route, the sidewalks were bright with yellow stars sewn to coats and jacket fronts. Men, women, and children wore the six-pointed star with the word *Jood* ("Jew") in the center. We were surprised, as we walked, at how many of the people we had passed each day were Jews. The man who read the *World Shipping News* in the Grote Markt wore a star on his neatly pressed business suit. So did The Bulldog, his jowly face more deeply lined than ever, his voice as he fussed at his dogs, sharp with strain.

Worst were the disappearances. A watch, repaired and ready, hanging on its hook in the back of the shop, month after month. A house in Nollie's block mysteriously deserted, grass growing in the rose garden. One day Mr. Kan's shop up the street did not open. Father knocked on his door as we passed that noon, to see if someone were ill, but there was no answer. The shop remained shuttered, the windows above dark and silent for several weeks. Then, although the shop stayed closed, an NSB family moved into the apartment above.

We never knew whether these people had been spirited away by the Gestapo or gone into hiding before this could happen. Certainly public arrests, with no attempt to conceal what was happening, were becoming more frequent. One day as Father and I were returning from our walk we found the Grote Markt cordoned off by a double ring of police and soldiers. A truck was parked in front of the fish mart; into the back were climbing men, women, and children, all wearing the yellow star. There was no reason we could see why this particular place at this particular time had been chosen.

"Father! Those poor people!" I cried.

The police line opened, the truck moved through. We watched till it turned the corner.

"Those poor people," Father echoed. But to my surprise I saw that he was looking at the soldiers now forming into ranks to march away. "I pity the poor Germans, Corrie. They have touched the apple of God's eye."

We talked often, Father, Betsie and I, about what we could do if a chance should come to help some of our Jewish friends. We knew that Willem had found hiding places at the beginning of the occupation for the German Jews who had been living in his house. Lately he had also moved some of the younger Dutch Jews away from the nursing home. "Not my old people," he would say. "Surely they will not touch my old people."

Willem had addresses. He knew of farms in rural areas where there were few occupying troops. Willem would be the one to ask.

It was a drizzly November morning in 1941, a year and a half after the invasion, as I stepped outside to fold back the shutters, that I saw a group of four German soldiers coming down the Barteljorisstraat. They were wearing combat helmets low over their ears, rifles strapped to their shoulders. I shrank back into the doorway and watched. They were checking shop numbers as they walked. At Weil's Furriers directly across the street the group stopped. One of the soldiers unstrapped his gun and with the butt banged on the door. He was drawing it back for another blow when the door opened and all four pushed inside.

I dashed back through our shop and up to the dining room where Betsie was setting out three places. "Betsie! Hurry! Something awful is happening at Weil's!" We reached the front door again in time to see Mr. Weil backing out of his shop, the muzzle of a gun pressed against his stomach. When he had prodded Mr. Weil a short way down the sidewalk, the soldier went back into the store and slammed the door. Not an arrest, then.

Inside, we could hear glass breaking. Soldiers began carrying out armloads of furs. A crowd was gathering in spite of the early morning hour. Mr. Weil had not moved from the spot on the sidewalk where the soldier had left him.

A window over his head opened and a small shower of clothes rained down on him—pajamas, shirts, underwear. Slowly, mechanically, the old furrier stooped and began to gather up his clothing. Betsie and I ran across the street to help him.

"Your wife!" Betsie whispered urgently. "Where is Mrs. Weil?"

The man only blinked at her.

"You must come inside!" I said, snatching socks and handkerchiefs from the sidewalk. "Quick, with us!"

And we propelled the bewildered old man across to the Beje. Father was in the dining room when we reached it and greeted Mr. Weil without the slightest sign of surprise. His natural manner seemed to relax the furrier a bit. His wife, he said, was visiting a sister in Amsterdam.

"We must find a telephone and warn her not to come home!" Betsie said.

Like most private telephones ours had been disconnected early in the occupation. There were public phones at several places in the city, but of course messages went to a public reception center at the other end. Was it right to connect a family in Amsterdam with the trouble here? And if Mrs. Weil could not come home, where was she to go? Where were the Weils to live? Certainly not with the sister where they could so easily be traced. Father and Betsie and I exchanged glances. Almost with a single breath we said, "Willem."

Again it was not the kind of matter that could be relayed through the public phone system. Someone had to go, and I was the obvious choice. Dutch trains were dirty and overcrowded under the occupation; the trip that should have taken under an hour took nearly three. Willem was not there when I finally reached the big nursing home just after noon, but Tine and their twenty-two-year-old son Kik were. I told them what had happened on the Barteljorisstraat and gave them the Amsterdam address.

"Tell Mr. Weil to be ready as soon as it's dark," Kik said.

But it was nearly 9:00 P.M.—the new curfew hour —before Kik rapped at the alley door. Tucking Mr. Weil's clothing bundle beneath his arm, he led the man away into the night.

It was more than two weeks before I saw Kik again to ask him what had happened. He smiled at me, the broad, slow smile I had loved since he was a child.

"If you're going to work with the underground, Tante Corrie, you must learn not to ask questions."

That was all we ever learned of the Weils. But Kik's words went round and round in my head. "The underground. . . . If you're going to work with the underground." Was Kik working with this secret and illegal group? Was Willem?

We knew of course that there was an underground in Holland—or suspected it. Most cases of sabotage were not reported in our controlled press, but rumors abounded. A factory had been blown up. A train carrying political prisoners had been stopped and seven, or seventeen, or seventy, had made it away. The rumors tended to get more spectacular with each repetition. But always they featured things we believed were wrong in the sight of God. Stealing, lying, murder. Was this what God wanted in times like these? How should a Christian act when evil was in power?

It was about a month after the raid on the fur shop that Father and I, on our usual walk, saw something so very unusual that we both stopped in midstride. Walking toward us along the sidewalk, as so many hundreds of times before, came The Bulldog with his rolling short-legged gait. The bright yellow star had by now ceased to look extraordinary, so what—and then I knew what was wrong. The dogs. The dogs were not with him!

He passed without seeming to see us. With one accord Father and I turned around and walked after him. He turned a number of corners while we grew more and more embarrassed at following him without any real excuse. Although Father and he had tipped their hats to each other for years, we had never spoken and did not even know his name.

At last the man stopped in front of a small second-hand shop, took out a ring of keys, and let himself in. We looked through the window at the cluttered interior. Only a glance showed us that this was more than the usual hodgepodge of bric-a-brac and hollow-seated chairs. Someone who loved beautiful things had chosen everything here. "We must bring Betsie!" I said.

A little bell over the door jingled as we stepped in. Astonishing to see The Bulldog hatless and indoors, unlocking a cash drawer at the rear of the store.

"Permit an introduction, Sir," Father began. "I am Casper ten Boom and this is my daughter, Cornelia."

The Bulldog shook hands and again.I noticed the deep creases in the sagging cheeks. "Harry de Vries," he said.

"Mr. de Vries, we've so often admired your—er—affection for your bulldogs. We hope they are well?"

The squat little man stared from one of us to the other. Slowly the heavy-rimmed eyes filled with tears. "Are they well?" he repeated. "I believe they are well. I hope that they are well. They are dead."

"Dead!" we said together.

"I put the medicine in their bowl with my own hands and I petted them to sleep. My babies. My little ones. If you could only have seen them eat! I waited, you know, till we had enough coupons for meat. They used to have meat all the time."

We stared at him dumbly. "Was it," I ventured at last, "was it because of the rationing?"

With a gesture of his hands the little man invited us into a small room in back of the shop and gave us chairs. "Miss ten Boom, I am a Jew. Who knows when they will come to take me away? My wife too—although she is a Gentile—is in danger because of her marriage."

The Bulldog raised his chin so high his jowls stretched taut. "It is not for ourselves we mind. We are Christians, Cato and I. When we die we will see Jesus, and this is all that matters.

"But I said to Cato, 'What about the dogs? If we are taken away who will feed them? Who will remember their water and their walk? They will wait and we will not come and they will not understand.' No! This way my mind is at ease."

"My dear friend!" Father grasped The Bulldog's hand in both of his. "Now that these dear companions may no longer walk with you, will you not do my daughter and me the great honor of accompanying us?"

But this The Bulldog would not do. "It would put you in danger," he kept saying. He did, however, accept an invitation to come to visit us. "After dark, after dark," he said.

And so one evening the following week Mr. de Vries came to the alley door of the Beje bringing his sweet, shy wife, Cato, and soon she and Harry were almost nightly visitors in Tante Jans's front room.

The Bulldog's chief delight at the Beje, after talking with Father, were the tomes of Jewish theology now housed in Tante Jans's big mahogany case. For he had become a Christian, some forty years earlier, without ceasing in the least to be a loyal Jew. "A completed Jew!" he would tell us smilingly. "A follower of the one perfect Jew."

The books belonged to the rabbi of Haarlem. He had brought them to Father more than a year before: "Just in case I should not be able to care for them—ah —indefinitely." He had waved a bit apologetically at the procession of small boys behind him, each staggering under the weight of several huge volumes. "My little hobby. Book collecting. And yet, old friend, books do not age as you and I do. They will speak still when we are gone, to generations we will never see. Yes, the books must survive."

The rabbi had been one of the first to vanish from Haarlem.

How often it is a small, almost unconscious event that marks a turning point. As arrests of Jews in the street became more frequent, I had begun picking up and delivering work for our Jewish customers myself so that they would not have to venture into the center of town. And so one evening in the early spring of 1942

I was in the home of a doctor and his wife. They were a very old Dutch family: the portraits on the walls could have been a textbook of Holland's history.

The Heemstras and I were talking about the things that were discussed whenever a group of people got together in those days, rationing and the news from England, when down the stairs piped a childish voice.

"Daddy! You didn't tuck us in!"

Dr. Heemstra was on his feet in an instant. With an apology to his wife and me he hurried upstairs and in a minute we heard a game of hide-and-seek going and the shrill laughter of two children.

That was all. Nothing had changed. Mrs. Heemstra continued with her recipe for stretching the tea ration with rose leaves. And yet everything was changed. For in that instant, reality broke through the numbness that had grown in me since the invasion. At any minute there might be a rap on this door. These children, this mother and father, might be ordered to the back of a truck.

Dr. Heemstra came back to the living room and the conversation rambled on. But under the words a prayer was forming in my heart.

"Lord Jesus, I offer myself for Your people. In any way. Any place. Any time."

And then an extraordinary thing happened.

Even as I prayed, that waking dream passed again before my eyes. I saw again those four black horses and the Grote Markt. As I had on the night of the invasion I scanned the passengers drawn so unwillingly behind them. Father, Betsie, Willem, myself—leaving Haarlem, leaving all that was sure and safe—going where?

6

The Secret Room

It was Sunday, May 10, 1942, exactly two years after the fall of Holland. The sunny spring skies, the flowers in the lamppost boxes, did not at all reflect the city's mood. German soldiers wandered aimlessly through the streets, some looking as if they had not yet recovered from a hard Saturday night, some already on the lookout for girls, a few hunting for a place to worship.

Each month the occupation seemed to grow harsher, restrictions more numerous. The latest heartache for Dutchmen was an edict making it a crime to sing the "Wilhelmus," our national anthem.

Father, Betsie, and I were on our way to the Dutch Reformed church in Velsen, a small town not far from Haarlem, where Peter had won the post of organist in competition against forty older and more experienced musicians. The organ at Velsen was one of the finest in the country; though the train seemed slower each time, we went frequently.

Peter was already playing, invisible in the tall organ loft, when we squeezed into the crowded pew. That was one thing the occupation had done for Holland: churches were packed.

After hymns and prayers came the sermon, a good one today, I thought. I wished Peter would pay closer attention. He regarded sermons as interesting only to venerable relics like his mother and me. I had reached fifty that spring, to Peter the age at which life had definitely passed by. I would beg him to remember that death and ultimate issues could come for any of us at any age—especially these days—but he would reply charmingly that he was too fine a musician to die young.

The closing prayers were said. And then, electrically, the whole church sat at attention. Without preamble, every stop pulled out to full volume, Peter was playing the "Wilhelmus"!

Father, at eighty-two, was the first one on his feet. Now everyone was standing. From somewhere in back of us a voice sang out the words. Another joined in, and another. Then we were all singing together, the full voice of Holland singing her forbidden anthem. We sang at the top of our lungs, sang our oneness, our hope, our love for Queen and country. On this anniversary of defeat it seemed almost for a moment that we were victors.

Afterward we waited for Peter at the small side door of the church. It was a long time before he was free to come away with us, so many people wanted to embrace him, to shake his hand and thump his back. Clearly he was enormously pleased with himself.

But now that the moment had passed I was, as usual, angry with him. The Gestapo was certain to hear about it, perhaps already had: their eyes and ears were everywhere. I thought of Nollie, home fixing Sunday dinner for us all. I thought of Peter's brothers and sisters. And Flip—what if he lost the principalship of the school for this? And for what had Peter risked so much? Not for people's lives but for a gesture. For a moment's meaningless defiance.

At Bos en Hoven Straat, however, Peter was a hero as one by one his family made us describe again what had happened. The only members of the household who felt as I did were the two Jewish women staying at Nollie's. One of these was an elderly Austrian lady whom Willem had sent into hiding here. "Katrien," as the family had rechristened her, was posing as the van Woerdens' housemaid—although Nollie confided to me that she had yet so much as to make her own bed. Probably she did not know how, as she came from a wealthy and aristocratic family.

The other woman was a young, blonde, blue-eyed Dutch Jew with flawless false identity papers supplied by the Dutch national underground itself. The papers were so good and Annaliese looked so unlike the Nazi stereotype of a Jew, that she went freely in and out of the house, shopping and helping out at the school, giving herself out to be a friend of the family whose husband had died in the bombing of Rotterdam. Katrien and Annaliese could not understand any more than I could Peter's deliberately doing something which would attract the attention of the authorities.

I spent an anxious afternoon, tensing at the sound of every motor, for only the police, Germans, and NSBers had automobiles nowadays. But the time came to go home to the Beje and still nothing had happened.

I worried two more days, then decided either Peter had not been reported or that the Gestapo had more important things to occupy them. It was Wednesday morning just as Father and I were unlocking our workbenches that Peter's little sister Cocky burst into the shop.

"Opa! Tante Corrie! They came for Peter! They took him away!"

"Who? Where?"

But she didn't know and it was three days before the family learned that he had been taken to the federal prison in Amsterdam.

It was 7:55 in the evening, just a few minutes before the new curfew hour of 8:00. Peter had been in prison for two weeks. Father and Betsie and I were seated around the dining room table, Father replacing watches in their pockets and Betsie doing needlework, our big, black, slightly-Persian cat curled contentedly in her lap. A knock on the alley door made me glance in the window mirror. There in the bright spring twilight stood a woman. She carried a small suitcase and— odd for the time of year—wore a fur coat, gloves, and a heavy veil.

I ran down and opened the door. "Can I come in?" she asked. Her voice was high-pitched in fear.

"Of course." I stepped back. The woman looked over her shoulder before moving into the little hallway.

"My name is Kleermaker. I'm a Jew."

"How do you do?" I reached out to take her bag, but she held onto it. "Won't you come upstairs?"

Father and Betsie stood up as we entered the dining room. "Mrs. Kleermaker, my father and my sister."

"I was about to make some tea!" cried Betsie. "You're just in time to join us!"

Father drew out a chair from the table and Mrs. Kleermaker sat down, still gripping the suitcase. The "tea" consisted of old leaves which had been crushed and reused so often they did little more than color the water. But Mrs. Kleermaker accepted it gratefully, plunging into the story of how her husband had been arrested some months before, her son gone into hiding. Yesterday the S.D.—the political police who worked under the Gestapo—had ordered her to close the family clothing store. She was afraid now to go back to the apartment above it. She had heard that we had befriended a man on this street. . . .

"In this household," Father said, "God's people are always welcome."

"We have four empty beds upstairs," said Betsie. "Your problem will be choosing which one to sleep in!" Then to my astonishment she added, "First though, give me a hand with the tea things."

I could hardly believe my ears. Betsie never let anyone help in her kitchen: "I'm just a fussy old maid," she'd say.

But Mrs. Kleermaker had jumped to her feet with pathetic eagerness and was already stacking plates and cups. . . .

Just two nights later the same scene was repeated. The time was again just before 8:00 on another bright May evening. Again there was a furtive knock at the side door. This time an elderly couple was standing outside.

"Come in!"

It was the same story: the same tight-clutched possessions, the same fearful glance and tentative tread. The story of neighbors arrested, the fear that tomorrow their turn would come.

That night after prayer-time the six of us faced our dilemma. "This location is too dangerous," I told our three guests. "We're half a block from the main police headquarters. And yet I don't know where else to suggest."

Clearly it was time to visit Willem again. So the next day I repeated the difficult trip to Hilversum. "Willem," I said, "we have three Jews staying right at the Beje. Can you get places for them in the country?"

Willem pressed his fingers to his eyes and I noticed suddenly how much white was in his beard. "It's getting harder," he said. "Harder every month. They're feeling the food shortage now even on the farms. I still have addresses, yes, a few. But they won't take anyone without a ration card."

"Without a ration card! But, Jews aren't issued ration cards!"

"I know." Willem turned to stare out the window. For the first time I wondered how he and Tine were feeding the elderly men and women in their care.

"I know," he repeated. "And ration cards can't be counterfeited. They're changed too often and they're too easy to spot. Identity cards are different. I know several printers who do them. Of course you need a photographer."

A photographer? Printers? What was Willem talking about? "Willem, if people need ration cards and there aren't any counterfeit ones, what do they do?"

Willem turned slowly from the window. He seemed to have forgotten me and my particular problem. "Ration cards?" He gestured vaguely. "You steal them."

I stared at this Dutch Reformed clergyman. "Then, Willem, could you steal . . . I mean . . . could you get three stolen cards?"

"No, Corrie! I'm watched! Don't you understand that? Every move I make is watched!"

He put an arm around my shoulder and went on

more kindly, "Even if I can continue working for a while, it will be far better for you to develop your own sources. The less connection with me—the less connection with anyone else—the better."

Joggling home on the crowded train I turned Willem's words over and over in my mind. "Your own sources." That sounded so—so professional. How was I going to find a source of stolen ration cards? Who in the world did I know. . . .

And at that moment a name appeared in my mind.

Fred Koornstra.

Fred was the man who used to read the electric meter at the Beje. The Koornstras had a retarded daughter, now a grown woman, who attended the "church" I had been conducting for the feeble-minded for some twenty years. And now Fred had a new job working for the Food Office. Wasn't it in the department where ration books were issued?

That evening after supper I bumped over the brick streets to the Koornstra house. The tires on my faithful old bicycle had finally given out and I had joined the hundreds clattering about town on metal wheel rims. Each bump reminded me jarringly of my fifty years.

Fred, a bald man with a military bearing, came to the door and stared at me blankly when I said I wanted to talk to him about the Sunday service. He invited me in, closed the door, and said, "Now Corrie, what is it you really came to see me about?"

("Lord," I prayed silently, "if it is not safe to confide in Fred, stop this conversation now before it is too late.")

"I must first tell you that we've had some unexpected company at the Beje. First it was a single woman, then a couple, when I got back this afternoon, another couple." I paused for just an instant. "They are Jews."

Fred's expression did not change.

"We can provide safe places for these people but they must provide something too. Ration cards."

coming to his house each month. What if he were to come to the Beje instead, dressed in his old meterman uniform?

The meter in the Beje was in the back hall at the foot of the stairs. When I got home that afternoon I pried up the tread of the bottom step, as Peter had done higher to hide the radio, and found a hollow space inside. Peter would be proud of me I thought as I worked—and was flooded by a wave of lonesomeness for that brave and cocksure boy. But even he would have to admit, I concluded as I stepped back at last to admire the completed hideaway, that a watchmaker's hand and eye were worth something. The hinge was hidden deep in the wood, the ancient riser undisturbed. I was ridiculously pleased with it.

We had our first test of the system on July 1. Fred was to come in through the shop as he always had, carrying the cards beneath his shirt. He would come at 5:30, when Betsie would have the back hall free of callers. To my horror at 5:25 the shop door opened and in stepped a policeman.

He was a tall man with close-cropped orange-red hair whom I knew by name—Rolf van Vliet—but little else. He had come to the Hundredth Birthday Party, but so had half the force. Certainly he was not one of Betsie's "regulars" for winter morning coffee.

Rolf had brought in a watch that needed cleaning, and he seemed in a mood to talk. My throat had gone dry, but Father chatted cheerfully as he took off the back of Rolf's watch and examined it. What were we going to do? There was no way to warn Fred Koornstra. Promptly at 5:30 the door of the shop opened and in he walked, dressed in his blue workclothes. It seemed to me that his chest was too thick by a foot at least.

With magnificent aplomb Fred nodded to Father, the policeman, and me. "Good evening." Courteous but a little bored.

He strode through the door at the rear of the shop and shut it behind him. My ears strained to hear him lift the secret lid. There! Surely Rolf must have heard

The door behind us opened again. So great was Fred's control that he had not ducked out the alleyway exit, but came strolling back through the shop.

"Good evening," he said again.

"Evening."

He reached the street door and was gone. We had got away with it this time, but somehow, some way, we were going to have to work out a warning system.

For meanwhile, in the weeks since Mrs. Kleermaker's unexpected visit, a great deal had happened at the Beje. Supplied with ration cards, Mrs. Kleermaker and the elderly couple and the next arrivals and the next had found homes in safer locations. But still the hunted people kept coming, and the needs were often more complicated than rations cards and addresses. If a Jewish woman became pregnant where could she go to have her baby? If a Jew in hiding died, how could he be buried?

"Develop your own sources," Willem had said. And from the moment Fred Koornstra's name had popped into my mind, an uncanny realization had been growing in me. We were friends with half of Haarlem! We knew nurses in the maternity hospital. We knew clerks in the Records Office. We knew someone in every business and service in the city.

We didn't know, of course, the political views of all these people. But—and here I felt a strange leaping of my heart—God did! My job was simply to follow His leading one step at a time, holding every decision up to Him in prayer. I knew I was not clever or subtle or sophisticated; if the Beje was becoming a meeting place for need and supply, it was through some strategy far higher than mine.

A few nights after Fred's first "meterman" visit the alley bell rang long after curfew. I sped downstairs expecting another sad and stammering refugee. Betsie and I had already made up beds for four new overnight guests that evening: a Jewish woman and her three small children.

But to my surprise, close against the wall of the dark alley, stood Kik. "Get your bicycle," he ordered with his usual young abruptness. "And put on a sweater. I have some people I want you to meet."

"Now? After curfew?" But I knew it was useless to ask questions. Kik's bicycle was tireless too, the wheel rims swathed in cloth. He wrapped mine also to keep down the clatter, and soon we were pedaling through the blacked-out streets of Haarlem at a speed that would have scared me even in daylight.

"Put a hand on my shoulder," Kik whispered. "I know the way."

We crossed dark side streets, crested bridges, wheeled round invisible corners. At last we crossed a broad canal and I knew we had reached the fashionable suburb of Aerdenhout.

We turned into a driveway beneath shadowy trees. To my astonishment Kik picked up my bicycle and carried both his and mine up the front steps. A serving girl with starched white apron and ruffled cap opened the door. The entrance hall was jammed with bicycles.

Then I saw him. One eye smiling at me, the other at the door, his vast stomach hastening ahead of him. Pickwick!

He led Kik and me into the drawing room where, sipping coffee and chatting in small groups, was the most distinguished-looking group of men and women I had ever seen. But all my attention, that first moment, was on the inexpressibly fragrant aroma in that room. Surely, was it possible, they were drinking real coffee?

Pickwick drew me a cup from the silver urn on the sideboard. It was coffee. After two years, rich, black, pungent Dutch coffee. He poured himself a cup too, dropping in his usual five lumps of sugar as though rationing had never been invented. Another starched and ruffled maid was passing a tray heaped high with cakes.

Gobbling and gulping I trailed about the room after Pickwick, shaking the hands of the people he singled out. They were strange introductions for no names were mentioned, only, occasionally, an address, and "Ask for Mrs. Smit." When I had met my fourth

Smit, Kik explained with a grin, "It's the only last name in the underground."

So this was really and truly the underground! But —where were these people from? I had never laid eyes on any of them. A second later I realized with a shiver down my spine that I was meeting the national group.

Their chief work, I gleaned from bits of conversation, was liaison with England and the Free Dutch forces fighting elsewhere on the continent. They also maintained the underground route through which downed Allied plane crews reached the North Sea coast.

But they were instantly sympathetic with my efforts to help Haarlem's Jews. I blushed to my hair roots to hear Pickwick describe me as "the head of an operation here in this city." A hollow space under the stairs and some haphazard friendships were not an operation. The others here were obviously competent, disciplined, and professional.

But they greeted me with grave courtesy, murmuring what they had to offer as we shook hands. False identity papers. The use of a car with official government plates. Signature forgery.

In a far corner of the room Pickwick introduced me to a frail-appearing little man with a wispy goatee. "Our host informs me," the little man began formally, "that your headquarters building lacks a secret room. This is a danger for all, those you are helping as well as yourselves and those who work with you. With your permission I will pay you a visit in the coming week...."

Years later I learned that he was one of the most famous architects in Europe. I knew him only as Mr. Smit.

Just before Kik and I started our dash back to the Beje, Pickwick slipped an arm through mine. "My dear, I have good news. I understand that Peter is about to be released."...

So he was, three days later, thinner, paler, and not a whit daunted by his two months in a concrete cell. Nollie, Tine, and Betsie used up a month's sugar ration baking cakes for his welcome home party.

And one morning soon afterward the first customer in the shop was a small thin-bearded man named Smit. Father took his jeweler's glass from his eye. If there was one thing he loved better than making a new acquaintance, it was discovering a link with an old one.

"Smit," he said eagerly. "I know several Smits in Amsterdam. Are you by any chance related to the family who——"

"Father," I interrupted, "this is the man I told you about. He's come to, ah, inspect the house."

"A building inspector? Then you must be the Smit with offices in the Grote Hout Straat. I wonder that I haven't——"

"Father!" I pleaded, "he's not a building inspector, and his name is not Smit."

"Not Smit?"

Together Mr. Smit and I attempted to explain, but Father simply could not understand a person's being called by a name not his own. As I led Mr. Smit into the back hall we heard him musing to himself, "I once knew a Smit on Koning Straat. . . ."

Mr. Smit examined and approved the hiding place for ration cards beneath the bottom step. He also pronounced acceptable the warning system we had worked out. This was a triangle-shaped wooden sign advertising "Alpina Watches" which I had placed in the dining room window. As long as the sign was in place, it was safe to enter.

But when I showed him a cubby hole behind the corner cupboard in the dining room, he shook his head. Some ancient redesigning of the house had left a crawl space in that corner and we'd been secreting jewelry, silver coins, and other valuables there since the start of the occupation. Not only the rabbi had brought us his library but other Jewish families had brought their treasures to the Beje for safekeeping. The space was large enough that we had believed a person could crawl in there if necessary, but Mr. Smit dismissed it without a second glance.

"First place they'd look. Don't bother to change it though. It's only silver. We're interested in saving people, not things."

He started up the narrow corkscrew stairs, and as he mounted so did his spirits. He paused in delight at the odd-placed landings, pounded on the crooked walls, and laughed aloud as the floor levels of the two old houses continued out of phase.

"What an impossibility!" he said in an awestruck voice. "What an improbable, unbelievable, unpredictable impossibility! Miss ten Boom, if all houses were constructed like this one, you would see before you a less worried man."

At last, at the very top of the stairs, he entered my room and gave a little cry of delight. "This is it!" he exclaimed.

"You want your hiding place as high as possible," he went on eagerly. "Gives you the best chance to reach it while the search is on below." He leaned out the window, craning his thin neck, the little faun's beard pointing this way and that.

"But . . . this is my bedroom. . . ."

Mr. Smit paid no attention. He was already measuring. He moved the heavy, wobbly old wardrobe away from the wall with surprising ease and pulled my bed into the center of the room. "This is where the false wall will go!" Excitedly he drew out a pencil and drew a line along the floor thirty inches from the back wall. He stood up and gazed at it moodily.

"That's as big as I dare," he said. "It will take a cot mattress, though. Oh yes. Easily!"

I tried again to protest, but Mr. Smit had forgotten I existed. Over the next few days he and his workmen were in and out of our house constantly. They never knocked. At each visit each man carried in something. Tools in a folded newspaper. A few bricks in a briefcase. "Wood!" he exclaimed when I ventured to wonder if a wooden wall would not be easier to build. "Wood sounds hollow. Hear it in a minute. No, no. Brick's the only thing for false walls."

After the wall was up, the plasterer came, then the carpenter, finally the painter. Six days after he had begun, Mr. Smit called Father, Betsie, and me to see.

We stood in the doorway and gaped. The smell of fresh paint was everywhere. But surely nothing in this room was newly painted! All four walls had that streaked and grimy look that old rooms got in coal-burning Haarlem. The ancient molding ran unbroken around the ceiling, chipped and peeling here and there, obviously undisturbed for a hundred and fifty years. Old water stains streaked the back wall, a wall that even I who had lived half a century in this room, could scarcely believe was not the original, but set back a precious two-and-a-half feet from the true wall of the building.

Built-in bookshelves ran along this false wall, old, sagging shelves whose blistered wood bore the same water stains as the wall behind them. Down in the far lefthand corner, beneath the bottom shelf, a sliding panel, two feet high and two wide, opened into the secret room.

Mr. Smit stooped and silently pulled this panel up. On hands and knees Betsie and I crawled into the narrow room behind it. Once inside we could stand up, sit, or even stretch out one at a time on the single mattress. A concealed vent, cunningly let into the real wall, allowed air to enter from outside.

"Keep a water jug there," said Mr. Smit, crawling in behind us. "Change the water once a week. Hardtack and vitamins keep indefinitely. Anytime there is anyone in the house whose presence is unofficial, all possessions except the clothes actually on his back must be stored in here."

Dropping to our knees again we crawled single file out into my bedroom. "Move back into this room," he told me. "Everything exactly as before."

With his fist he struck the wall above the bookshelves.

"The Gestapo could search for a year," he said. "They'll never find this one."

7

Eusie

Peter was home, yet he was not safe, any more than any healthy young male was safe. In Germany the munitions factories were desperate for workers. Without warning soldiers would suddenly surround a block of buildings and sweep through them, herding every male between sixteen and thirty into trucks for transport. This method of lightning search and seizure was called "the razzia," and every family with young men lived in dread of it.

Flip and Nollie had rearranged their kitchen to give them an emergency hiding place as soon as the razzias started. There was a small potato cellar beneath the kitchen floor: they enlarged the trapdoor letting into it, put a large rug on top of it and moved the kitchen table to stand on this spot.

Since Mr. Smit's work at the Beje I realized that this hole under the kitchen floor was a totally inadequate hiding place. Too low in the house for one thing, and probably as Mr. Smit would say, "the first place they'd look." However, it was not a sustained search by trained people it was intended for, but a swoop by soldiers, a place to get out of sight for half an hour. And for that, I thought, it was probably sufficient. . . .

It was Flip's birthday when the razzia came to that quiet residential street of identical attached homes. Father, Betsie, and I had come early with a quarter-pound of real English tea from Pickwick.

Nollie, Annaliese, and the two older girls were not yet back when we arrived. A shipment of men's shoes had been announced by one of the department stores and Nollie had determined to get Flip a pair "if I have to stand in line all day."

We were chatting in the kitchen with Cocky and Katrien when all at once Peter and his older brother, Bob, raced into the room, their faces white. "Soldiers! Quick! They're two doors down and coming this way!"

They jerked the table back, snatched away the rug and tugged open the trapdoor. Bob lowered himself first, lying down flat, and Peter tumbled in on top of him. We dropped the door shut, yanked the rug over it and pulled the table back in place. With trembling hands Betsie, Cocky, and I threw a long tablecloth over it and started laying five places for tea.

There was a crash in the hall as the front door burst open and a smaller crash close by as Cocky dropped a teacup. Two uniformed Germans ran into the kitchen, rifles leveled.

"Stay where you are. Do not move."

We heard boots storming up the stairs. The soldiers glanced around disgustedly at this room filled with women and one old man. If they had looked closer at Katrien she would surely have given herself away: her face was a mask of terror. But they had other things on their minds.

"Where are your men?" the shorter soldier asked Cocky in clumsy, thick-accented Dutch.

"These are my aunts," she said, "and this is my grandfather. My father is at his school, and my mother is shopping and——"

"I didn't ask about the whole tribe!" the man exploded in German. Then in Dutch: "Where are your brothers?"

Cocky stared at him a second, then dropped her eyes. My heart stood still. I knew how Nollie had trained her children—but surely, surely now of all times a lie was permissible!

"Do you have brothers?" the officer asked again.

"Yes," Cocky said softly. "We have three."

"How old are they?"

"Twenty-one, nineteen, and eighteen."

Upstairs we heard the sounds of doors opening and shutting, the scrape of furniture dragged from walls.

"Where are they now?" the soldier persisted.

Cocky leaned down and began gathering up the broken bits of cup. The man jerked her upright. "Where are your brothers?"

"The oldest one is at the Theological College. He doesn't get home most nights because——"

"What about the other two?"

Cocky did not miss a breath.

"Why, they're under the table."

Motioning us all away from it with his gun, the soldier seized a corner of the cloth. At a nod from him the taller man crouched with his rifle cocked. Then he flung back the cloth.

At last the pent-up tension exploded: Cocky burst into spasms of high hysterical laughter. The soldiers whirled around. Was this girl laughing at them?

"Don't take us for fools!" the short one snarled. Furiously he strode from the room and minutes later the entire squad trooped out—not, unfortunately, before the silent soldier had spied and pocketed our precious packet of tea.

It was a strange dinner party that evening, veering as it did from heartfelt thanksgiving to the nearest thing to a bitter argument our close-knit family had ever had. Nollie stuck by Cocky, insisting she would have answered the same way. "God honors truth-telling with perfect protection!"

Peter and Bob, from the viewpoint of the trapdoor, weren't so sure. And neither was I. I had never had Nollie's bravery—no, nor her faith either. But I could spot illogic. "And it isn't logical to *say* the truth and *do* a lie! What about Annaliese's false papers—and that maid's uniform on Katrien?"

" 'Set a watch, O Lord, before my mouth,' " Nollie quoted. " 'Keep the door of my lips.' Psalm One Hundred Forty-one!" she finished triumphantly.

"All right, what about the radio? I had to lie with my lips to keep that!"

"And yet whatever came from your lips, Corrie, I am sure it was spoken in love!" Father's kindly voice reproached my flushed face.

Love. How did one show it? How could God Himself show truth and love at the same time in a world like this?

By dying. The answer stood out for me sharper and chiller than it ever had before that night: the shape of a Cross etched on the history of the world.

It was getting harder and harder to find safe homes in the country for the scores of Jews who were passing through our underground station by early 1943. Even with ration cards and forged papers there were not enough places for them all. Sooner or later we knew we were going to have to start hiding people here in the city. How sad that the very first should have been the dearest of all.

It was in the middle of a busy morning in the shop when Betsie slipped through the workshop door. "Harry and Cato are here!" she said.

We were surprised. Harry had never come to the Beje in the daytime because he feared his yellow star would cause awkwardness for us. Father and I hurried behind Betsie up the stairs.

Harry de Vries related the familiar story. The visit the evening before from an NSB quisling. The announcement that the shop was confiscated. Who cared if Harry were a Christian? Any Jew can convert to avoid trouble, the NSBer said. This morning the appearance of a uniformed German to make it official: the shop was closed "in the interest of national security."

"But—if I am a security risk," said poor Harry, "surely they will not stop with taking my store."

Doubtless they would not. But just then there was absolutely no available place outside the city. In fact the only underground address we had at the moment was the home of a woman named De Boer, not four blocks from the Beje.

That afternoon I knocked on Mrs. De Boer's door. She was a dumpy woman dressed in a blue cotton smock and bedroom slippers. We supplied Mrs. De Boer with ration cards and had arranged an emergency appendectomy from there. She showed me the living quarters in her attic. Eighteen Jews were staying there, most of them in their early twenties. "They've been cooped up too long," she said. "They sing and dance and make all sorts of noise."

"If you think one more couple is too much. . . ."

"No. No . . . how can I turn them away? Bring them tonight. We'll manage."

And so Harry and Cato began their life at Mrs. De Boer's, living in one of the narrow dormers in the attic. Betsie went every day to take them some home-made bread, a bit of tea, a slice of sausage. But Betsie's main concern was not for the morale of Harry and Cato, it was for their very lives.

"They're in danger, you know," she told Father and me. "It's true that these young people are at the bursting point. This afternoon they were making such a commotion I could hear them down on the street!"

There were other concerns, that bitter gray winter. Though there was little snow, the cold came early and stayed late, and fuel was scarce. Here and there in the parks and along the canals trees began to disappear as people cut them down to heat cookstoves and fireplaces.

The damp unheated rooms were hardest on the very young and the very old. One morning Christoffels did not appear for Bible reading in the dining room, nor later in the workshop. His landlady found him dead in his bed, the water in his washbasin frozen solid. We buried the old clockmaker in the splendid suit and vest he had worn to the Hundredth Birthday Party, six years and another lifetime ago.

Spring came slowly. We celebrated my fifty-first birthday with a little party in the de Vrieses' alcove home.

It was one week later, April 22, that Cato arrived alone at the Beje. Inside the door she burst into tears. "Those foolish young people went crazy! Last night eight of them left the house. Naturally they were stopped and arrested—the boys hadn't even bothered to cut their sideburns. The Gestapo didn't have any trouble getting information out of them."

The house had been raided, she said, at 4:00 that morning. Cato was released when they discovered she was not Jewish. "But everyone else—Harry, Mrs. De Boer too—oh what will become of them!"

For the next three days Cato was at the Haarlem police station from early morning until curfew, pestering Dutch and Germans alike to let her see her husband. When they sent her away, she stepped across the street and waited silently on the sidewalk.

Friday just before the noon closing when the shop was crowded a policeman pushed open the street door, hesitated, then continued back into the rear room. It was Rolf van Vliet, the officer who had been here when our ration cards were first delivered. He took off his cap and I noticed again that startling orange-red hair.

"This watch is still not keeping time," Rolf said. He took off his wristwatch, placed it on my workbench, and leaned forward. Was he saying something? It was all I could do to hear. "Harry de Vries will be taken to Amsterdam tomorrow. If you want to see him, come promptly at three this afternoon." And then, "Do you see? The second hand still hesitates at the top of the dial."

At three that afternoon Cato and I stepped through the tall double doors of the police station. The policeman on duty at the guard post was Rolf himself.

"Come with me," he said gruffly. He led us through a door and along a high-ceilinged corridor. At a locked metal gate he stopped. "Wait here," Rolf said.

Someone on the other side opened the gate and Rolf passed through. He was gone several minutes. Then the door opened again and we were face to face with Harry. Rolf stood back as Harry took Cato into his arms.

"You have only a few seconds," whispered Rolf.

They drew apart, looking into each other's eyes. "I'm sorry," said Rolf. "He'll have to go back." Harry kissed his wife. Then he took my hand and shook it solemnly. Tears filled our eyes. For the first time Harry spoke. "I shall use this place—wherever they're taking us," he said. "It will be my witness stand for Jesus."

Rolf took Harry by the elbow.

"We will pray for you many times every day, Harry!" I cried as the gate swung shut.

An instinct which I shared with no one told me that this was the last time I would ever see our friend The Bulldog.

That night we held a meeting about Rolf: Betsie and I and the dozen or so teenage boys and girls who acted as messengers for this work. If Rolf had risked his own safety to tell us about Harry's transport, perhaps he should work with us.

"Lord Jesus," I said aloud, "this could be a danger for all of us and for Rolf too." But even with the words came a flood of assurance about this man. How long, I wondered, would we be led by this Gift of Knowledge.

I assigned one of our younger boys to follow Rolf home from work next day and learn where he lived. The older boys, the ones susceptible to the factory draft, we sent out only after dark now, and then most often dressed as girls.

The following week I visited Rolf at home. "You have no idea how much it meant to see Harry," I said when I was safe inside. "How can we repay this kindness?"

Rolf ran his hands through his bright hair. "Well, there is a way. The cleaning woman at the jail has a teenage son and they've almost picked him up twice. She's desperate to find another place for him to live."

"Perhaps I can help," I said. "Do you think she could find that her watch needs repairing?"

The next day Toos came to the door of Tante Jans's room where I was talking with two new volunteers for our work. More and more I was leaving the watch shop to her and Father as our underground "operation" required more time. "There's a funny looking little woman downstairs," Toos said. "She says her name is Mietje. She says to tell you 'Rolf sent her.'"

I met Mietje in the dining room. The hand that I shook was ridged and leathery from years of scrubbing floors. A tuft of hair grew from her chin. "I understand," I said, "that you have a son you're very proud of."

"Oh yes!" Mietje's face lit up at the mention of him.

I took the bulky old alarm clock she had brought with her. "Come for your clock tomorrow afternoon and I'll hope to have good news."

That night we listened to our messengers' reports. The long, cruel winter had opened up places at several addresses. There was a place on a nearby tulip farm, but the farmer had decided he must be paid for the risk he was taking. We would have to provide a fee—in silver rijksdaalders, not paper money—plus an additional ration card. It didn't happen often that a "host" would require money for his services; when one did we paid gladly.

When Mietje appeared the following morning I took a small banknote from my purse and tore off a corner. "This is for your son," I said. "Tonight he is to go to the Gravenstenenbrug. There is a tree stump right next to the bridge—they cut down the tree last winter. He is to wait beside it, looking into the canal. A man will come up and ask if he has change for a bankbill. Your son is to match the missing corner, and then follow this man without asking questions."

Betsie came into the dining room as Mietje was grasping my hand in her two sandpaper ones. "I'll make it up to you! Somehow, some day, I'll find a way to repay you!"

Betsie and I exchanged smiles. How could this simple little soul help with the kind of need we faced?

And so the work grew. As each new need arose, a new answer was found, too. Through Pickwick, for example, we met the man at the central telephone exchange whose department handled orders to connect and disconnect lines. With a little rewiring and juggling of numbers, he soon had our instrument in operation.

What a day it was when the old wall phone in the rear hall jangled joyously for the first time in three years! And how we needed it! For by now there were eighty Dutchmen—elderly women and middle-aged men along with our teenagers—working in "God's underground" as we sometimes laughingly called ourselves. Most of these people never saw one another; we kept face-to-face contacts as few as possible. But all knew the Beje. It was headquarters, the center of a spreading web: the knot where all threads crossed.

But if the telephone was a boon, it was also a fresh risk—as was each added worker and connection. We set the phone's ring as low as we could and still hear it; but who might happen to be passing through the hall when it rang?

For that matter how long would curious eyes up and down the street continue to believe that one small watch shop was quite as busy as it appeared? It was true that repair work was in demand: plenty of legitimate customers still passed in and out. But there was altogether too much coming and going, especially in the early evening. The curfew was now 7:00 P.M., which in spring and summer left no nighttime hours at all in which workers could move legally through the streets.

It was an hour and a half before that time on the first of June, 1943, and I was thinking of all this as I sat impatiently behind my workbench. Six workers still not back and so many loose ends to tie up before 7:00. For one thing, being the first of the month, Fred Koornstra should be arriving with the new ration cards. The hundred cards which had seemed such an extravagant request a year ago were now far too few for our needs and Fred was only one of our suppliers, some of the stolen cards coming from as far away as Delft. How long can we go on this way? I wondered. How long can we continue to count on this strange protection?

My thoughts were interrupted by the side entrance bell. Betsie and I reached it at the same instant.

In the alley stood a young Jewish woman cradling a tiny blanketed bundle in her arms. Behind her I recognized an intern from the maternity hospital.

The baby, he told us in the hallway, had come prematurely. He had kept mother and child in the hospital longer than permitted already because she had nowhere else to go.

Betsie held out her arms for the baby and at that moment Fred Koornstra opened the door from the shop. He blinked a moment at seeing people in the hall, then turned with great deliberation to the meter on the wall. The young doctor, seeing what he took to be an actual meterman, turned as white as his own collar. I longed to reassure both him and Fred, but knew that the fewer of the group who knew one another the safer it was for all. The poor intern gulped a hasty goodbye while Betsie and I got mother and baby up to the dining room and closed the door on Fred and his work.

Betsie poured a bowl of the soup she had cooked for supper from a much-boiled bone. The baby began a thin high wail; I rocked it while the mother ate. Here was a new danger, a tiny fugitive too young to know the folly of making a noise. We had had many Jewish children over a night or several nights at the Beje and even the youngest had developed the uncanny silence of small hunted things. But at two weeks this one had yet to discover how unwelcoming was its world: we would need a place for them far removed from other houses.

And the very next morning into the shop walked the perfect solution. He was a clergyman friend of ours, pastor in a small town outside of Haarlem, and his home was set back from the street in a large wooded park.

"Good morning, Pastor," I said, the pieces of the puzzle falling together in my mind. "Can we help you?"

I looked at the watch he had brought in for repair. It required a very hard-to-find spare part. "But for you, Pastor, we will do our very best. And now I have something I want to confess."

The pastor's eyes clouded. "Confess?"

I drew him out the back door of the shop and up the stairs to the dining room.

"I confess that I too am searching for something." The pastor's face was now wrinkled with a frown. "Would you be willing to take a Jewish mother and her baby into your home? They will almost certainly be arrested otherwise."

Color drained from the man's face. He took a step back from me. "Miss ten Boom! I do hope you're not involved with any of this illegal concealment and undercover business. It's just not safe! Think of your father! And your sister—she's never been strong!"

On impulse I told the pastor to wait and ran upstairs. Betsie had put the newcomers in Willem's old room, the farthest from windows on the street. I asked the mother's permission to borrow the infant: the little thing weighed hardly anything in my arms.

Back in the dining room I pulled back the coverlet from the baby's face.

There was a long silence. The man bent forward, his hand in spite of himself reaching for the tiny fist curled round the blanket. For a moment I saw compassion and fear struggle in his face. Then he straightened. "No. Definitely not. We could lose our lives for that Jewish child!"

Unseen by either of us, Father had appeared in the doorway. "Give the child to me, Corrie," he said.

Father held the baby close, his white beard brushing its cheek, looking into the little face with eyes as blue and innocent as the baby's own. At last he looked up at the pastor. "You say we could lose our lives for this child. I would consider that the greatest honor that could come to my family."

The pastor turned sharply on his heels and walked out of the room.

So we had to accept a bad solution to our problem. On the edge of Haarlem was a truck farm which hid refugees for short periods of time. It was not a good location, since the Gestapo had been there already. But there was nowhere else available on short notice. Two workers took the woman and child there that afternoon.

A few weeks later we heard that the farm had been raided. When the Gestapo came to the barn where the woman was hidden, not the baby but the mother began to shriek with hysteria. She, the baby, and her protectors were all taken.

We never learned what happened to them.

Although we had a friend at the telephone exchange, we could never be sure that our line was not tapped. So we developed a system for coding our underground messages in terms of watches.

"We have a woman's watch here that needs repairing. But I can't find a mainspring. Do you know who might have one?" (We have a Jewish woman in need of a hiding place and we can't find one among our regular contacts.)

"I have a watch here with a face that's causing difficulty. One of the numbers has worked loose and it's holding back the hand. Do you know anyone who does this kind of repair work?" (We have a Jew here whose features are especially Semitic. Do you know anyone who would be willing to take an extra risk?)

"I'm sorry, but the child's watch you left with us is not repairable. Do you have the receipt?" (A Jewish child has died in one of our houses. We need a burial permit.)

One morning in the middle of June the telephone rang with this message. "We have a man's watch here that's giving us trouble. We can't find anyone to repair it. For one thing, the face is very old-fashioned. . . ."

So, a Jew whose features gave him away. This was the hardest kind of person to place. "Send the watch over and I'll see what we can do in our own shop," I said.

Promptly at 7:00 that evening the side doorbell rang. I glanced at the mirror in the window of the dining room where we were still sitting over tea of rose leaves and cherry stems. Even from the side of his head I could tell that this was our old-fashioned watch. His form, his clothes, his very stance were music-hall-comedy Jewish.

I ran down to the door. "Do come in."

The smiling slender man in his early thirties, with his protruding ears, balding head, and miniscule glasses, gave an elaborate bow. I liked him instantly.

Once the door was closed he took out a pipe. "The very first thing I must ask," he said, "is whether or not I should leave behind my good friend the pipe? Meyer Mossel and his pipe are not easily separated. But for you, kind lady, should the smell get into your drapes, I would gladly say goodbye to my friend nicotine."

I laughed. Of all the Jews who had come to our house this was the first to enter gaily and with a question about our own comfort.

"Of course you must keep your pipe!" I said. "My father smokes a cigar—when he can get one these days."

"Ah! These days!" Meyer Mossel raised arms and shoulders in an enormous shrug. "What do you expect, when the barbarians have overrun the camp?"

I took him up to the dining room. There were seven seated at the table, a Jewish couple waiting placement and three underground workers in addition to Father and Betsie. Meyer Mossel's eyes went straight to Father.

"But," he cried. "One of the Patriarchs!"

It was exactly the right thing to say to Father. "But," he returned with equal good humor, "a brother of the Chosen People!"

"Can you recite the One Hundred and Sixty-sixth Psalm, Opa?" Meyer said.

Father beamed. Of course there is no Psalm 166; the Psalter stops with 150. It must be a joke, and nothing could please Father better than a scriptural joke. "The Hundred and Sixty-sixth Psalm?"

"Shall I recite it for you?" Meyer asked.

Father gave a bow of assent and Meyer plunged into verse.

"But that's Psalm One Hundred!" Father interrupted. And then his face lit up. Of course! Psalm 66 started with the identical words. Meyer had asked for the One Hundredth *and* the Sixty-sixth Psalm. For the rest of the evening I could hear Father chuckling, "Psalm One Hundred and Sixty-six!"

At 8:45 Father took the old brass-bound Bible from its shelf. He opened to the reading in Jeremiah where we had left off the night before, then with sudden inspiration passed the Bible across the table to Meyer.

"I would consider it an honor if you would read for us tonight," Father said.

Lifting the Book lovingly, Meyer rose to his feet. From a pocket came a small prayer cap, and then, from deep in his throat, half-sung, half-pleaded, came the words of the ancient prophet, so feelingly and achingly that we seemed to hear the cry of the Exile itself.

Meyer Mossel, he told us afterward, had been cantor in the synagogue in Amsterdam. For all his lightheartedness he had suffered much. Most of his family had been arrested; his wife and children were in hiding on a farm in the north which had declined to accept Meyer—"for obvious reasons," he said with a grimace at his own unmistakable features.

And gradually it dawned on all of us that this endearing man was at the Beje to stay. It was certainly not an ideal place, but for Meyer nothing could be ideal right now.

"At least," I told him one evening, "your name doesn't have to give you away too." Ever since the days when Willem was studying church history, I had remembered the venerable fourth-century church father, Eusebius.

"I think we'll call you Eusebius," I decided. We were sitting in Tante Jans's front room with Kik and some other young men who had made us a delivery of forged travel-permits too late to get home by curfew.

Meyer leaned back and stared at the ceiling pensively. He took his pipe out of his mouth. "Eusebius Mossel," he said, tasting the words. "No, it doesn't sound quite right. Eusebius Gentile Mossel."

We all laughed. "Don't be a goose," Betsie said. "You must change both names!"

Kik looked slyly at Father. "Opa! How about Smit? That seems a popular name these days."

"It does seem so!" said Father, not catching the joke. "Extraordinarily popular!"

And Eusebius Smit it became.

Changing Meyer's name was easy—at once he became "Eusie." But getting Eusie to eat non-kosher food was something else. The problem of course was that we were grateful for food of any kind: we stood in line for hours, this third year of the occupation, to get whatever was available.

One day the paper announced that coupon number four was good for pork sausage. It was the first meat we'd had in weeks. Lovingly Betsie prepared the feast, saving every drop of fat for flavoring other foods later.

"Eusie," Betsie said as she carried the steaming casserole of pork and potatoes to the table, "the day has come."

Eusie knocked the ashes out of his pipe and considered his plight out loud. He, who had always eaten kosher, he, the oldest son of an oldest son of a respected family, in fact, he Meyer Mossel Eusebius Smit, was seriously being asked to eat pork.

Betsie placed a helping of sausage and potato before him. "Bon appetit."

The tantalizing odor reached our meat-starved palates. Eusie wet his lips with his tongue. "Of course," he said, "there's a provision for this in the Talmud." He speared the meat with his fork, bit hungrily and rolled his eyes heavenward in pure pleasure. "And I'm going to start hunting for it, too," he said, "just as soon as dinner's over."

As if Eusie's arrival had broken down a last hesitation, within a week there were three new permanent additions to the household. First there was Jop, our current apprentice, whose daily trip from his parents' home in the suburbs had twice nearly ended in seizure for the factory transport. The second time it happened his parents asked if he could stay at the Beje and we agreed. The other two were Henk, a young lawyer, and Loendert, a schoolteacher. Leendert made an especially important contribution to the secret life of the Beje. He installed our electric warning system.

By now I had learned to make the nighttime trip out to Pickwick's almost as skillfully as could Kik. One evening when I had gratefully accepted a cup of coffee, my wall-eyed friend sat me down for a lecture.

"Cornelia," he said, settling his bulk on a velvet chair too small for him, "I understand you have no alarm system in your house. This is purest folly. Also I am given to believe that you are not carrying on regular drills for your guests."

I was always amazed at how well Pickwick knew what went on at the Beje.

"You know that a raid may come any day," Pickwick continued. "I don't see how you can avoid one. Scores of people in and out—and an NSB agent living over Kan's up the street.

"Your secret room is no good to you if people can't get to it in time. I know this Leendert. He's a good man and a very passable electrician. Get him to put a buzzer in every room with a door or a window on the street. Then hold practice drills until your people can disappear into that room without a trace in less than a minute. I'll send someone to get you started."

Leendert did the electrical work that weekend. He installed a buzzer near the top of the stairs—loud enough to be heard all over the house but not outside. Then he placed buttons to sound the buzzer at every vantage point where trouble might first be spotted. One button went beneath the dining room windowsill, just below the mirror which gave onto the side door. Another went in the downstairs hall just inside that door and a third inside the front door on the Barteljorisstraat. He also put a button behind the counter in the shop and one in each workbench as well as beneath the windows in Tante Jans's rooms.

We were ready for our first trial run. The four unacknowledged members of our household were already climbing up to the secret room two times a day: in the morning to store their night clothes, bedding and toilet articles, and in the evening to put away their day things. Members of our group, too, who had to spend the night, kept raincoats, hats, anything they had brought with them, in that room. Altogether that made a good deal of traffic in and out of my small bedroom— smaller now indeed by nearly a yard. Many nights my last waking sight would be Eusie in long robe and tasseled nightcap, handing his day clothes through the secret panel.

But the purpose of the drills was to see how rapidly people could reach the room at any hour of the day or night without prior notice. A tall sallow-faced young man arrived from Pickwick one morning to teach me how to conduct the drills.

"Smit!" Father exclaimed when the man introduced himself. "Truly it's most astonishing! We've had one Smit after another here lately. Now you bear a great resemblance to. . . ."

Mr. Smit disentangled himself gently from Father's genealogical inquiries and followed me upstairs.

"Mealtimes," he said. "That's a favorite hour for a raid. Also the middle of the night." He strode from room to room pointing everywhere to evidence that more than three people lived in the house. "Watch wastebaskets and ashtrays."

He paused in a bedroom door. "If the raid comes at night they must not only take their sheets and blankets but get the mattress turned. That's the S.D.'s favorite trick—feeling for a warm spot on a bed."

Mr. Smit stayed for lunch. There were eleven of us at the table that day, including a Jewish lady who had arrived the night before and a Gentile woman and her small daughter, members of our underground, who acted as "escorts." The three of them were leaving for a farm in Brabant right after lunch.

Betsie had just passed around a stew so artfully prepared you scarcely missed the meat when, without warning, Mr. Smit leaned back in his chair and pushed the button below the window.

Above us the buzzer sounded. People sprang to their feet, snatching up glasses and plates, scrambling for the stairs, while the cat clawed halfway up the curtain in consternation. Cries of "Faster!" "Not so loud!" and "You're spilling it!" reached us as Father, Betsie, and I hastily rearranged table and chairs to look like a lunch for three in progress.

"No, leave my place," Mr. Smit instructed. "Why shouldn't you have a guest for lunch? The lady and the little girl could have stayed too."

At last we were seated again and silence reigned upstairs.

The whole process had taken four minutes.

A little later we were all gathered again around the dining room table. Mr. Smit set out before him the incriminating evidence he had found: two spoons and a piece of carrot on the stairs, pipe ashes in an "unoccupied" bedroom. Everyone looked at Eusie who blushed to the tips of his large ears.

"Also those," he pointed to the hats of mother and daughter still dangling from the pegs on the dining room wall. "If you have to hide, stop and think what you arrived with. Besides which, you're all simply too slow."

The next night I sounded the alarm again and this time we shaved a minute thirty-three seconds off our run. By our fifth trial we were down to two minutes. We never did achieve Pickwick's ideal of under a minute, but with practice we learned to jump up from whatever we were doing and get those who had to hide into the secret room in seventy seconds. Father, Toos, and I worked on "stalling techniques" which we would use if the Gestapo came through the shop door; Betsie invented a similar strategy for the side door. With these delaying tactics we hoped we could gain a life-saving seventy ticks of a second hand.

Because the drills struck so close to the fear which haunted each of our guests—never spoken, always present—we tried to keep these times from becoming altogether serious. "Like a game!" we'd tell each other: "a race to beat our own record!" One of our group owned the bakery in the next street. Early in the month I would deposit a supply of sugar coupons with him. Then when I decided it was time for a drill I would go to him for a bag of cream puffs—an inexpressible treat in those sweetless days—to be secreted in my workbench and brought out as a reward for a successful practice.

Each time the order of cream puffs was larger. For by now, in addition to the workers whom we wanted to initiate into the system, we had three more permanent boarders: Thea Dacosta, Meta Monsanto, and Mary Itallie.

Mary Itallie, at seventy-six the oldest of our guests, was also the one who posed the greatest problem. The moment Mary stepped through our door I heard the asthmatic wheezing which had made other hosts unwilling to take her in.

Since her ailment compromised the safety of the others, we took up the problem in caucus. The seven most concerned—Eusie, Jop, Henk, Leendert, Meta, Thea, and Mary herself—joined Father, Betsie, and me in Tante Jans's front room.

"There is no sense in pretending," I began. "Mary has a difficulty—especially after climbing stairs—that could put you all in danger."

In the silence that followed, Mary's labored breathing seemed especially loud.

"Can I speak?" Eusie asked.

"Of course."

"It seems to me that we're all here in your house because of some difficulty or other. We're the orphan children—the ones nobody else wanted. Any one of us is jeopardizing all the others. I vote that Mary stay."

"Good," said lawyer Henk, "let's put it to the vote."

Hands began rising but Mary was struggling to speak. "Secret ballots," she brought out at last. "No one should be embarrassed."

Henk brought a sheet of paper from the desk in the next room and tore it into nine small strips. "You too," he said, handing ballots to Betsie, Father, and me. "If we're discovered, you suffer the same as us."

He handed around pencils. "Mark 'No' if it's too great a risk, 'Yes' if you think she belongs here."

For a moment pencils scratched, then Henk collected the folded ballots. He opened them in silence, then reached over and dropped them into Mary's lap.

Nine little scraps of paper, nine times the word, "Yes."

And so our "family" was formed. Others stayed with us a day or a week, but these seven remained, the nucleus of our happy household.

That it could have been happy, at such a time and in such circumstances, was largely a tribute to Betsie. Because our guests' physical lives were so very restricted, evenings under Betsie's direction became the door to the wide world. Sometimes we had concerts, with Leendert on the violin, and Thea, a truly accomplished musician, on the piano. Or Betsie would announce "an evening of Vondel" (the Dutch Shakespeare), with each of us reading a part. One night a week she talked Eusie into giving Hebrew lessons, another night Meta taught Italian.

The evening's activity had to be kept brief because the city now had electricity only a short while each night, and candles had to be hoarded for emergencies. When the lamps flickered and dimmed we would wind back down to the dining room where my bicycle was set up on its stand. One of us would climb onto it, the others taking chairs, and then while the rider pedaled furiously to make the headlight glow bright, someone would pick up the chapter from the night before. We changed cyclist and reader often as legs or voice grew tired, reading our way through histories, novels, plays.

Father always went upstairs after prayers at 9:15, but the rest of us lingered, reluctant to break the circle, sorry to see the evening end. "Oh well," Eusie would say hopefully as we started at last to our rooms, "maybe there'll be a drill tonight! I haven't had a cream puff in nearly a week. . . ."

8

Storm Clouds Gather

If evenings were pleasant, daytimes grew increasingly tense. We were too big; the group was too large, the web too widespread. For a year and a half now we had got away with our double lives. Ostensibly we were still an elderly watchmaker living with his two spinster daughters above his tiny shop. In actuality the Beje was the center of an underground ring that spread now to the farthest corners of Holland. Here daily came dozens of workers, reports, appeals. Sooner or later we were going to make a mistake.

It was mealtimes especially when I worried. There were so many now for every meal that we had to set the chairs diagonally around the dining room table. The cat loved this arrangement. Eusie had given him the Hebrew name "Maher Shalal Hashbaz," meaning appropriately enough, "hastening to the spoils, hurrying to the prey." With the chairs set so close M. S. Hashbaz could circle the entire table on our shoulders, purring furiously, traveling round and round.

But I was uneasy at being so many. The dining room was only five steps above street-level; a tall passerby could see right in the window. We'd hung a white curtain across it providing a kind of screen while letting in light. Still, only when the heavy blackout shades were drawn at night did I feel truly private.

At lunch one day, looking through the thin curtain I thought I saw a figure standing just outside in the alley. When I looked again a minute later it was still there. There was no reason for anyone to linger there unless he was curious about what went on in the Beje. I got up and parted the curtain an inch.

Standing a few feet away, seemingly immobilized by some terrible emotion, was old Katrien from Nollie's house!

I bolted down the stairs, threw open the door, and pulled her inside. Although the August day was hot, the old lady's hands were cold as ice. "Katrien! What are you doing here? Why were you just standing there?"

"She's gone mad!" she sobbed. "Your sister's gone mad!"

"Nollie? Oh, what's happened!"

"They came!" she said. "The S.D.! I don't know what they knew or who told them. Your sister and Annaliese were in the living room and I heard her!" The sobs broke out again. "I heard her!"

"Heard what?" I nearly screamed.

"Heard what she told them! They pointed at Annaliese and said, 'Is this a Jew?' And your sister said, 'Yes.'"

I felt my knees go weak. Annaliese, blonde, beautiful young Annaliese with the perfect papers. And she'd trusted us! Oh Nollie, Nollie, what has your rigid honesty done! "And then?" I asked.

"I don't know. I ran out the back door. She's gone mad!"

I left Katrien in the dining room, wheeled my bicycle down the stairs and bumped as fast as I could the mile and a half to Nollie's. Today the sky did not seem larger above the Wagenweg. At the corner of Bos en Hoven Straat I leaned my bike against a lamppost and stood panting, my heart throbbing in my throat. Then, as casually as I was able, I strolled up the sidewalk toward the house. Except for a car parked at the street curb directly in front, everything looked deceptively normal. I walked past. Not a sound from behind the white curtains. Nothing to distinguish this house from the replicas of it on either side.

When I got to the corner I turned around. At that

moment the door opened and Nollie came out. Behind her walked a man in a brown business suit. A minute later a second man appeared, half pulling, half supporting Annaliese. The young woman's face was white as chalk; twice before they reached the car I thought she would faint. The car doors slammed, the motor roared, and they were gone.

I pedaled back to the Beje fighting back tears of anxiety. Nollie, we soon learned, had been taken to the police station around the corner, to one of the cells in back. But Annaliese had been sent to the old Jewish theater in Amsterdam from which Jews were transported to extermination camps in Germany and Poland.

It was Mietje, stooped, care-worn little Mietje whose offer of help we had discounted, who kept us in touch with Nollie. She was in wonderful spirits, Mietje said, singing hymns and songs in her high sweet soprano.

How could she sing when she had betrayed another human being! Mietje delivered the bread that Betsie baked for Nollie each morning, and the blue sweater Nollie asked for, her favorite, with flowers embroidered over the pocket.

Mietje relayed another message from Nollie, one especially for me: "No ill will happen to Annaliese. God will not let them take her to Germany. He will not let her suffer because I obeyed Him."

Six days after Nollie's arrest, the telephone rang. Pickwick's voice was on the other end. "I wonder, my dear, if I could trouble you to deliver that watch yourself?"

A message, then, that he could not relay over the phone. I biked at once out to Aerdenhout, taking along a man's watch for safe measure.

Pickwick waited until we were in the drawing room with the door shut. "The Jewish theater in Amsterdam was broken into last night. Forty Jews were rescued. One of them—a young woman—was most insistent that Nollie know: 'Annaliese is free.'"

He fixed me with one of his wide-set eyes. "Do you understand this message?"

I nodded, too overcome with relief and joy to speak. How had Nollie known? How had she been so sure?

After ten days in the Haarlem jail, Nollie was transferred to the federal prison in Amsterdam.

Pickwick said that the German doctor in charge of the prison hospital was a humane man who occasionally arranged a medical discharge. I went at once to Amsterdam to see him. But what could I say, I wondered, as I waited in the entrance hall of his home. How could I get into the good graces of this man?

Lolling about the foyer, sniffing from time to time at my legs and hands, were three perfectly huge Doberman pinschers. I remembered the book we were reading aloud by bicycle lamp, *How to Win Friends and Influence People*. One of the techniques advocated by Dale Carnegie was: find the man's hobby. Hobby, dogs . . . I wonder. . . .

At last the maid returned and showed me into a small sitting room. "How smart of you, Doctor!" I said in German to the grizzle-haired man on the sofa.

"Smart?"

"Yes, to bring these lovely dogs with you. They must be good company when you have to be away from your family."

The doctor's face brightened. "You like dogs then?"

About the only dogs I had ever known were Harry de Vries' bulldogs. "Bulls are my favorite. Do you like bulls?"

"People don't realize it," the doctor said eagerly, "but bulldogs are very affectionate."

For perhaps ten minutes, while I racked my brain for everything I had ever heard or read on the subject, we talked about dogs. Then abruptly the doctor stood up. "But I'm sure you haven't come here to talk about dogs. What's on your mind?"

I met his eye. "I have a sister in prison here in Amsterdam. I was wondering if . . . I don't think she's well."

The doctor smiled. "So, you aren't interested in dogs at all."

"I'm interested now," I said, smiling too. "But I'm far more interested in my sister."

"What's her name?"

"Nollie van Woerden."

The doctor went out of the room and came back with a brown notebook. "Yes. One of the recent arrivals. Tell me something about her. What is she in prison for?"

Taking a chance, I told the doctor that Nollie's crime had been hiding a Jew. I also told him that she was the mother of six children, who if left without aid could become a burden to the State. (I did not mention that the youngest of these children was now seventeen.)

"Well, we'll see." He walked to the door of the sitting room. "You must excuse me now."

I was more encouraged than at any time since Nollie's arrest as I rode the train back to Haarlem. But days, then a week, then two weeks passed and there was no further news. I went back to Amsterdam. "I've come to see how those Dobermans are," I told the doctor.

He was not amused. "You mustn't bother me. I know that you have not come to talk about dogs. You must give me time."

So there was nothing to do but wait.

It was a bright September noon when seventeen of us were squeezed around the dining room table. All of a sudden Nils, seated across from me, turned pale. Nils, one of our workers, had come to report old Katrien safely arrived at a farm north of Alkmaar. Now Nils spoke in a low normal voice.

"Do not turn around. Someone is looking over the curtain."

Over the curtain! But—that was impossible! He'd have to be ten feet high. The table fell silent.

"He's on a ladder, washing the window," Nils said.

"I didn't order the windows washed," said Betsie.

Whoever it was, we mustn't sit here in this frozen, guilty silence! Eusie had an inspiration. "Happy Birthday!" he sang. "Happy Birthday to you!" We all got the idea and joined in lustily. "Happy Birthday, dear Opa . . . ," the song was still echoing through the Beje when I went out the side door and stood next to the ladder, looking up at the man holding bucket and sponge.

"What are you doing? We didn't want the windows washed. Especially not during the party!"

The man took a piece of paper from his hip pocket and consulted it. "Isn't this Kuiper's?"

"They're across the street. But—anyhow, come in and help us celebrate." The man shook his head. He thanked me, but he had work to do. I watched him crossing the Barteljorisstraat with his ladder to Kuiper's candy store.

"Did it work?" a clamor of voices asked when I got back to the dining room. "Do you think he was spying?"

I didn't answer. I didn't know.

That was the hardest. Never knowing. And one of the biggest unknowns was my own performance under questioning. As long as I was awake I felt fairly sure of myself. But if they should come at night . . . Over and over again the group worked with me— Nils, Henk, Leendert—bursting into my room without warning, shaking me awake, hurling questions at me.

The first time it happened I was sure the real raid had come. There was a terrific pounding on my door, then the beam of a flashlight in my eyes. "Get up! On your feet!" I could not see the man who was speaking.

"Where are you hiding your nine Jews?"

"We only have six Jews now."

There was an awful silence. The room light came on to show Rolf clutching his head with his hands. "Oh no. Oh no," he kept saying. "It can't be that bad."

"Think now," said Henk just behind him. "The Gestapo is trying to trap you. The answer is, 'What Jews! We don't have Jews here.' "

"Can I try again?"

"Not now," said Rolf. "You're wide-awake now."

They tried again a few nights later. "The Jews you're hiding, where do they come from?"

I sat up groggily. "I don't know. They just come to the door."

Rolf flung his hat to the floor. "No, no, no!" he shouted. " 'What Jews! There are no Jews!' Can't you learn?"

"I'll learn," I promised. "I'll do better."

And sure enough the next time I woke a little more completely. Half a dozen shadowy forms filled the room. "Where do you hide the ration cards?" a voice demanded.

Under the bottom stair, of course. But this time I would not be trapped into saying so. A crafty reply occurred to me: "In the Frisian clock on the stairwell!"

Kik sat down beside me on the bed and put an arm around me. "That was better, Tante Corrie," he said. "You tried, this time. But remember—you *have* no cards except the three for you, Opa, and Tante Betsie. There *is* no underground activity here, you don't understand what they're talking about. . . ."

Gradually, with repeated drills, I got better. Still, when the time actually came, when they were real Gestapo agents really trained in getting the truth from people, how would I perform?

Willem's underground work brought him frequently to Haarlem. There was an expression of something like despair mingled now with the worry lines in his face. Twice soldiers had been to the nursing home, and although he had managed to deceive them about most of the Jews still in residence there, one sick blind old woman had been taken away.

"Ninety-one!" Willem kept saying. "She couldn't even walk—they had to carry her to the car."

So far, Willem's position as a minister had prevented direct action against him and Tine, but he was watched, he said, more closely than ever. To provide an official reason for his visits to Haarlem he started conducting a weekly prayer fellowship at the Beje each Wednesday morning.

But Willem could do nothing routinely—especially pray—and soon the meeting was attended by dozens of Haarlemers hungry for something to believe in, this fourth year of the occupation. Most of those coming to the services had no idea of the double life of the Beje. In a way they posed a fresh danger as they passed workers and couriers from other underground groups coming and going on the narrow stairs. But in another way, we thought, it might be an advantage to have these flocks of obviously innocent people in and out. That, at least, was our hope.

We were sitting around the supper table after curfew one night, three ten Booms, the seven "permanent guests," and two Jews for whom we were seeking homes, when the shop doorbell chimed.

A customer after closing? And one bold enough to stand on the Barteljorisstraat after curfew? Taking the keys from my pocket I hurried down to the hall, unlocked the workshop door, and felt my way through the dark store. At the front door I listened a moment.

"Who's there?" I called.

"Do you remember me?"

A man's voice speaking German. "Who is it?" I asked in the same language.

"An old friend, come for a visit. Open the door!"

I fumbled with the lock and drew the door gingerly back. It was a German soldier in uniform. Before I could reach the alarm button behind the door, he had pushed his way inside. Then he took off his hat and in the October twilight I recognized the young German watchmaker whom Father had discharged four years ago.

"Otto!" I cried.

"Captain Altschuler," he corrected me. "Our positions are slightly reversed, Miss ten Boom, are they not?"

I glanced at his insignia. He was not a captain or anything close to it, but I said nothing. He looked around the shop.

"Same stuffy little place," he said. He reached for the wall switch, but I put my hand over it.

"No! We don't have blackout shades in the shop!"

"Well, let's go upstairs where we can talk over old times. That old clock cleaner still around?"

"Christoffels? He died in the fuel shortage last winter."

Otto shrugged. "Good riddance then! What about the pious old Bible reader?"

I was edging my way to the sales counter where another bell was located. "Father is very well, thank you."

"Well, aren't you going to invite me up to pay my respects?"

Why was he so eager to go upstairs? Had the wretched fellow come just to gloat, or did he suspect something? My finger found the button.

"What was that!" Otto whirled around suspiciously.

"What was what?"

"That sound! I heard a kind of buzzing."

"I didn't hear anything."

But Otto had started back through the workshop.

"Wait!" I shouted. "Let me get the front door locked and I'll go up with you! I—I want to see how long it takes them to recognize you."

I dawdled at the door as long as I dared: definitely his suspicions were aroused. Then I followed him through the rear door into the hall. Not a sound from the dining room or the stairs. I dashed past him up the steps and rapped on the door.

"Father! Betsie!" I cried in what I hoped was a playful voice. "I'll give you three—no, uh—six guesses who's standing here!"

"No guessing games!" Otto reached past me and flung open the door.

Father and Betsie looked up from their meal. The table was set for three, my unfinished plate on the other side. It was so perfect that even I, who had just seen twelve people eating here, could scarcely believe this was anything but an innocent old man dining with his daughters. The "Alpina" sign stood on the sideboard: they had remembered everything.

Uninvited, Otto pulled out a chair. "Well!" he crowed. "Things happened just like I said, didn't they?"

"So it would seem," said Father mildly.

"Betsie," I said, "give Captain Altschuler some tea!"

Otto took a sip of the brew Betsie poured him and glared round the table at us. "Where did you get real tea! No one else in Holland has tea."

How stupid of me. The tea had come from Pickwick.

"If you must know," I said, "it comes from a German officer. But you mustn't ask any further questions." I tried to imply clandestine dealings with a high occupation official.

Otto lingered another fifteen minutes. And then, feeling perhaps that he had underlined his victory sufficiently, sauntered out into the empty streets.

It was only after another half-hour that we dared give the all clear to nine cramped and shaky people.

The second week in October, during a particularly hectic morning with underground problems, the secret telephone number rang downstairs in the hall. I hurried down to pick it up; only Father, Betsie, or I ever answered it.

"Well!" said a voice. "Aren't you coming to pick me up?"

It was Nollie.

"Nollie! When——How——Where are you?"

"At the train station in Amsterdam! Only I have no money for the trainfare."

"Stay right there! Oh, Nollie, we're coming!"

I biked to Bos en Hoven Straat and then with Flip and the children who happened to be at home, hurried to the Haarlem station. We saw Nollie even before our train came to a stop in Amsterdam——her bright blue sweater like a patch of blue sky in the big dark shed.

Seven weeks in prison had left her pallid-faced,

A chilling photodrama of Corrie's courageous struggle against Nazi Germany.

Photographs by Pat Prince

"Achtung! Achtung! By order of the Reich Commissioner, all citizens are ordered to surrender their radios..."

As the Nazi madness swept across Europe, a gentle family of watchmakers — the ten Booms saw the lights go out of a free Holland. And with the growth of discrimination... of hatred... they were motivated by love to become involved... to care.

The ten Boom family did all they could. They provided food, strength, and a place to hide from the terrors of Hitler's forces. They were a channel of God's love in a world torn by fear.

"Aunt Betsie, how many times have I told you? Take the sign out of the window when it isn't safe!"

Bricks, mortar, paint, to build a secret room in which to hide during raids were carried into their house in the case of an old grandfather's clock. They narrowly escaped discovery by a German officer who was having a watch repaired in the shop.

A trap was set. And the bait—
a cry for help. They answered
the plea, and the Gestapo
closed around them. Betsie
sounded the alarm, and
everyone dropped what they
were doing. The door to
the secret room was sealed just
seconds before the soldiers
broke into the house.

'Ten Boom, give me your
word you will behave yourself,
and you can die in your bed
old man, where you belong."

'If I stay behind, I will
open my door to <u>anyone</u> who
knocks for help."

The ten Booms paid the price for caring...in the darkness of prison. Alone. And yet...not alone.

A break in the months of solitary confinement...Corrie was summoned by the prison warden.

"Tell me, Miss ten Boom. How can you believe in a God who lets an old man die in prison...his body forgotten somewhere in a pauper's grave?"

"My father?"

"I understand he was taken ill after about ten days. He was taken to a hospital in The Hague. Unfortunately, there were no beds available... he seemingly died in the hallway. Under such circumstances — when no one claims the body — it is difficult to trace."

"I <u>know</u> where my father is, Lieutenant."

The transfer to Ravensbrück. Hundreds of human beings, treated as less than cattle, cramped together in a train bound for Germany. Day melted into night...into day. Hunger...disease...filth. And yet, Corrie and Betsie somehow knew that God was with them.

"Corrie, we are in Hell."

"One small observation on which your life depends—there is only one road to freedom — <u>work.</u>"

Betsie's poor health prevented her from meeting her "quota" — a fact which did not go unnoticed by a brutal prison guard. Without thinking, Corrie moved to avenge the beating of her sister.

"No hate, Corrie, no hate."

"We must go everywhere. We must tell people that no pit is so deep that He is not deeper still. They will believe us, because we were here."

Life in Ravensbrück was a faith-building experience. Corrie and Betsie were able to share His strength...and the power of His forgiveness ...with the other prisoners.

Betsie's last words...her last words before she was set free...were the words that compelled Corrie to tell in the light what she learned in the darkness of that dreaded place.

"Papa, what is it like to die?"

"When you and I go to Amsterdam, when do I give you your ticket?"

"Just before we get on the train."

"So it is with death. When the time comes, our wise heavenly Father will give you all the strength you need."

Corrie was startled to hear her number called out by a prison guard. Why did they single her out? What was going to happen to her?

In that brief moment, she thought back to her childhood. She thought about that time in her life when she was filled with questions. She thought about how Papa always seemed to have the right answers.

Corrie had many questions right now. But she knew her heavenly Father would give her all the strength she would need. For whatever was ahead...

Photos by Patrick Prince

but as radiantly Nollie as ever. A prison doctor, she said, had pronounced her low blood pressure a serious condition, one that might leave her permanently disabled and her six children a burden to society. Her face wrinkled in puzzlement as she said it.

Christmas, 1943, was approaching. The light snow which had fallen was the only festive quality of the season. Every family it seemed had someone in jail, in a work camp, or in hiding. For once the religious side of the holidays was uppermost in every mind.

At the Beje, we had not only Christmas to celebrate but also Hanukkah, the Jewish "Festival of Lights." Betsie found a Hanukkah candlestand among the treasures stored with us behind the dining room cupboard and set it up on the upright piano. Each night we lighted one more candle as Eusie read the story of the Maccabees. Then we would sing, haunting, melancholy desert music. We were all very Jewish those evenings.

About the fifth night of the Festival, as we were gathered round the piano, the doorbell in the alley rang. I opened it to find Mrs. Beukers, wife of the optician next door, standing in the snow. Mrs. Beukers was as round and placid as her husband was thin and worried, but tonight her plump face was twisted with anxiety.

"Do you think," she whispered, "your Jews could sing a little more softly? We can hear them right through the walls and—well, there are all kinds of people on this street. . . ."

Back in Tante Jans's rooms we considered this news in consternation. If the Beukers family knew all about our affairs, how many other people in Haarlem did too?

It wasn't long before we discovered that one who did was the chief of police himself. One dark January morning when it was trying to snow again, Toos burst into underground "headquarters" in Tante Jans's rear room clutching a letter in her hand. The envelope bore the seal of the Haarlem police.

I tore it open. Inside, on the police chief's stationery, was a handwritten note. I read it silently, then aloud.

"You will come to my office this afternoon at three o'clock."

For twenty minutes we tried to analyze that note. Some felt it was not a prelude to arrest. Why would the police give you a chance to escape? Still, it was safest to prepare for search and imprisonment. Workers slipped out of the house, one at a time. Boarders emptied wastebaskets and picked up scraps of sewing in preparation for a quick fight in the secret room. I burned incriminating papers in the long-empty coal hearth in the dining room. The cat caught the tension in the air and sulked beneath the sideboard.

Then I took a bath, perhaps the last for months and packed a prison bag according to what Nollie and others had learned: a Bible, a pencil, needle and thread, soap—or what we called soap these days—toothbrush, and comb. I dressed in my warmest clothes with several sets of underwear and a second sweater beneath the top one. Just before 3:00 I hugged Father and Betsie tight, and walked through the gray slush to the Smedestraat.

The policeman on duty was an old acquaintance. He looked at the letter, then at me with a curious expression. "This way," he said.

He knocked at a door marked "Chief." The man who sat behind the desk had red-gray hair combed forward over a bald spot. A radio was playing. The chief reached over and twisted the volume knob not down but up.

"Miss ten Boom," he said. "Welcome."

"How do you do, Sir."

The chief had left his desk to shut the door behind me. "Do sit down," he said. "I know all about you, you know. About your work."

"The watchmaking you mean. You're probably thinking more about my father's work than my own."

The chief smiled. "No, I mean your other work."

"Ah, then you're referring to my work with retarded children? Yes. Let me tell you about that——"

"No, Miss ten Boom," the chief lowered his voice. "I am not talking about your work with retarded children. I'm talking about still another work, and I want you to know that some of us here are in sympathy."

The chief was smiling broadly now. Tentatively I smiled back. "Now, Miss ten Boom," he went on, "I have a request."

The chief sat down on the edge of his desk and looked at me steadily. He dropped his voice until it was just audible. He was, he said, working with the underground himself. But an informer in the police department was leaking information to the Gestapo. "There's no way for us to deal with this man but to kill him."

A shudder went down my spine.

"What alternative have we?" the chief went on in a whisper. "We can't arrest him—there are no prisons except those controlled by the Germans. But if he remains at large many others will die. That is why I wondered, Miss ten Boom, if in your work *you* might know of someone who could——"

"Kill him?"

"Yes."

I leaned back. Was this all a trap to trick me into admitting the existence of a group, into naming names?

"Sir," I said at last, seeing the chief's eyes flicker impatiently, "I have always believed that it was my role to save life, not destroy it. I understand your dilemma, however, and I have a suggestion. Are you a praying man?"

"Aren't we all, these days?"

"Then let us pray together now that God will reach the heart of this man so that he does not continue to betray his countrymen."

There was a long pause. Then the chief nodded. "That I would very much like to do."

And so there in the heart of the police station, with the radio blaring out the latest news of the German advance, we prayed. We prayed that this Dutchman would come to realize his worth in the sight of God and the worth of every other human being on earth.

At the end of the prayer the chief stood up. "Thank you, Miss ten Boom." He shook my hand. "Thank you again. I know now that it was wrong to ask you."

Still clutching my prison bag, I walked through the foyer and around the corner to the Beje.

Upstairs, people crowded around wanting to know everything. But I did not tell them. Not everything— I did not want Father and Betsie to know that we had been asked to kill. It would have been an unnecessary burden for them to bear.

The episode with the chief of police should have been encouraging. Apparently we had friends in high places. As a matter of fact the news had the opposite effect upon us. Here was one more illustration of how our secret was no secret at all. All of Haarlem seemed to know what we were up to.

We knew we should stop the work, but how could we? Who would keep open the network of supplies and information on which the safety of hundreds depended? If a hideaway had to be abandoned, as happened all the time, who would coordinate the move to another address? We had to go on, but we knew that disaster could not be long in coming.

As a matter of fact, it came first to Jop, the seventeen-year-old apprentice who had sought a safe home at the Beje.

Late one afternoon near the end of January, 1944, Rolf stepped stealthily into the workshop. He glanced at Jop. I nodded: Jop was party to everything that went on in the house.

"There's an underground home in Ede that is going to be raided this evening. Do you have anyone who can go?"

But I did not. Not a single courier or escort person was at the Beje this late in the day.

"I'll go," Jop said.

I opened my mouth to protest that he was inexperienced, and liable to the factory transport himself if stopped on the street. Then I thought of the unsus-

pecting people at Ede. We had a wardrobe of girls'
scarves and dresses upstairs. . . .

"Then quickly, boy," Rolf said. "You must
leave immediately." He gave Jop the details and hurried away. In a few moments Jop reappeared, making
a very pretty brunette in long coat and kerchief, a fur
muff hiding his hands. Did the lad have some kind of
premonition? To my astonishment he turned at the
door and kissed me.

Jop was supposed to be back by the 7:00 P.M.
curfew. Seven came and went. Perhaps he had been
delayed and would return in the morning.

We did have a visitor early the next day but it
was not Jop. I knew the minute Rolf stepped through
the door that bad news was weighing him down.

"It's Jop, isn't it?"

"Yes."

"What happened?"

Rolf had learned the story from the sergeant at
the night desk. When Jop got to the address in Ede the
Gestapo was already there. Jop had rung the bell;
the door opened. Pretending to be the owner of the
house, the S.D. man had invited Jop in.

"And Corrie," Rolf said, "we must face it. The
Gestapo will get information out of Jop. They have
already taken him to Amsterdam. How long will he be
able to hold his tongue?"

Once again we considered stopping the work.
Once again we discovered we could not.

That night Father and Betsie and I prayed long
after the others had gone to bed. We knew that in
spite of daily mounting risks we had no choice but to
move forward. This was evil's hour: we could not
run away from it. Perhaps only when human effort
had done its best and failed, would God's power alone
be free to work.

9

The Raid

At the sound of someone in my room I opened my eyes painfully. It was Eusie, carrying up his bedding and night clothes to store in the secret room. Behind him came Mary and Thea with their bundles.

I shut my eyes again. It was the morning of February 28, 1944. For two days I had been in bed with influenza. My head throbbed, my joints were on fire. Every little sound, Mary's wheeze, the scrape of the secret panel, made me want to shriek. I heard Henk and Meta come in, then Eusie's laugh as he handed the day things out to the others through the low door.

Go away all of you! Leave me alone! I bit my lip to keep from saying it.

At last they collected their clothes and belongings and trooped out, closing the door behind them. Where was Leendert? Why hadn't he come up? Then I remembered that Leendert was away for a few days setting up electrical warning systems like ours in several of our host homes. I drifted back into a feverish sleep.

The next thing I knew, Betsie was standing at the foot of the bed, a steaming cup of herb tea in her hand. "I'm sorry to wake you, Corrie. But there's a man down in the shop who insists he will talk only to you."

"Who is he?"

"He says he's from Ermelo. I've never seen him before."

I sat up shakily. "That's all right. I have to get up anyway. Tomorrow the new ration cards come."

I sipped the scalding tea, then struggled to my feet. There by the bed lay my prison bag, packed and ready as it had been since the summons from the chief of police. In fact I'd been adding to it. Besides the Bible, clothing, and toilet things, it now held vitamins, aspirins, iron pills for Betsie's anemia and much else. It had become a kind of talisman for me, a safeguard against the terrors of prison.

I got slowly into my clothes and stepped out onto the landing. The house seemed to reel around me. I crept down, clinging to the handrail. At the door to Tante Jans's rooms I was surprised to hear voices. I looked in. Of course, I'd forgotten. It was Wednesday morning, people were gathering for Willem's weekly service. I saw Nollie passing around "occupation coffee" as we called the current brew of roots and dried figs. Peter was already at the piano, as he was most weeks to provide the music. I continued down around the stairs, passing new arrivals streaming up.

As I arrived, wobble-kneed, in the shop, a small sandy-haired man sprang forward to meet me. "Miss ten Boom!"

"Yes?" There was an old Dutch expression: you can tell a man by the way he meets your eyes. This man seemed to concentrate somewhere between my nose and my chin. "Is it about a watch?" I asked.

"No, Miss ten Boom, something far more serious!" His eyes seemed to make a circle around my face. "My wife has just been arrested. We've been hiding Jews, you see. If she is questioned, all of our lives are in danger."

"I don't know how *I* can help," I said.

"I need six hundred guilders. There's a policeman at the station in Ermelo who can be bribed for that amount. I'm a poor man—and I've been told you have certain contacts."

"Contacts?"

"Miss ten Boom! It's a matter of life and death!

If I don't get it right away she'll be taken to Amsterdam and then it will be too late."

Something about the man's behavior made me hesitate. And yet how could I risk being wrong? "Come back in half an hour. I'll have the money," I said.

For the first time the man's eyes met mine.

"I'll never forget this," he said.

The amount was more than we had at the Beje so I sent Toos to the bank with instructions to hand the man the money, but not to volunteer any information.

Then I struggled back up the stairs. Where ten minutes earlier I'd been burning with fever, now I was shaking with cold. I stopped at Tante Jans's rooms just long enough to take a briefcase of papers from the desk. Then with apologies to Willem and the others I continued to my room. I undressed again, refilled the vaporizer where it was hissing on its small spirit-stove, and climbed back into bed. For a while I tried to concentrate on the names and addresses in the briefcase. Five cards needed this month in Zandvoort. None in Overveen. We would need eighteen in. . . . The flu roared behind my eyes, the papers swam in front of me. The briefcase slipped from my hand and I was asleep.

In my fevered dream a buzzer kept ringing. On and on it went. Why wouldn't it stop? Feet were running, voices whispering. "Hurry! Hurry!"

I sat bolt upright. People were running past my bed. I turned just in time to see Thea's heels disappear through the low door. Meta was behind her, then Henk.

But—I hadn't planned a drill for today! Who in the world—unless—unless it wasn't a drill. Eusie dashed past me, white-faced, his pipe rattling in the ashtray that he carried in shaking hands.

And at last it penetrated my numbed brain that the emergency had come. One, two, three people already in the secret room; four as Eusie's black shoes and scarlet socks disappeared. But Mary—where was Mary? The old woman appeared in the bedroom door, mouth open, gasping for air. I sprang from my bed and half-pulled, half-shoved her across the room.

I was sliding the secret panel down behind her when a slim white-haired man burst into the room. I recognized him from Pickwick's, someone high in the national Resistance. I'd had no idea he was in the house. He dived after Mary. Five, six. Yes, that was right with Leendert away.

The man's legs vanished and I dropped the panel down and leapt back into bed. Below I heard doors slamming, heavy footsteps on the stairs. But it was another sound that turned my blood to water: the strangling, grating rasp of Mary's breathing.

"Lord Jesus!" I prayed. "You have the power to heal! Heal Mary now!"

And then my eye fell on the briefcase, stuffed with names and addresses. I snatched it up, yanked up the sliding door again, flung the case inside, shoved the door down and pushed my prison bag up against it. I had just reached the bed again when the bedroom door flew open.

"What's your name?"

I sat up slowly and—I hoped—sleepily.

"What?"

"Your name!"

"Cornelia ten Boom." The man was tall and heavy-set with a strange, pale face. He wore an ordinary blue business suit. He turned and shouted down the stairs, "We've got one more up here, Willemse."

He turned back to me. "Get up! Get dressed!"

As I crawled out from under the covers, the man took a slip of paper from his pocket and consulted it. "So you're the ring leader!" He looked at me with new interest. "Tell me now, where are you hiding the Jews?"

"I don't know what you're talking about."

The man laughed. "And you don't know anything about an underground ring, either. We'll see about that!"

He had not taken his eyes off me, so I began to pull on my clothes over my pajamas, ears straining for a sound from the secret room.

"Let me see your papers!"

I pulled out the little sack that I wore around my neck. When I took out my identification folder, a roll of bills fell out with it. The man stooped, snatched up the money from the floor, and stuffed it into his pocket. Then he took my papers and looked at them. For a moment the room was silent. Mary Itallie's wheeze—why wasn't I hearing it?

The man threw the papers back at me. "Hurry up!"

But he was not in half the hurry I was to get away from that room. I buttoned my sweater all wrong in my haste and stuffed my feet into my shoes without bothering to tie them. Then I was about to reach for my prison bag.

Wait.

It stood where I had shoved it in my panic: directly in front of the secret panel. If I were to reach down under the shelf to get it now, with this man watching my every move, might not his attention be attracted to the last place on earth I wanted him to look?

It was the hardest thing I had ever done to turn and walk out of that room, leaving the bag behind.

I stumbled down the stairs, my knees shaking as much from fear as from flu. A uniformed soldier was stationed in front of Tante Jans's rooms; the door was shut. I wondered if the prayer meeting had ended, if Willem and Nollie and Peter had got away. Or were they all still in there? How many innocent people might be involved?

The man behind me gave me a little push and I hurried on down the stairs to the dining room. Father, Betsie, and Toos were sitting on chairs pulled back against the wall. Beside them sat three underground workers who must have arrived since I had gone upstairs. On the floor beneath the window, broken in three pieces, lay the "Alpina" sign. Someone had managed to knock it from the sill.

A second Gestapo agent in plain clothes was pawing eagerly through a pile of silver rijksdaalders and jewelry heaped on the dining room table. It was the cache from the space behind the corner cupboard: it had been indeed the first place they looked.

"Here's the other one listed at the address," said the man who had brought me down. "My information says she's the leader of the whole outfit."

The man at the table, the one called Willemse, glanced at me, then turned back to the loot in front of him. "You know what to do, Kapteyn."

Kapteyn seized me by the elbow and shoved me ahead of him down the remaining five steps and into the rear of the shop. Another soldier in uniform stood guard just inside this door. Kapteyn prodded me through to the front room and pushed me against the wall.

"Where are the Jews?"

"There aren't any Jews here."

The man struck me hard across the face.

"Where do you hide the ration cards?"

"I don't know what you're——"

Kapteyn hit me again. I staggered up against the astronomical clock. Before I could recover he slapped me again, then again, and again, stinging blows that jerked my head backward.

"Where are the Jews?"

Another blow.

"Where is your secret room?"

I tasted blood in my mouth. My head spun, my ears rang—I was losing consciousness. "Lord Jesus," I cried out, "protect me!"

Kapteyn's hand stopped in midair.

"If you say that name again I'll kill you!"

But instead his arm slowly dropped to his side. "If you won't talk, that skinny one will."

I stumbled ahead of him up the stairs. He pushed me into one of the chairs against the dining room wall. Through a blur I saw him lead Betsie from the room.

Above us hammer blows and splintering wood showed where a squad of trained searchers was probing for the secret room. Then down in the alley the door-bell rang. But the sign! Didn't they see the "Alpina" sign was gone and—I glanced at the window and caught my breath. There on the sill, the broken pieces fitted carefully together, sat the wooden triangle.

Too late I looked up to see Willemse staring intently at me. "I thought so!" he said. "It was a signal, wasn't it?"

He ran down the stairs. Above us the hammering and the tramp of boots had stopped. I heard the alley door open and Willemse's voice, smooth and ingratiating.

"Come in, won't you?"

"Have you heard!" A woman's voice. "They've got Oom Herman!"

Pickwick? Not Pickwick!

"Oh?" I heard Willemse say. "Who was with him?" He pumped her as hard as he could, then placed her under arrest. Blinking with fright and confusion, the woman was seated with us along the wall. I recognized her only as a person who occasionally took messages for us about the city. I stared in anguish at the sign in the window announcing to the world that all was as usual at the Beje. Our home had been turned into a trap: how many more would fall into it before this day was over? And Pickwick! Had they really caught Pickwick!

Kapteyn appeared with Betsie in the dining room door. Her lips were swollen and puffy, a bruise was darkening on her cheek. She half fell into the chair next to mine.

"Oh Betsie! He hurt you!"

"Yes." She dabbed at the blood on her mouth. "I feel so sorry for him."

Kapteyn whirled, his white face even paler. "Prisoners will remain silent!" he shrieked. Two men were clumping down the stairs and into the dining room carrying something between them. They had discovered the old radio beneath the stairs.

"Law-abiding citizens, are you?" Kapteyn went on. "You! The old man there. I see you believe in the Bible." He jerked his thumb at the well-worn book on its shelf. "Tell me, what does it say in there about obeying the government?"

" 'Fear God,' " Father quoted, and on his lips in that room the words came as blessing and reassurance. " 'Fear God and honor the Queen.' "

Kapteyn stared at him. "It doesn't say that. The Bible doesn't say that."

"No." Father admitted. "It says, 'Fear God, honor the King.' But in our case, that is the Queen."

"It's not King or Queen!" roared Kapteyn. "We're the legal government now, and you're all lawbreakers!"

The doorbell rang again. Again there were the questions and the arrest. The young man—one of our workers—had barely been assigned a chair when again the bell sounded. It seemed to me that we had never had so many callers: the dining room was getting crowded. I felt sorriest for those who had come simply on social visits. An elderly retired missionary was brought in, jaw quivering with fear. At least, from the banging and thumping above, they had not yet discovered the secret room.

A new sound made me jump. The phone down in the hall was ringing.

"That's a telephone!" cried Willemse.

He glared around the room, then grabbing me by the wrist yanked me down the stairs behind him. He thrust the receiver up against my ear but kept his own hand on it.

"Answer!" he said with his lips.

"This is the ten Boom residence and shop," I said as stiffly as I dared.

But the person on the other end did not catch the strangeness. "Miss ten Boom, you're in terrible danger! They've arrested Herman Sluring! They know everything! You've got to be careful!" On and on the woman's voice babbled, the man at my side hearing everything.

She had scarcely hung up when the phone rang again. A man's voice, and again the message, "Oom Herman's been taken to the police station. That means they're on to everything. . . ."

At last, the third time I repeated my formal and untypical little greeting, there was a click on the other end. Willemse snatched the earpiece from my hand.

"Hello! Hello!" he shouted. He jiggled the cradle on the wall. The line had gone dead. He shoved me back up the stairs and into my chair again. "Our friends wised up," he told Kapteyn. "But I heard enough."

Apparently Betsie had received permission to leave her chair: she was slicing bread at the sideboard. I was surprised to realize it was already lunchtime. Betsie passed the bread around the room but I shook my head. The fever was raging again. My throat ached and my head throbbed.

A man appeared in the doorway. "We've searched the whole place, Willemse," he said. "If there's a secret room here, the devil himself built it."

Willemse looked from Betsie to Father to me. "There's a secret room," he said quietly. "And people are using it or they would have admitted it. All right. We'll set a guard around the house till they've turned to mummies."

In the hush of horror which followed there was a gentle pressure on my knees. Maher Shalal Hashbaz had jumped up into my lap to rub against me. I stroked the shining black fur. What would become of him now? I would not let myself think about the six people upstairs.

It had been half an hour since the doorbell had rung last. Whoever had caught my message over the phone must have spread the alarm. Word was out: no one else would walk into the trap at the Beje.

Apparently Willemse had come to the same conclusion because abruptly he ordered us on our feet and down to the hallway with our coats and hats. Father, Betsie, and me he held in the dining room till last. In front of us down the stairs came the people from Tante Jans's rooms. I held my breath scanning them. Apparently most of those at the prayer service had left before the raid. But by no means all. Here came Nollie, behind her, Peter. Last in the line came Willem.

The whole family then. Father, all four of his children, one grandchild. Kapteyn gave me a shove.

"Get moving."

Father took his tall hat from the wall peg. Outside the dining room door he paused to pull up the weights on the old Frisian clock.

"We mustn't let the clock run down," he said.

Father! Did you really think we would be back home when next the chain ran out?

The snow had gone from the streets; puddles of dirty water stood in the gutters as we marched through the alley and into the Smedestraat. The walk took only a minute, but by the time we got inside the double doors of the police station I was shaking with cold. I looked anxiously around the foyer for Rolf and the others we knew, but saw no one. A contingent of German soldiers seemed to be supplementing the regular police force.

We were herded along a corridor and through the heavy metal door where I had last seen Harry de Vries. At the end of this hall was a large room that had obviously been a gymnasium. Windows high in the walls were covered with wire mesh; rings and basketball hoops were roped to the ceiling. Now a desk stood in the center of the room with a German army officer seated behind it. Tumbling mats had been spread out to cover part of the floor and I collapsed onto one of them.

For two hours the officer took down names, addresses, and other statistics. I counted those who had been arrested with us: thirty-five people from the raid on the Beje.

People from previous arrests were sitting or lying about on the mats too, some of them faces we knew. I looked for Pickwick but he was not among them. One of them, a fellow watchmaker who often came to the Beje on business, seemed especially distressed at what had happened to us. He came and sat down beside Father and me.

At last the officer left. For the first time since the alarm buzzer sounded we could talk among ourselves. I struggled to sit up. "Quick!" I croaked.

"We've got to agree on what to say! Most of us can simply tell the truth but——" My voice died in my throat. It seemed to my flu-addled brain that Peter was giving me the most ferocious frown I had ever seen.

"But if they learn that Uncle Willem was teaching this morning from the Old Testament, it could make trouble for him," Peter finished for me.

He jerked his head to one side and I clamored unsteadily to my feet. "Tante Corrie!" he hissed when we were on the other side of the room. "That man, the watchmaker! He's a Gestapo plant." He patted my head as though I were a sick child. "Lie down again, Tante Corrie. Just for heaven's sake don't do any talking."

I was waked by the heavy door of the gym slamming open. In strode Rolf.

"Let's have it quiet in here!" he shouted. He leaned close to Willem and said something I could not hear. "Toilets are out back," he continued in a loud voice. "You can go one at a time under escort."

Willem sat down beside me. "He says we can flush incriminating papers if we shred them fine enough." I fumbled through my coat pockets. There were several scraps of paper and a billfold containing a few paper rijksdaalders. I went over each item, trying to think how I would explain it in a court process. Beside the row of outdoor toilets was a basin with a tin cup on a chain. Gratefully I took a long drink—the first since the tea Betsie had brought me that morning.

Toward evening a policeman carried into the gym a large basket of fresh hot rolls. I could not swallow mine. Only the water tasted good to me, though I grew embarrassed at asking again and again to be taken outside.

When I got back the last time, a group had gathered around Father for evening prayers. Every day of my life had ended like this: that deep steady voice, that sure and eager confiding of us all to the care of God. The Bible lay at home on its shelf, but much of it was stored in his heart. His blue eyes seemed to be

seeing beyond the locked and crowded room, beyond
Haarlem, beyond earth itself, as he quoted from memory: "Thou art my hiding place and my shield: I
hope in thy word. . . . Hold thou me up, and I shall
be safe. . . ."

None of us slept much. Each time someone left
the room he had to step over a dozen others. At last
light crept through the high, screened windows at the
top of the room. The police again brought rolls. As
the long morning wore on I dozed with my back up
against the wall; the worst pain now seemed to be in
my chest. It was noon when soldiers entered the room
and ordered us on our feet. Hastily we struggled into
our coats and filed again through the cold corridors.

In the Smedestraat a wall of people pressed
against police barricades set across the street. As Betsie and I stepped out with Father between us, a mur-
mur of horror greeted the sight of "Haarlem's Grand
Old Man" being led to prison. In front of the door
stood a green city bus with soldiers occupying the rear
seats. People were climbing aboard while friends and
relatives in the crowd wept or simply stared. Betsie and
I gripped Father's arms to start down the steps. Then
we froze. Stumbling past us between two soldiers, hatless and coatless, came Pickwick. The top of his bald
head was a welter of bruises, dried blood clung to the
stubble on his chin. He did not look up as he was
hauled onto the bus.

Father, Betsie, and I squeezed into a double seat
near the front. Through the window I caught a glimpse
of Tine standing in the crowd. It was one of those
radiant winter days when the air seemed to shimmer
with light. The bus shuddered and started up. Police
cleared a path and we inched forward. I gazed hungrily out the window, holding onto Haarlem with my
eyes. Now we were crossing the Grote Markt, the
walls of the great cathedral glowing a thousand shades
of gray in the crystal light. In a strange way it seemed
to me that I had lived through this moment before.

Then I recalled.

The vision. The night of the invasion. I had seen

it all. Willem, Nollie, Pickwick, Peter—all of us here —drawn against our wills across this square. It had all been in the dream—all of us leaving Haarlem, unable to turn back. Going where?

10

Scheveningen

Outside Haarlem the bus took the south road, parallel-ing the sea. On our right rose the low sandy hills of the dune country, soldiers silhouetted on the ridges. Clearly we were not being taken to Amsterdam.

A two-hour drive brought us instead into the streets of The Hague. The bus stopped in front of a new, functional building; word was whispered back that this was Gestapo headquarters for all of Holland. We were marched—all but Pickwick, who seemed un-able to rise out of his seat—into a large room where the endless process of taking down names, addresses, and occupations began all over again.

On the other side of the high counter running the length of the room I was startled to see both Willemse and Kapteyn. As each of the prisoners from Haarlem reached the desk, one or the other would lean forward and speak to a man seated at a typewriter and there would be a clatter of sound from the machine.

Suddenly the chief interrogator's eye fell on Fa-ther. "That old man!" he cried. "Did he have to be arrested? You, old man!"

Willem led Father up to the desk. The Gestapo chief leaned forward. "I'd like to send you home, old fellow," he said. "I'll take your word that you won't cause any more trouble."

I could not see Father's face, only the erect carriage of his shoulders and the halo of white hair above them. But I heard his answer.

"If I go home today," he said evenly and clearly, "tomorrow I will open my door again to any man in need who knocks."

The amiability drained from the other man's face. "Get back in line!" he shouted. *"Schnell!* This court will tolerate no more delays!"

But delays seemed all that this court existed for. As we inched along the counter there were endless repetitions of questions, endless consulting of papers, endless coming and going of officials. Outside the windows the short winter day was fading. We had not eaten since the rolls and water at dawn.

Ahead of me in line, Betsie answered, "Unmarried," for the twentieth time that day.

"Number of children?" droned the interrogator.

"I'm unmarried," Betsie repeated.

The man did not even look up from his papers. "Number of children!" he snapped.

"No children," said Betsie resignedly.

Toward nightfall a stout little man wearing the yellow star was led past us to the far end of the room. A sound of scuffling made us all look up. The wretched man was attempting to hold onto something clutched in his hands.

"It's mine!" he kept shouting. "You can't take it! You can't take my purse!"

What madness possessed him? What good did he imagine money would do him now? But he continued to struggle, to the obvious glee of the men around him.

"Here Jew!" I heard one of them say. He lifted his booted foot and kicked the small man in the back of his knees. "This is how we take things from a Jew."

It made so much noise. That was all I could think as they continued to kick him. I clutched the counter to keep from falling myself as the sounds continued. Wildly, unreasonably, I hated the man being kicked, hated him for being so helpless and so hurt. At last I heard them drag him out.

Then all at once I was standing in front of the chief

questioner. I looked up and met Kapteyn's eyes, just behind him.

"This woman was the ringleader," he said.

Through the turmoil inside me I realized it was important for the other man to believe him. "What Mr. Kapteyn says is true," I said. "These others—they know nothing about it. It was all my——"

"Name?" the interrogator inquired imperturbably.

"Cornelia ten Boom, and I'm the——"

"Age?"

"Fifty-two. The rest of these people had nothing to do——"

"Occupation?"

"But I've told you a dozen times!" I burst out in desperation.

"Occupation?" he repeated.

It was dark night when we were marched at last out of the building. The green bus was gone. Instead we made out the bulk of a large canvas-roofed army truck. Two soldiers had to lift Father over the tailgate. There was no sign of Pickwick. Father, Betsie, and I found places to sit on a narrow bench that ran around the sides.

The truck had no springs and bounced roughly over the bomb-pitted streets of The Hague. I slipped my arm behind Father's back to keep him from striking the edge. Willem, standing near the back, whispered back what he could see of the blacked-out city. We had left the downtown section and seemed to be headed west toward the suburb of Scheveningen. That was our destination then, the federal penitentiary named after this seaside town.

The truck jerked to a halt; we heard a screech of iron. We bumped forward a few feet and stopped again. Behind us massive gates clanged shut.

We climbed down to find ourselves in an enormous courtyard surrounded by a high brick wall. The truck had backed up to a long low building; soldiers prodded us inside. I blinked in the white glare of bright ceiling lights.

"Nasen gegen Mauer!"—"Noses to the wall!"

I felt a shove from behind and found myself staring at cracked plaster. I turned my eyes as far as I could, first left and then right. There was Willem. Two places away from him, Betsie. Next to me on the other side was Toos. All like me standing with their faces to the wall. Where was Father?

There was an endless wait while the scars on the wall before my eyes became faces, landscapes, animal shapes. Then somewhere to the right a door opened.

"Women prisoners follow me!"

The matron's voice sounded as metallic as the squealing door. As I stepped away from the wall I glanced swiftly round the room for Father. There he was—a few feet out from the wall, seated in a straight-backed chair. One of the guards must have brought it for him.

Already the matron was starting down the long corridor that I could see through the door. But I hung back, gazing desperately at Father, Willem, Peter, all our brave underground workers.

"Father!" I cried suddenly. "God be with you!"

His head turned toward me. The harsh overhead light flashed from his glasses.

"And with you, my daughters," he said.

I turned and followed the others. Behind me the door slammed closed. And with you! And with you! Oh Father, when will I see you next?

Betsie's hand slipped around mine. A strip of coconut-palm matting ran down the center of the wide hall. We stepped onto it off the damp concrete.

"Prisoners walk to the side" It was the bored voice of the guard behind us. "Prisoners must not step on the matting."

Guiltily we stepped off the privileged path.

Ahead of us in the corridor was a desk, behind it a woman in uniform. As each prisoner reached this point she gave her name for the thousandth time that day and placed on the desk whatever she was wearing of value. Nollie, Betsie, and I unstrapped our beautiful wristwatches. As I handed mine to the officer, she pointed to the simple gold ring that had belonged to Mama. I wriggled it from my finger and laid it on the desk along with my wallet and paper guilders.

The procession down the corridor continued. The walls on both sides of us were lined with narrow metal doors. Now the column of women halted: the matron was fitting a key into one of them. We heard the thud of a bolt drawn back, the screech of hinges. The matron consulted a list in her hand, then called the name of a lady I didn't even know, one of those who had been at Willem's prayer meeting.

Was it possible that that had been only yesterday? Was this only Thursday night? Already the events at the Beje seemed part of another lifetime. The door banged shut; the column moved on. Another door unlocked, another human being closed behind it. No two from Haarlem in the same cell.

Among the very first names read from the list was Betsie's. She stepped through the door; before she could turn or say goodbye, it had closed. Two cells farther on, Nollie left me. The clang of those two doors rang in my ears as the slow march continued.

Now the corridor branched and we turned left. Then right, then left again, an endless world of steel and concrete.

"Ten Boom, Cornelia."

Another door rasped open. The cell was deep and narrow, scarcely wider than the door. A woman lay on the single cot, three others on straw ticks on the floor. "Give this one the cot," the matron said. "She's sick."

And indeed, even as the door slammed behind me a spasm of coughing seized my chest and throat.

"We don't want a sick woman in here!" someone shouted. They were stumbling to their feet, backing as far from me as the narrow cubicle would allow.

"I'm . . . I'm so very sorry——" I began, but another voice interrupted me.

"Don't be. It isn't your fault. Come on, Frau Mikes, give her the cot." The young woman turned to me. "Let me hang up your hat and coat."

Gratefully I handed her my hat, which she added to a row of clothes hanging from hooks along one wall.

But I kept my coat wrapped right around me. The cot had been vacated and I moved shakily toward it, trying not to sneeze or breathe as I squeezed past my cellmates. I sank down on the narrow bed, then went into a fresh paroxysm of coughs as a cloud of choking black dust rose from the filthy straw mattress. At last the attack passed and I lay down. The sour straw smell filled my nostrils. I felt each slat of wood through the thin pallet.

"I will never be able to sleep on such a bed," I thought, and the next thing I knew it was morning and there was a clattering at the door. "Food call," my cellmates told me. I struggled to my feet. A square of metal had dropped open in the door, forming a small shelf. Onto this someone in the hall was placing tin plates filled with a steaming gruel.

"There's a new one here!" the woman called Frau Mikes called through the aperture. "We get five portions!" Another tin plate was slammed onto the shelf. "If you're not hungry," Frau Mikes added, "I'll help you with it."

I picked up my plate, stared at the watery gray porridge and handed it silently to her. In a little while the plates were collected and the pass-through in the door slammed shut.

Later in the morning a key grated in the lock, the bolt banged, and the door opened long enough for the sanitary bucket to be passed out. The wash basin was also emptied and returned with clean water. The women picked up their straw pallets from the floor and piled them in a corner, raising a fresh storm of dust which started me coughing helplessly again.

Then a prison boredom—which I soon learned to fear above all else—settled over the cell. At first I attempted to relieve it by talking with the others, but though they were as courteous as people can be who are living literally on top of one another, they turned aside my questions and I never learned much about them.

The young woman who had spoken kindly to me the night before, I did discover, was a baroness, only seventeen years old. This young girl paced constantly, from morning until the overhead light bulb went off at night, six steps to the door, six steps back, dodging those sitting on the floor, back and forth like an animal in a cage.

Frau Mikes turned out to be an Austrian woman who had worked as a charwoman in an office building. She often cried for her canary. "Poor little thing! What will become of him? They'll never think to feed him."

This would start me thinking of our cat. Had Maher Shalal Hashbaz made his escape into the street— or was he starving inside the sealed house? I would picture him prowling among the chairlegs in the dining room, missing the shoulders he loved to walk on. I tried not to let my mind venture higher in the house, not to let it climb the stairs to see if Thea, Mary, Eusie—no! I could do nothing for them here in this cell. God knew they were there.

One of my cellmates had spent three years here in Scheveningen. She could hear the rattle of the meal cart long before the rest of us and tell by the footstep who was passing in the corridor. "That's the trusty from medical supply. Someone's sick" . . . "This is the fourth time someone in 316 has gone for a hearing."

Her world consisted of this cubicle and the corridor outside—and soon I began to see the wisdom of this narrowed vision, and why prisoners instinctively shied away from questions about their larger lives. For the first days of my imprisonment I stayed in a frenzy of anxiety about Father, Betsie, Willem, Pickwick. Was Father able to eat this food? Was Betsie's blanket as thin as this one?

But these thoughts led to such despair that I soon learned not to give in to them. In an effort to fix my mind on something I asked Frau Mikes to teach me the card game that she played hour after hour. She had made the cards herself with the squares of toilet paper that were issued two a day to each prisoner; all day she sat on a corner of the cot endlessly laying them out in front of her and gathering them up again.

I was a slow learner, since no cards of any kind had been played at the Beje. Now as I began to grasp the solitaire game I wondered what Father's resistance

to them had been—surely nothing could be more innocent than this succession of shapes called clubs, spades,
diamonds. . . .

But as the days passed I began to discover a subtle
danger. When the cards went well my spirits rose. It
was an omen: someone from Haarlem had been released! But if I lost. . . . Maybe someone was ill. The
people in the secret room had been found. . . .

At last I had to stop playing. In any case I was
finding it hard to sit up so long. Increasingly I was
spending the days as I did the nights, tossing on the
thin straw pallet trying in vain to find a position in
which all aches at once were eased. My head throbbed
continually, pain shot up and down my arms, my cough
brought up blood.

I was thrashing feverishly on the cot one morning
when the cell door opened and there stood the steel-
voiced matron I had seen the night I entered the cell
two weeks before.

"Ten Boom, Cornelia."

I struggled to my feet.

"Bring your hat and your coat and come with
me."

I looked around at the others for a hint as to what
was happening. "You're going to the outside," our prison expert said. "When you take your hat you always
go outside."

My coat I was wearing already, but I took my hat
from its hook and stepped out into the corridor. The
matron relocked the door then set off so rapidly that my
heart hammered as I trotted after her, careful to stay
off the precious matting. I stared yearningly at the
locked doors on either side of us; I could not remember behind which ones my sisters had disappeared.

At last we stepped out into the broad, high-walled
courtyard. Sky! For the first time in two weeks, blue
sky! How high the clouds were, how inexpressibly
white and clean. I remembered suddenly how much
sky had meant to Mama.

"Quick!" snapped the matron.

I hurried to the shiny black automobile beside
which she was standing. She opened the rear door and

I got in. Two others were already in the back seat, a soldier and a woman with a gaunt gray face. In front next to the driver slumped a desperately ill-looking man whose head lolled strangely on the seat back. As the car started up the woman beside me lifted a blood-stained towel to her mouth and coughed into it. I understood the three of us were ill. Perhaps we were going to a hospital!

The massive prison gate opened and we were in the outside world, spinning along broad city streets. I stared in wonderment through the window. People walking, looking in store windows, stopping to talk with friends. Had I truly been as free as that only two weeks ago?

The car parked before an office building; it took both the soldier and the driver to get the sick man up three flights of stairs. We entered a waiting room jammed with people and sat down under the watchful eyes of the soldier. When nearly an hour had passed I asked permission to use the lavatory. The soldier spoke to the trim white-uniformed nurse behind the reception desk.

"This way," she said crisply. She took me down a short hall, stepped into the bathroom with me and shut the door. "Quick! Is there any way I can help?"

I blinked at her. "Yes. Oh yes! A Bible! Could you get me a Bible? And—a needle and thread! And a toothbrush! And soap!"

She bit her lip doubtfully. "So many patients to-day—and the soldier—but I'll do what I can." And she was gone.

But her kindness shone in the little room as brightly as the gleaming white tiles and shiny faucets. My heart soared as I scrubbed the grime off my neck and face.

A man's voice at the door: "Come on! You've been in there long enough!"

Hastily I rinsed off the soap and followed the soldier back to the waiting room. The nurse was back at her desk, coolly efficient as before; she did not look up. After another long wait my name was called. The doctor asked me to cough, took my temperature and blood pressure, applied his stethoscope, and announced that I had pleurisy with effusion, pre-tubercular.

He wrote something on a sheet of paper. Then with one hand on the doorknob he laid the other for an instant on my shoulder. "I hope," he said in a low voice, "that I am doing you a favor with this diagnosis."

In the waiting room the soldier was on his feet ready for me. As I crossed the room the nurse rose briskly from her desk and swished past me. In my hand I felt a small knobby something wrapped in paper.

I slid it into my coat pocket as I followed the soldier down the stairs. The other woman was already back in the car; the sick man did not reappear. All during the return ride my hand kept straying to the object in my pocket, stroking it, tracing the outline. "Oh Lord, it's so small, but still it could be—let it be a Bible!"

The high walls loomed ahead, the gate rang shut behind us. At last, at the end of the long echoing corridors, I reached my cell and drew the package from my pocket. My cellmates crowded round me as I unwrapped the newspaper and trembling hands. Even the baroness stopped her pacing to watch.

As two bars of precious prewar soap appeared, Frau Mikes clapped her hand over her mouth to suppress her yelp of triumph. No toothbrush or needle but —unheard-of wealth—a whole packet of safety pins! And, most wonderful of all, not indeed a whole Bible, but in four small booklets, the four Gospels.

I shared the soap and pins among the five of us but, though I offered to divide the books as well, they refused. "They catch you with those," the knowledgeable one said, "and it's double sentence and *kalte kost* as well." *Kalte kost*—the bread ration alone without the daily plate of hot food—was the punishment constantly held over our heads. If we made too much noise we'd have *kalte kost*. If we were slow with the bucket it would be *kalte kost*. But even *kalte kost* would be a small price to pay, I thought as I stretched my aching body on the foul straw, for the precious books I clutched between my hands.

It was two evenings later, near the time when the light bulb usually flickered off, that the cell door banged open and a guard strode in.

"Ten Boom, Cornelia," she snapped. "Get your things."

I stared at her, an insane hope rising in me. "You mean——"

"Silence! No talking!"

It did not take long to gather my "things": my hat and an undervest that was drying after a vain attempt to get it clean in the much-used basin water. My coat with the precious contents of its pockets had never yet been off my back. Why such strict silence, I wondered. Why should I not be allowed even a goodbye to my cellmates? Would it be so very wrong for a guard to smile now and then, or give a few words of explanation?

I said farewell to the others with my eyes and followed the stiff-backed woman into the hall. She paused to lock the door, then marched off down the corridor. But—the wrong way! We were not heading toward the outside entrance at all, but deeper into the maze of prison passageways.

Still without a word she halted in front of another door and opened it with a key. I stepped inside. The door clanged behind me. The bolt slammed shut.

The cell was identical with the one I had just left, six steps long, two wide, a single cot at the back. But this one was empty. As the guard's footsteps died away down the corridor I leaned against the cold metal of the door. Alone. Alone behind these walls. . . .

I must not let my thoughts run wildly; I must be very mature and very practical. Six steps. Sit down on the cot. This one reeked even worse than the other: the straw seemed to be fermenting. I reached for the blanket: someone had been sick on it. I thrust it away but it was too late. I dashed for the bucket near the door and leaned weakly over it.

At that moment the light bulb in the ceiling went

out. I groped back to the cot and huddled there in the dark, setting my teeth against the stink of the bedding, wrapping my coat tighter about me. The cell was bitter cold, wind hammered against the wall. This must be near the outside edge of the prison: the wind had never shrieked so in the other one.

What had I done to be separated from people this way? Had they discovered the conversation with the nurse at the doctor's office? Or perhaps some of the prisoners from Haarlem had been interrogated and the truth about our group was known. Maybe my sentence was solitary confinement for years and years. . . .

In the morning my fever was worse. I could not stand even long enough to get my food from the shelf in the door and after an hour or so the plate was taken away untouched.

Toward evening the pass-through dropped open again and the hunk of coarse prison bread appeared. By now I was desperate for food but less able to walk than ever. Whoever was in the hall must have seen the problem. A hand picked up the bread and hurled it toward me. It landed on the floor beside the cot where I clawed for it and gnawed it greedily.

For several days while the fever raged my supper was delivered in this manner. Mornings the door squealed open and a woman in a blue smock carried the plate of hot gruel to the cot. I was as starved for the sight of a human face as for the food and tried in a hoarse croak to start a conversation. But the woman, obviously a fellow prisoner, would only shake her head with a fearful glance toward the hall.

The door also opened once a day to let in the trusty from Medical Supply with a dose of some stinging yellow liquid from a very dirty bottle. The first time he entered the cell I clutched at his sleeve. "Please!" I rasped. "Have you seen an eighty-four-year-old man—white hair, a long beard? Casper ten Boom! You must have taken medicine to him!"

The man tugged loose. "I don't know! I don't know anything!"

The cell door slammed back against the wall, framing the guard. "Solitary prisoners are not permitted to talk! If you say another word to one of the work-duty prisoners it will be *kalte kost* for the duration of your sentence!" And the door banged behind the two of them.

This same trusty was also charged with recording my temperature each time he came. I had to take off my shirt and place the thermometer between my arm and the side of my body. It did not look to me like an accurate system: sure enough, by the end of the week an irritable voice called through the food slot, "Get up and get the food yourself! Your fever's gone—you won't be waited on again!"

I felt sure that the fever had not gone, but there was nothing for it but to creep, trembling, to the door for my plate. When I had replaced it I would lie down again on the smelly straw, steeling myself for the bawling out I knew would come. "Look at the great lady, back in bed again! Are you going to lie there all day long?" Why lying down was such a crime I could never understand. Nor indeed what one was supposed to accomplish if one got up. . . .

Thoughts, now that I was alone, were a bigger problem than ever. I could no longer even pray for family and friends by name, so great was the fear and longing wrapped round each one. "Those I love, Lord," I would say. "You know them. You see them. Oh— bless them all!"

Thoughts were enemies. That prison bag . . . how many times I opened it in my mind and pawed through all the things I had left behind. A fresh blouse. Aspirin, a whole bottle of them. Toothpaste with a kind of pepperminty taste, and——

Then I would catch myself. How ridiculous, such thoughts! If I had it to do again would I really put these little personal comforts ahead of human lives? Of course not. But in the dark nights, as the wind howled and the fever pulsed, I would draw that bag out of some dark corner of my mind and root through it once again. A towel to lay on this scratchy straw. An aspirin . . .

In only one way was this new cell an improvement over the first one. It had a window. Seven iron bars ran across it, four bars up and down. It was high in the wall, much too high to look out of, but through those twenty-eight squares I could see the sky.

All day I kept my eyes fixed on that bit of heaven. Sometimes clouds moved across the squares, white or pink or edged with gold, and when the wind was from the west I could hear the sea. Best of all, for nearly an hour each day, gradually lengthening as the spring sun rose higher, a shaft of checkered light streamed into the dark little room. As the weather turned warmer and I grew stronger I would stand up to catch the sunshine on my face and chest, moving along the wall with the moving light, climbing at last onto the cot to stand on tiptoe in the final rays.

As my health returned, I was able to use my eyes longer. I had been sustaining myself from my Scriptures a verse at a time; now like a starving man I gulped entire Gospels at a reading, seeing whole the magnificent drama of salvation.

And as I did, an incredible thought prickled the back of my neck. Was it possible that this—all of this that seemed so wasteful and so needless—this war, Scheveningen prison, this very cell, none of it was unforeseen or accidental? Could it be part of the pattern first revealed in the Gospels? Hadn't Jesus—and here my reading became intent indeed—hadn't Jesus been defeated as utterly and unarguably as our little group and our small plans had been?

But . . . if the Gospels were truly the pattern of God's activity, then defeat was only the beginning. I would look around at the bare little cell and wonder what conceivable victory could come from a place like this.

The prison expert in the first cell had taught me to make a kind of knife by rubbing a corset stay against the rough cement floor. It seemed to me strangely important not to lose track of time. And so with a sharp-boned stay I scratched a calendar on the wall behind the cot. As each long featureless day crawled to a close,

I checked off another square. I also started a record of special dates beneath the calendar:

February 28, 1944   Arrest
February 29, 1944   Transport to Scheveningen
March 16, 1944   Beginning of Solitary

And now a new date:

April 15, 1944   My Birthday in Prison

A birthday had to mean a party, but I searched in vain for a single cheerful object. At least in the other cell there had been bright bits of clothing: the baroness' red hat, Frau Mikes' yellow blouse. How I regretted now my own lack of taste in clothes.

At least I would have a song at my party! I chose one about the Bride of Haarlem tree—she would be in full bloom now. The child's song brought it all close: the bursting branches, the petals raining like snow on the brick sidewalk——

"Quite in there!" A volley of blows sounded on my iron door. "Solitary prisoners are to keep silent!"

I sat on the cot, opened the Gospel of John, and read until the ache in my heart went away.

Two days after my birthday I was taken for the first time to the big, echoing shower room. A grim-faced guard marched beside me, her scowl forbidding me to take pleasure in the expedition. But nothing could dim the wonder of stepping into that wide corridor after so many weeks of close confinement.

At the door to the shower room several women were waiting. Even in the strict silence this human closeness was joy and strength. I scanned the faces of those coming out, but neither Betsie nor Nollie was there, nor anyone else from Haarlem. And yet, I thought, they are all my sisters. How rich is anyone who can simply see human faces!

The shower too was glorious: warm clean water over my festering skin, streams of water through my matted hair. I went back to my cell with a new resolve: the next time I was permitted a shower I would take with me three of my Gospels. Solitary was teaching me that it was not possible to be rich alone.

And I was not alone much longer: into my solitary cell came a small busy black ant. I had almost put my foot where he was one morning as I carried my bucket to the door when I realized the honor being done me. I crouched down and admired the marvelous design of legs and body. I apologized for my size and promised I would not so thoughtlessly stride about again.

After a while he disappeared through a crack in the floor. But when my evening piece of bread appeared on the door shelf, I scattered some crumbs and to my joy he popped out almost at once. He picked up a heroic piece, struggled down the hole with it and came back for more. It was the beginning of a relationship.

Now in addition to the daily visit of the sun I had the company of this brave and handsome guest—in fact soon of a whole small committee. If I was washing out clothes in the basin or sharpening the point on my homemade knife when the ants appeared, I stopped at once to give them my full attention. It would have been unthinkable to squander two activities on the same bit of time!

One evening as I was crossing another long, long day from the calendar scratched on my wall, I heard shouts far down the corridor. They were answered closer by. Now noisy voices came from every direction. How unusual for the prisoners to be making a racket! Where were the guards?

The shelf in my door had not been closed since the bread came two hours ago. I pressed my ear to it and listened but it was hard to make sense of the tumult outside. Names were being passed from cell to cell. People were singing, others pounding on their doors. The guards must all be away!

"Please! Let's be quiet!" a voice nearby pleaded. "Let's use this time before they get back!"

"What's happening?" I cried through the open slot. "Where are the guards?"

"At the party," the same voice answered me. "It's Hitler's birthday."

Then—these must be their own names people were shouting down the corridor. This was our chance to tell where we were, to get information.

"I'm Corrie ten Boom!" I called through the food shelf. "My whole family is here somewhere! Oh, has anyone seen Casper ten Boom! Betsie ten Boom! Nollie van Woerden! Willem ten Boom!" I shouted names until I was hoarse and heard them repeated from mouth to mouth down the long corridor. I passed names too, to the right and left, as we worked out a kind of system.

After a while answers began to filter back. "Mrs. van der Elst is in Cell 228. . . ." "Pietje's arm is much better. . . ." Some of the messages I could hardly bear to relay: "The hearing was very bad: he sits in the cell without speaking." "To my husband Joost: our baby died last week. . . ."

Along with personal messages were rumors about the world outside, each more wildly optimistic than the last.

"There is a revolution in Germany!"

"The Allies have invaded Europe!"

"The war cannot last three weeks longer!"

At last some of the names I had shouted out began to return. "Betsie ten Boom is in cell 312. She says to tell you that God is good."

Oh, that was Betsie! That was every inch Betsie!

Then: "Nollie van Woerden was in cell 318, but she was released more than a month ago." Released! Oh, thank God!

Toos, too, released!

News from the men's section was longer returning, but as it did my heart leapt higher and higher.

Peter van Woerden. Released!

Herman Sluring. Released!

Willem ten Boom. Released!

As far as I could discover, every single one taken in the raid on the Beje—with the exception of Betsie and me—had been freed. Only about Father could I discover no news at all, although I called his name over and over into the murmuring hall. No one seemed to have seen him. No one seemed to know. . . .

It was perhaps a week later that my cell door opened and a prison trusty tossed a package wrapped in brown paper onto the floor. I picked it up, hefted it, turned it over and over. The wrapping paper had been torn open and carelessly retied, but even through the disarray I could spot Nollie's loving touch. I sat on the cot and opened it.

There, familiar and welcoming as a visit from home, was the light blue embroidered sweater. As I put it on I seemed to feel Nollie's arms circling my shoulders. Also inside the package were cookies and vitamins, needle and thread, and a bright red towel. How Nollie understood the gray color-hunger of prison! She had even wrapped the cookies in gay red cellophane.

I was biting into the first one when an inspiration came to me. I dragged the cot out from the wall to stand under the naked overhead bulb. Climbing on it I fashioned a lampshade with the paper: a cheery red glow at once suffused the bleak little room.

I was rewrapping the cookies in the brown outer paper when my eyes fell on the address written in Nollie's careful hand, slanting upward toward the postage stamp. But—Nollie's handwriting did not slant. . . . The stamp! Hadn't a message once come to the Beje under a stamp, penciled in the tiny square beneath? Laughing at my own overwrought imagination I moistened the paper in the basin water and worked the stamp gently free.

Words! There was definitely writing there—but so tiny I had to climb again onto the cot and hold the paper close to the shaded bulb.

"All the watches in your closet are safe."

Safe. Then—then Eusie, and Henk, and Mary, and—they'd got out of the secret room! They'd escaped! They were free!

I burst into racking sobs, then heard heavy footsteps bearing down the corridor. Hastily I jumped down from the cot and shoved it back to the wall. The pass-through clattered open.

"What's the commotion in here!"

"It's nothing. I—won't do it again."

The slot in the door snapped shut. How had they managed it? How had they got past the soldiers? Never mind, dear Lord. You were there, and that was all that mattered. . . .

The cell door opened to let in a German officer followed by the head matron herself. My eyes ran hungrily over the well-pressed uniform with its rows of brilliant-colored battle ribbons.

"Miss ten Boom," the officer began in excellent Dutch. "I have a few questions I believe you can help me with."

The matron was carrying a small stool which she leapt to set down for the officer. I stared at her. Was this obsequious creature the terrible-voiced terror of the women's wing?

The officer sat down, motioning me to take the cot. There was something in that gesture that belonged to the world outside the prison. As he took out a small notebook and began to read names from it I was suddenly conscious of my rumpled clothes, my long, ragged fingernails.

To my relief I honestly did not know any of the names he read—now I understood the wisdom of the ubiquitous "Mr. Smit." The officer stood up. "Will you be feeling well enough to come for your hearing soon?"

Again that ordinary human manner. "Yes—I—I hope so." The officer stepped out into the hall, the matron bobbing and scurrying after him with the stool.

It was the third of May; I was sitting on my cot sewing. Since Nollie's package had been delivered I had a wonderful new occupation: one by one I was pulling the threads from the red towel and with them embroidering bright figures on the pajamas that I had only recently stopped wearing beneath my clothes. A window with ruffled curtains. A flower with an impossible number of petals and leaves. I had just started work on the head of a cat over the right pocket when the food shelf in the door banged open and shut with a single motion.

And there on the floor of the cell lay a letter.

I dropped the pajamas and sprang forward. Nollie's writing. Why should my hand tremble as I picked it up?

The letter had been opened by the censors—held by them too: the postmark was over a week old. But it was a letter, a letter from home—the very first one! Why this sudden fear?

I unfolded the paper. "Corrie, can you be very brave?"

No! No, I couldn't be brave! I forced my eyes to read on.

"I have news that is very hard to write you. Father survived his arrest by only ten days. He is now with the Lord. . . ."

I stood with the paper between my hands so long that the daily shaft of sunlight entered the cell and fell upon it. Father . . . Father . . . the letter glittered in the criss-cross light as I read the rest. Nollie had no details, not how or where he had died, not even where he was buried.

Footsteps were passing on the coconut matting. I ran to the door and pressed my face to the closed pass-through. "Please! Oh please!"

The steps stopped. The shelf dropped open. "What's the matter?"

"Please! I've had bad news—oh please, don't go away!"

"Wait a minute." The footsteps retreated, then returned with a jangle of keys. The cell door opened.

"Here." The young woman handed me a pill with a glass of water. "It's a sedative."

"This letter just came," I explained. "It says that my father—it says my father has died."

The girl stared at me. "Your father!" she said in astonished tones.

I realized how very old and decrepit I must look to this young person. She stood in the doorway a while, obviously embarrassed at my tears. "Whatever happens," she said at last, "you brought it on yourself by breaking the laws!"

Dear Jesus, I whispered as the door slammed and her footsteps died away, how foolish of me to have called for human help when You are here. To think that Father sees You now, face to face! To think that he and Mama are together again, walking those bright streets. . . .

I pulled the cot from the wall and below the calendar scratched another date:

March 9, 1944   Father. Released.

11

The Lieutenant

I was walking with a guard—behind and a little to the right of her so my feet would not touch the sacrosanct mat—down a corridor I had not seen before. A turn to the right, a few steps down, right again . . . what an endless labyrinth this prison was. At last we stepped out into a small interior courtyard. A drizzle of rain was falling. It was a chill raw morning in late May: after three months in prison I had been called for my first hearing.

Barred windows stared from tall buildings on three sides of the courtyard, along the fourth was a high wall and against this stood a row of small huts. So these were where the infamous interrogations took place. My breath came short and hard as I thought back to the reports I had passed on, the night of Hitler's birthday.

"Lord Jesus, You were called to a hearing too. Show me what to do."

And then I saw something. Whoever used the fourth of the huts had planted a row of tulips along the side. They were wilted now, only tall stems and yellowing leaves, but . . . "Dear Lord, let me go to hut number four!"

The guard had paused to unstrap a long military cape fastened to the shoulder of her uniform. Protected from the rain, she crunched up the gravel path. Past the first hut, the second, the third. She halted in front of the hut with the flowerbed and rapped on the door.

"Ja! Herrein!" called a man's voice.

The guard pushed open the door, gave a straight-armed salute and marched smartly off. The man wore a gun in a leather holstered and a beribboned uniform. He removed his hat and I was staring into the face of the gentle-mannered man who had visited me in my cell.

"I am Lieutenant Rahms," he said, stepping to the door to close it behind me. "You're shivering! Here, let me get a fire going."

He filled a pot-bellied stove from a small coal scuttle, for all the world a kindly German householder entertaining a guest. What if this were a subtle trap? This kind, human manner—perhaps he had simply found it more effective than brutality in tricking the truth from affection-starved people. "Oh Lord, let no weak gullibility on my part endanger another's life."

"I hope," the officer was saying, "we won't have many more days this spring as cold as this one." He drew out a chair for me to sit on.

Warily I accepted it. How strange after three months, to feel a chair-back behind me, chair-arms for my hands! The heat from the stove was quickly warming the little room. In spite of myself I began to relax. I ventured a timid comment about the tulips. "So tall, they must have been beautiful."

"Oh they were!" he seemed ridiculously pleased. "The best I've ever grown. At home we always have Dutch bulbs."

We talked about flowers for a while and then he said, "I would like to help you, Miss ten Boom. But you must tell me everything. I may be able to do something, but only if you do not hide anything from me."

So there it was already. All the friendliness, the kindly concern that I had half-believed in—all a device to elicit information. Well, why not? This man was a professional with a job to do. But I, too, in a small way, was a professional.

For an hour he questioned me, using every psychological trick that the young men of our group had drilled me in. In fact, I felt like a student who has crammed for a difficult exam and then is tested on only the most elementary material. It soon became clear that they believed the Beje had been a headquarters for raids on food ration offices around the country. Of all the illegal activities I had on my conscience, this was probably the one I knew least about. Other than receiving the stolen cards each month and passing them on, I knew no details of the operation. Apparently my real ignorance began to show; after a while Lieutenant Rahms stopped making notes of my hopelessly stupid answers.

"Your other activities, Miss ten Boom. What would you like to tell me about them?"

"Other activities? Oh, you mean—you want to know about my church for mentally retarded people!" And I plunged into an eager account of my efforts at preaching to the feeble-minded.

The lieutenant's eyebrows rose higher and higher. "What a waste of time and energy!" he exploded at last. "If you want converts, surely one normal person is worth all the half-wits in the world!"

I stared into the man's intelligent blue-gray eyes: true National-Socialist philosophy I thought, tulip bed or no. And then to my astonishment I heard my own voice saying boldly, "May I tell you the truth, Lieutenant Rahms?"

"This hearing, Miss ten Boom, is predicated on the assumption that you will do me that honor."

"The truth, Sir," I said, swallowing, "is that God's viewpoint is sometimes different from ours—so different that we could not even guess at it unless He had given us a Book which tells us such things."

I knew it was madness to talk this way to a Nazi officer. But he said nothing so I plunged ahead. "In the Bible I learn that God values us not for our strength or our brains but simply because He has made us. Who knows, in His eyes a half-wit may be worth more than a watchmaker. Or—a lieutenant."

Lieutenant Rahms stood up abruptly. "That will

be all for today." He walked swiftly to the door.
"Guard!"

I heard footsteps on the gravel path.

"The prisoner will return to her cell."

Following the guard through the long cold corridors, I knew I had made a mistake. I had said too much. I had ruined whatever chance I had that this man might take an interest in my case.

And yet the following morning it was Lieutenant Rahms himself who unlocked my cell door and escorted me to the hearing. Apparently he did not know of the regulation that forbade prisoners to step on the mat, for he indicated that I was to walk ahead of him down the center of the hall. I avoided the eyes of the guards along the route, guilty as a well-trained dog discovered on the living room sofa.

In the courtyard this time a bright sun was shining. "Today," he said, "we will stay outside. You are pale. You are not getting enough sun."

Gratefully I followed him to the farthest corner of the little yard where the air was still and warm. We settled our backs against the wall. "I could not sleep last night," the lieutenant said, "thinking about that Book where you have read such different ideas. What else does it say in there?"

On my closed eyelids the sun glimmered and blazed. "It says," I began slowly, "that a Light has come into this world, so that we need no longer walk in the dark. Is there darkness in your life, Lieutenant?"

There was a very long silence.

"There is great darkness," he said at last. "I cannot bear the work I do here."

Then all at once he was telling me about his wife and children in Bremen, about their garden, their dogs, their summer hiking vacations. "Bremen was bombed again last week. Each morning I ask myself are they still alive?"

"There is One Who has them always in His sight, Lieutenant Rahms. Jesus is the Light the Bible shows to me, the Light that can shine even in such darkness as yours."

The man pulled the visor of his hat lower over his eyes; the skull-and-crossbones glinted in the sunlight. When he spoke it was so low I could hardly hear. "What can you know of darkness like mine. . . ."

Two more mornings the hearings continued. He had dropped all pretense of questioning me on my underground activities and seemed especially to enjoy hearing about my childhood. Mama, Father, the aunts —he wanted to hear stories about them again and again. He was incensed to learn that Father had died right here in Scheveningen; the documents on my case made no mention of it.

These documents did answer one question: the reason for solitary confinement. "Prisoner's condition contagious to others in cell." I stared at the brief typed words where Lieutenant Rahms's finger rested. I thought of the long wind-haunted nights, the scowling guards, the rule of silence. "But, if it wasn't punishment, why were they so angry with me? Why couldn't I talk?"

The lieutenant squared the edges of the papers in front of him. "A prison is like any institution, Miss ten Boom, certain rules, certain ways of doing things——"

"But I'm not contagious now! I've been better for weeks and weeks, and my own sister is so close! Lieutenant Rahms, if I could only see Betsie! If I could just talk with her a few minutes!"

He lifted his eyes from the desk and I saw anguish in them. "Miss ten Boom, it is possible that I appear to you a powerful person. I wear a uniform. I have a certain authority over those under me. But I am in prison, dear lady from Haarlem, a prison stronger than this one."

It was the fourth and final hearing, and we had come back into the small hut for the signing of the *procès-verbal*. He gathered up the completed transcript and went out with it, leaving me alone. I was sorry to say goodbye to this man who was struggling so earnestly for truth. The hardest thing for him seemed to be that Christians should suffer. "How can you believe in God

now?" he'd ask. "What kind of a God would have let
that old man die here in Scheveningen?"

I got up from the chair and held my hands out
to the squat little stove. I did not understand either why
Father had died in such a place. I did not understand
a great deal.

And suddenly I was thinking of Father's own
answer to hard questions: "Some knowledge is too
heavy . . . you cannot bear it . . . your Father will carry
it until you are able." Yes! I would tell Lieutenant
Rahms about the traincase—he always liked stories
about Father.

But when the lieutenant returned to the room a
guard from the women's wing was with him. "Prisoner
ten Boom has completed her hearings," he said, "and
will return to her cell."

The young woman snapped to attention. As I
stepped through the door, Lieutenant Rahms leaned
forward.

"Walk slowly," he said, "in Corridor F."

Walk slowly? What did he mean? The guard
strode down the long door-lined halls so swiftly I had
to trot to keep up with her. Ahead of us a prison trusty
was unlocking the door to a cell. I trailed behind the
guard as much as I dared, my heart thumping wildly.
It would be Betsie's cell—I knew it!

Then I was abreast of the door. Betsie's back
was to the corridor. I could see only the graceful up-
swept bun of her chestnut hair. The other women in
the cell stared curiously into the corridor; her head
remained bent over something in her lap. But I had
seen the home Betsie had made in Scheveningen.

For unbelievably, against all logic, this cell was
charming. My eyes seized only a few details as I inched
reluctantly past. The straw pallets were rolled instead
of piled in a heap, standing like little pillars along
the walls, each with a lady's hat atop it. A headscarf
had somehow been hung along the wall. The contents
of several food packages were arranged on a small shelf;
I could just hear Betsie saying, "The red biscuit tin
here in the center!" Even the coats hanging on their

hooks were part of the welcome of that room, each sleeve draped over the shoulder of the coat next to it like a row of dancing children——

"*Schneller! Aber schnell!*"

I jumped and hurried after my escort. It had been a glimpse only, two seconds at the most, but I walked through the corridors of Scheveningen with Betsie's singing spirit at my side.

All morning I heard doors opening and closing. Now keys rattled outside my own: a very young guard in a very new uniform bounded in.

"Prisoner stand at attention!" she squeaked. I stared at her wide, blinking eyes; the girl was in mortal fear of something or someone.

Then a shadow filled the doorway and the tallest woman I had ever seen stepped into the cell. Her features were classically handsome, the face and height of a goddess—but one carved in marble. Not a flicker of feeling registered in her eyes.

"No sheets here either, I see," she said in German to the guard. "See that she has two by Friday. One to be changed every two weeks."

The ice-cold eyes appraised me exactly as they had the bed. "How many showers does the prisoner get?"

The guard wet her lips. "About one a week, *Wachtmeisterin.*"

One a week! One shower a month was closer!

"She will go twice a week."

Sheets! Regular showers! Were conditions going to be better? The new head matron took two strides into the cell; she did not need the cot to reach the overhead bulb. Rip! Off came my red-cellophane lampshade. She pointed to a box of soda crackers that had come in a second package from Nollie.

"No boxes in the cells!" cried the little guard in Dutch, as indignantly as though this had been a long-standing rule.

Not knowing what else to do I dumped the crackers out onto the cot. At the matron's unspoken command I emptied a bottle of vitamins and a sack of peppermint drops the same way.

Unlike the former head matron, who shrieked and scolded endlessly in her rusted-hinge voice, this woman worked in a terrifying silence. With a gesture she directed the guard to feel beneath the mattress. My heart wedged in my throat; my precious remaining Gospel was hidden there. The guard knelt and ran her hands the length of the cot. But whether she was too nervous to do a thorough job or whether there was a more mysterious explanation, she straightened up empty-handed.

And then they were gone.

I stood gazing numbly at the jumble of food on my cot. I thought of this woman reaching Betsie's cell, reducing it again to four walls and a prison cot. A chill wind was blowing through Scheveningen, cleaning, ordering, killing.

It was this tall, ramrod-straight woman who unlocked the door to my cell one afternoon in the second half of June and admitted Lieutenant Rahms. At the severity in his face I swallowed the greeting that had almost burst from me.

"You will come to my office," he said briefly. "The notary has come."

We might as well have been total strangers. "Notary?" I asked stupidly.

"For the reading of your Father's will." He made an impatient gesture; obviously this minor matter had interrupted a busy day. "It's the law—family present when a will is opened."

Already he was heading from the cell and down the corridor. I broke into a clumsy run to keep up with the strides of the silent woman beside me. The law? What law? And since when had the German occupation government concerned itself with Dutch legal procedures? Family. Family present. . . . No, don't let yourself think of it!

At the door to the courtyard the matron turned, erect and impassive, back along the corridor. I followed Lieutenant Rahms into the dazzling early summer afternoon. He opened the door for me into the fourth hut. Before my eyes adjusted to the gloom I was drowning in Willem's embrace.

"Corrie! Corrie! Baby sister!" It was fifty years since he had called me that.

Now Nollie's arm was around me too, the other one still clinging to Betsie, as though by the strength of her grip she would hold us together forever. Betsie! Nollie! Willem! I did not know which name to cry first. Tine was in that little room too—and Flip! And another man; when I had time to look I recognized the Haarlem notary who had been called in on the watchshop's few legal consultations. We held each other at arm's length to look, we babbled questions all at once.

Betsie was thin and prison-pale. But it was Willem who shocked me. His face was gaunt, yellow, and pain-haunted. He had come home this way from Scheveningen, Tine told me. Two of the eight men crowded into his tiny cell had died of jaundice while he was there.

Willem! I could not bear to see him this way. I crooked my arm through his, standing close so that I did not have to look at him, loving the sound of his deep rolling voice. Willem did not seem aware of his own illness: his concern was all for Kik. This handsome blond son had been seized the month before while helping an American parachutist reach the North Sea. They believed he had been on one of the recent prison trains into Germany.

As for Father, they had learned a few more facts about his last days. He had apparently become ill in his cell and been taken by car to the municipal hospital in The Hague. There, no bed had been available. Father had died in a corridor, separated somehow from his records or any clue as to his identity. Hospital authorities had buried the unknown old man in the paupers' cemetery. The family believed they had located the particular grave.

I glanced over at Lieutenant Rahms. He was standing with his back to us as we talked, staring down at the cold unlit stove. Swiftly I opened the package that Nollie had pressed into my hand with the first embrace. It was what my leaping heart had told me: a

Bible, the entire Book in a compact volume, tucked inside a small pouch with a string for wearing around the neck as we had once carried our identity cards. I dropped it quickly over my head and down my back beneath my blouse. I couldn't even find words with which to thank her: the day before, in the shower line, I had given away my last remaining Gospel.

"We don't know all the details," Willem was saying in a low voice to Betsie, "just that after a few days the soldiers were taken off guard duty at the Beje and police stationed there instead." The fourth night, he believed, the chief had succeeded in assigning Rolf and another of our group to the same shift. They had found all the Jews well, though cramped and hungry, and seen them to new hiding places.

"And now?" I whispered back. "They're all right now?"

Willem lowered his deep-sunk eyes to mine. He had never been good at concealing difficult truths. "They're all right, Corrie—all except Mary." Old Mary Itallie, he said, had been arrested one day walking down a city street. Where she had been going and why she had exposed herself this way in broad daylight, nobody knew.

"The time is up." Lieutenant Rahms left his perusal of the stove and nodded to the notary. "Proceed with the reading of the will."

It was a brief, informal document: the Beje was to be home for Betsie and me as long as we wanted it; should there ever be any money realized from the sale of house or watch shop, he knew we would recall his equal love for us all; he committed us with joy to the constant care of God.

In the silence which followed, we all suddenly bowed our heads. "Lord Jesus," Willem said, "we praise You for these moments together under the protection of this good man. How can we thank him? We have no power to do him any service. Lord, allow us to share this inheritance from our father with him as well. Take him too, and his family, into Your constant care."

Outside, a guard's footsteps sounded on the crunchy gravel walk.

12

Vught

"Get your things together! Get ready to evacuate! Collect all possessions in pillowcases!" The shouts of the guards echoed up and down the long corridor.

I stood in the center of my cell in a frenzy of excitement. Evacuate! Then—then something was happening! We were leaving the prison! The counter-invasion must have begun.

I snatched the pillowcase from the little wad of straw I had stuffed into it. What riches this coarse bit of muslin had been in the two weeks since it had been provided: a shield for my head from the scratch and smell of the bedding. It almost didn't matter that the promised sheets had never arrived.

With trembling hands I dropped my few belongings into it, the blue sweater, the pajamas—covered now back and front with embroidered figures—toothbrush, comb, a few remaining crackers wrapped in toilet paper. My Bible was in its pouch on my back where it remained except when I was reading it.

I put on my coat and hat and stood at the iron door clutching the pillowcase in both hands. It was still early in the morning; the tin breakfast plate had not yet been removed from the shelf in the door. Getting ready had taken no time at all.

An hour passed. I sat on the cot. Two hours. Three. It was warm in the cell this late June day. I took off my hat and coat and folded them next to me on the cot.

More time passed. I kept my eyes on the ant hole, hoping for a last visit from my small friends, but they did not appear. Probably I had frightened them by my early dashing about. I reached into the pillowcase, took one of the crackers and crumbled it about the little crack. No ants. They were staying safely hidden.

And suddenly I realized that this too was a message, a last wordless communication among neighbors. For I too had a hiding place when things were bad. Jesus was this place, the Rock cleft for me. I pressed a finger to the tiny crevice.

The afternoon sun appeared on the wall and moved slowly across the cell. And then all at once there was a clanging out in the corridor. Doors scraped. Bolts banged. "Out! *Schnell!* All out! No talking!"

I snatched up my hat and coat.

My door screeched open. "Form ranks of five ——" the guard was already at the next cell.

I stepped out into the hall. It was jammed from wall to wall: I had never dreamed so many women occupied this corridor. We exchanged looks. "In-vasion," we mouthed silently, the soundless word sweeping through the massed women like an electric charge. Surely the invasion of Holland had begun! Why else would they be emptying the prison!

Where would we be taken? Where were we headed? Not into Germany! Dear Jesus, not Germany.

The command was given and we shuffled forward down the long chill halls, each carrying a pillowcase, with her belongings forming a little bulge at the bottom. At last we emerged into the wide courtyard inside the front gate of the prison and another long wait began. But this wait was pleasant with the late afternoon sun on our backs. Far to the right I could see the columns of the men's section. But crane my neck though I would, I could not see Betsie anywhere.

At last the huge gate swung in and a convoy of gray transport buses drove through. I was herded aboard the third one. The seats had been removed, the windows painted over. The bus lurched dreadfully as it started up but we were standing too close together to fall. When the bus ground to a stop we were at a freight yard somewhere on the outskirts of the city.

Again we were formed into ranks. The guards' voices were tense and shrill. We had to keep our heads facing forward, eyes front. Behind us we could hear buses arriving, then lumbering away again. It was still light, but I knew by the ache in my stomach that it was long past suppertime.

And then, ahead and to the left of me, in the newest group of arriving prisoners, I spotted a chestnut bun. Somehow, some way, I was going to get to her! Now instead of wanting the day to end, I prayed that we stay where we were until dark.

Slowly the long June day faded. Thunder rumbled and a few drops of rain fell. At last a long row of unlit coaches rolled slowly over the tracks in front of us. They banged to a stop, rolled forward a little farther, then stopped again. After a while they began backing. For an hour or more the train switched back and forth.

By the time the order came to board, it was pitch dark. The ranks of prisoners surged forward. Behind us the guards shouted and cursed: obviously they were nervous at transporting so many prisoners at one time. I wriggled and shoved to the left. Elbows and shoulders were in my way but I squirmed past. At the very steps of the train I reached out and seized Betsie's hand.

Together we climbed onto the train, together found seats in a crowded compartment, together wept tears of gratitude. The four months in Scheveningen had been our first separation in fifty-three years; it seemed to me that I could bear whatever happened with Betsie beside me.

More hours passed as the loaded train sat on the siding. For us they flew, there was so much to share. Betsie told me about each of her cellmates—and I told her about mine and the little hole into which they scrambled at any emergency. As always, Betsie had given to others everything she had. The Bible that

Nollie had smuggled to her she had torn up and passed around, book by book.

It must have been 2:00 or 3:00 in the morning that the train at last began to move. We pressed our faces to the glass, but no lights showed and clouds covered the moon. The thought uppermost in every mind was: Is it Germany? At one point we made out a tower that Betsie was sure was the cathedral at Delft. An hour or more later the clack of the train changed pitch: we were crossing a trestle. But—a very long one! As the minutes passed and still we had not reached the other side Betsie and I exchanged looks. The Moerdijk Bridge! Then we were headed south. Not east into Germany, but south to Brabant. For the second time that night we wept tears of joy.

I leaned my head back against the wooden slats of the seat and shut my eyes; reliving another train trip to Brabant. Mama's hand had gripped Father's, then, as the train swayed. Then, too, it was June—the June of the First Sermon, of the garden back of the manse, of Karel. . . .

I must have fallen asleep, back in that other June, for when I opened my eyes the train had stopped. Voices were shouting at us to move: *Schneller! Aber Schnell!* An eerie glare lit the windows. Betsie and I stumbled after the others along the aisle and down the iron steps. We seemed to have stopped in the middle of a woods. Floodlights mounted in trees lit a broad rough-cleared path lined by soldiers with leveled guns.

Spurred by the shouts of the guards Betsie and I started up the path between the gun barrels. *"Schneller! Close ranks! Keep up! Five abreast!"* Betsie's breath was coming short and hard and still they yelled at us to go faster. It had rained hard here, for there were deep puddles in the path. Ahead of us a white-haired woman stepped to the side to avoid one; a soldier struck her in the back with a gun butt. I took Betsie's pillowcase along with mine, hooked my other arm through hers and hauled her along beside me.

The nightmare march lasted a mile or more. At last we came to a barbed-wire fence surrounding a row of wooden barracks. There were no beds in the one we entered, only long tables with backless benches pulled up to them. Betsie and I collapsed onto one of these. Under my arm I could feel the irregular flutter of her heart. We fell into an exhausted sleep, our heads on the table.

The sun was streaming through the barracks windows when we woke up. We were thirsty and hungry: we had had nothing to eat or drink since the early meal at Scheveningen the morning before. But all that day no guard or any official person appeared inside the barracks. At last, when the sun was low in the sky, a prisoner crew arrived with a great vat of some thick steamy substance that we gobbled ravenously.

And so began our stay in this place that, we learned, was named Vught after the nearest small village. Unlike Scheveningen, which had been a regular Dutch prison, Vught had been constructed by the occupation especially as a concentration camp for political prisoners. We were not yet in the camp proper but in a kind of quarantine compound outside. Our biggest problem was idleness, wedged together as we were around the long rows of tables with nothing to do. We were guarded by the same young women who had patrolled the corridors at Scheveningen. They had been adequate enough as long as we were behind locked doors; here they seemed at a loss. Their only technique for maintaining discipline was to shriek obscenities and hand out punishments to all alike. Half rations for the entire barracks. An extra roll call at rigid attention. A ban on talking for twenty-four hours.

Only one of our overseers never threatened or raised her voice. This was the tall, silent head matron from Scheveningen. She appeared in Vught the third morning during the predawn roll call and at once something like order seized our rebellious and untidy ranks. Lines straightened, hands were clamped to sides, whispers ceased as those cold blue eyes swept across us.

Among ourselves we nicknamed her "The General." During one long roll call a pregnant woman at our table slumped to the floor, striking her head against the edge of the bench. The General did not so much as pause in her expressionless reading of names.

We had been in this outer camp at Vught almost two weeks when Betsie and I along with a dozen others were called out by name during morning roll call. When the rest had been dismissed The General distributed typewritten forms among us and instructed us to present them at the administration barracks at 9:00 o'clock.

A worker on the food crew—a long-term prisoner from the main camp—smiled encouragingly as he ladled out our breakfast. "You're free!" he whispered. "Those pink forms mean release!"

Betsie and I stared disbelievingly at the sheets of paper in our hands. Free? Free to leave—free to go home? Others crowded around, congratulating us, embracing us. The women from Betsie's cell at Scheveningen wept unabashedly. How cruel to have to leave all these behind!

"Surely the war will be over very soon," we told them. We emptied our pillowcases, passing out our few belongings among those who had to stay.

Long before 9:00 we were standing in the big wooden anteroom of Administration. At last we were summoned to an inner office where our forms were examined, stamped, and handed over to a guard. We followed this man down a corridor into another office. For hours the process continued as we were shuttled from one room and official to another, questioned, fingerprinted, sent on to the next post. The group of prisoners grew until there were forty or fifty of us standing in line beside a high anchor-chain fence topped with barbed wire. On the other side of the fence was a white birch woods, above our heads the blue Brabant sky. We too belonged to that wide free world.

The next barracks we entered held a row of desks with women clerks seated behind them. At one of these I was handed a brown paper envelope. I emptied it into my hand and the next moment was staring in disbelief at my Alpina watch. Mama's ring. Even my paper guilders. I had not seen these things since the night we arrived at Scheveningen. Money . . . why, that belonged to the world of shops and trolley cars. We could go to a train station with this money. Two fares to Haarlem, please. . . .

We marched along a path between twisted rolls of barbed wire and through a wide gate into a compound of low tin-roofed barracks. There were more lines, more waits, more shuffling from desk to desk, but already the camp and its procedures had become unreal to me.

Then we were standing before a high counter and a young male clerk was saying, "Leave all personal effects at the window marked 'C' "

"But they just gave them back to me!"

"Watches, purses, jewelry . . ."

Mechanically, like a machine with no will of its own, I handed watch, ring, and money through the small barred window. A uniformed woman swept them into a metal box. "Move along! Next!"

Then—were we not to be released? Outside this building a florid-faced officer formed us into a double column and marched us across a broad parade ground. At one end of it a crew of men with shaved heads and striped overalls were digging a ditch. What did it mean? What did any of it mean, this whole long day of lines and waits? Betsie's face was gray with weariness and she stumbled as we marched.

Through another fence we arrived in a yard surrounded on three sides by low concrete buildings. A young woman in a military cape was waiting for us.

"Prisoners halt!" barked the red-faced officer. "Explain to the newcomers, *Fraulein*, the function of the bunkers."

"The bunkers," the girl began in the bored voice of a museum guide, "are for the accommodation of those who fail to cooperate with camp rules. The rooms are cozy, if a bit small: about the size of a gym locker. To hasten the educational process the hands are tied above the head. . . ."

Even as the horrid recital continued, two guards came out of the bunkers, carrying between them the form of a man. He was alive, for his legs were moving, but he seemed to have no conscious control over them. His eyes were sunken and rolled back in his head.

"Not everyone," the girl observed in the same detached drawl, "seems to appreciate the accommodations at the bunkers."

I seized Betsie's arm as the command to march came again, more to steady myself than her. It was Father's traincase once again. Such cruelty was too much to grasp, too much to bear. Heavenly Father, carry it for me!

We followed the officer down a wide street lined with barracks on either side and halted at one of the gray, featureless sheds. It was the end of the long day of standing, waiting, hoping: we had simply arrived in the main camp at Vught.

The barracks appeared almost identical with the one we had left this morning, except that this one was furnished with bunks as well as tables and benches. And still we were not allowed to sit: there was a last wait while the matron with maddening deliberateness checked off our documents against a list.

"Betsie!" I wailed, "how long will it take?"

"Perhaps a long, long time. Perhaps many years. But what better way could there be to spend our lives?"

I turned to stare at her. "Whatever are you talking about?"

"These young women. That girl back at the bunkers. Corrie, if people can be taught to hate, they can be taught to love! We must find the way, you and I, no matter how long it takes. . . ."

She went on, almost forgetting in her excitement to keep her voice to a whisper, while I slowly took in the fact that she was talking about our guards. I glanced at the matron seated at the desk ahead of us. I saw a gray uniform and a visored hat; Betsie saw a wounded human being.

And I wondered, not for the first time, what sort of a person she was, this sister of mine . . . what kind of road she followed while I trudged beside her on the all-too-solid earth.

A few days later Betsie and I were called up for work assignments. One glance at Betsie's pallid face and fragile form, and the matron waved her contemptuously back inside the barracks where the elderly and infirm spent the day sewing prison uniforms. The women's uniform here in Vught was a blue overall with a red stripe down the side of the leg, practical and comfortable, and a welcome change after our own clothes that we had worn since the day of our arrest.

Apparently I looked strong enough for harder work; I was told to report to the Phillips factory. This "factory" turned out to be no more than another large barracks inside the camp complex. Early in the morning though it was, the tar beneath the shingled roof was beginning to bubble in the hot July sun. I followed my escort into the single large room where several hundred men and women sat at long plank tables covered with thousands of tiny radio parts. Two officers, one male, one female, were strolling the aisles between the benches while the prisoners bent to their tasks.

I was assigned a seat at a bench near the front and given the job of measuring small glass rods and arranging them in piles according to lengths. It was monotonous work. The heat from the roof pressed like a weight on my head. I longed to exchange at least names and home towns with my neighbors on either side, but the only sound in the room was the clink of metal parts and the squeak of the officers' boots. They reached the door across from where I sat.

"Production was up again last week," the male officer said in German to a tall slender man with a shaved head and a striped uniform. "You are to be commended for this increase. However we continue to receive complaints of defective wiring. Quality control must improve."

The shaved-headed man made an apologetic gesture. "If there were more food, *Herr Officier*," he murmured. "Since the cutback in rations I see a difference. They grow sleepy, they have trouble concentrating. . . . " His voice reminded me a little of Willem's, deep, cultivated, the German with only a trace of Dutch accent.

"Then you must wake them up! Make them concentrate on the penalties! If the soldiers on the front can fight on half-rations, then these lazy——"

At a terrible look from the woman officer, he stopped and ran his tongue over his lips. "Ah—that is —I speak of course merely as an example. There is naturally no truth in the rumor that rations at the front are reduced. So! I—I hold you responsible!" And together they stalked from the building.

For a moment the prisoner-foreman watched them from the doorway. Slowly he raised his left hand, then dropped it with a slap to his side. The quiet room exploded. From under tables appeared writing paper, books, knitting yarn, tins of biscuits. People left their benches and joined little knots of chattering friends all over the room. Half a dozen crowded around me: Who was I? Where was I from? Did I have any news of the war?

After perhaps half an hour of visiting among the tables, the foreman reminded us that we had a day's quota to meet and people drifted back to their places. The foreman's name, I learned, was Moorman and he had been headmaster of a Roman Catholic boys' school. He himself came over to my workbench the third day I was there; he had heard that I had followed the entire assembly line through the barracks, tracing what became of my dull little piles of rods. "You're the first woman worker," he said, "who has ever shown any interest in what we are making here."

"I am very interested," I said. "I'm a watchmaker."

He stared at me with new interest. "Then I have work you will enjoy more." He took me to the opposite end of the huge shed where the final assembly of relay switches was done. It was intricate and exacting work, though not nearly so hard as watch repair, and Mr. Moorman was right. I enjoyed it and it helped make the eleven-hour workday go faster.

Not only to me but to all the Phillips workers,

Mr. Moorman acted more as a kindly older brother than a crew boss. I would watch him, ceaselessly moving among his hundreds of charges, counseling, encouraging, finding a simpler job for the weary, a harder one for the restless. We had been at Vught more than a month before I learned that his twenty-year-old son had been shot here at the camp the week Betsie and I arrived.

No trace of this personal tragedy showed in his care for the rest of us. He stopped frequently at my bench, the first weeks, more to check my frame of mind than my work. But eventually his eyes would travel to the row of relay switches in front of me. . . .

"Dear watch lady! Can you not remember for whom you are working? These radios are for their fighter planes!" And reaching across me he would yank a wire from its housing or twist a tiny tube from an assembly.

"Now solder them back wrong. And not so fast! You're over the day's quota and it's not yet noon."

Lunchtime would have been the best time of day if I could have spent it with Betsie. However, Phillips workers were not allowed to leave the factory compound until the workday ended at 6:00. Prisoners on kitchen detail lugged in great buckets of gruel made of wheat and peas, tasteless but nourishing. Apparently there had been a cutback in rations recently: still the food was better and more plentiful than at Scheveningen where there had been no noonday meal at all.

After eating we were free for a blessed half hour to stroll about within the Phillips compound in the fresh air and the glorious Brabant sun. Most days I found a spot along the fence and stretched out on the warm ground to sleep (the days started with roll call at 5:00 A.M.). Sweet summer smells came in the breezes from the farms around the camp; sometimes I would dream that Karel and I were walking hand in hand along a country lane.

At 6:00 in the evening there was another roll call, then we marched back to our various sleeping barracks. Betsie always stood in the doorway of ours waiting for me; each evening it was as though a week had passed, there was so much to tell one another.

"That Belgian boy and girl at the bench next to mine? This noon they became engaged!"

"Mrs. Heerma—whose granddaughter was taken to Germany—today she let me pray with her."

One day Betsie's news touched us directly. "A lady from Ermelo was transferred to the sewing detail today. When I introduced myself, she said, 'Another one!'"

"What did she mean?"

"Corrie, do you remember, the day we were arrested, a man came to the shop? You were sick and I had to wake you up."

I remembered very well. Remembered the strange roving eyes, the uneasiness in the pit of my stomach that was more than fever.

"Apparently everyone in Ermelo knew him. He worked with the Gestapo from the first day of occupation. He reported this woman's two brothers for Resistance work, and finally herself and her husband too." When Ermelo had finally caught on to him he had come to Haarlem and teamed up with Willemse and Kapteyn. His name was Jan Vogel.

Flames of fire seemed to leap around that name in my heart. I thought of Father's final hours, alone and confused, in a hospital corridor. Of the underground work so abruptly halted. I thought of Mary Itallie arrested while walking down a street. And I knew that if Jan Vogel stood in front of me now I could kill him.

Betsie drew the little cloth bag from beneath her overalls and held it out to me, but I shook my head. Betsie kept the Bible during the day, since she had more chance to read and teach from it here than I did at the Phillips barracks. In the evenings we held a clandestine prayer meeting for as many as could crowd around our bunk.

"You lead the prayers tonight, Betsie. I have a headache."

More than a headache. All of me ached with the

violence of my feelings about the man who had done us so much harm. That night I did not sleep and the next day at my bench scarcely heard the conversation around me. By the end of the week I had worked myself into such a sickness of body and spirit that Mr. Moorman stopped at my bench to ask if something were wrong.

"Wrong? Yes, something's wrong!" And I plunged into an account of that morning. I was only too eager to tell Mr. Moorman and all Holland how Jan Vogel had betrayed his country.

What puzzled me all this time was Betsie. She had suffered everything I had and yet she seemed to carry no burden of rage. "Betsie!" I hissed one dark night when I knew that my restless tossing must be keeping her awake. Three of us now shared this single cot as the crowded camp daily received new arrivals. "Betsie, don't you feel anything about Jan Vogel? Doesn't it bother you?"

"Oh yes, Corrie! Terribly! I've felt for him ever since I knew—and pray for him whenever his name comes into my mind. How dreadfully he must be suffering!"

For a long time I lay silent in the huge shadowy barracks restless with the sighs, snores, and stirrings of hundreds of women. Once again I had the feeling that this sister with whom I had spent all my life belonged somehow to another order of beings. Wasn't she telling me in her gentle way that I was as guilty as Jan Vogel? Didn't he and I stand together before an all-seeing God convicted of the same sin of murder? For I had murdered him with my heart and with my tongue.

"Lord Jesus," I whispered into the lumpy ticking of the bed, "I forgive Jan Vogel as I pray that You will forgive me. I have done him great damage. Bless him now, and his family. . . ." That night for the first time since our betrayer had a name I slept deep and dreamlessly until the whistle summoned us to roll call.

The days in Vught were a baffling mixture of good and bad. Morning roll call was often cruelly long. If the smallest rule had been broken, such as a single prisoner late for evening check-in, the entire barracks would be punished by a 4:00 A.M. or even a 3:30 call and made to stand at parade attention until our backs ached and our legs cramped. But the summer air was warm and alive with birds as the day approached. Gradually, in the east, a pink-and-gold sunrise would light the immense Brabant sky as Betsie and I squeezed each other's hands in awe.

At 5:30 we had black bread and "coffee," bitter and hot, and then fell into marching columns for the various work details. I looked forward to this hike to the Phillips factory. Part of the way we walked beside a small woods, separated only by a roll of barbed wire from a glistening world of dewdrops. We also marched past a section of the men's camp, many of our group straining to identify a husband or a son among the ranks of shaved heads and striped overalls.

This was another of the paradoxes of Vught. I was endlessly, daily grateful to be again with people. But what I had not realized in solitary confinement was that to have companions meant to have their griefs as well. We all suffered with the women whose men were in this camp: the discipline in the male section was much harsher than in the women's; executions were frequent. Almost every day a salvo of shots would send the anguished whispers flying: How many this time? Who were they?

The woman next to me at the relay bench was an intense Communist woman named Floor. She and her husband had managed to get their two small children to friends before their arrest, but she worried aloud all day about them and about Mr. Floor, who had tuberculosis. He worked on the rope-making crew in the compound next to Phillips and each noon they managed to exchange a few words through the barbed wire separating the two enclosures. Although she was expecting a third child in September she would never eat her morning allotment of bread but passed it through the fence to him. She was dangerously thin, I felt, for an expectant mother, and several times I brought her a portion of my own breakfast bread. But this too was always set aside for Mr. Floor.

And yet in spite of sorrow and anxiety—and no

one in that place was without both—there was laughter too in the Phillips barracks. An impersonation of the pompous, blustering second lieutenant. A game of blind-man's bluff. A song passed in rounds from bench to bench until——

"Thick clouds! Thick clouds!" The signal might come from any bench which faced a window. The factory barracks was set in the center of the broad Phillips compound; there was no way a camp official could approach it without crossing this open space. In an instant every bench would be filled, the only sound the businesslike rattle of radio parts.

One morning the code words were still being relayed down the long shed when a rather hefty *Aufseherin* stepped through the door. She glanced furiously about, face flushing scarlet as she applied "thick clouds" to her appearance. She shrieked and ranted for a quarter of an hour, then deprived us of our noontime break in the open air that day. After this we adopted the more neutral signal, "fifteen."

"I've assembled fifteen dials!"

During the long hot afternoons pranks and talk died down as each one sat alone with his own thoughts. I scratched on the side of the table the number of days until September 1. There was nothing official about that date, just a chance remark by Mrs. Floor to the effect that six months was the usual prison term for ration-card offenders. Then, if that were the charge and if they included the time served at Scheveningen, September 1 would be our release date!

"Corrie," Betsie warned one evening when I announced triumphantly that August was half over, "we don't know for sure."

I had the feeling, almost, that to Betsie it didn't matter. I looked at her, sitting on our cot in the last moments before lights out, sewing up a split seam in my overalls as she'd so often sat mending under the lamplight in the dining room. Betsie by the very way she sat evoked a high-backed chair behind her and a carpet at her feet instead of this endless row of metal cots on a bare pine floor. The first week we were here she had added extra hooks to the neck of her overalls so that she could fasten the collar high around her throat and, this propriety taken care of, I had the feeling she was as content to be reading the Bible here in Vught to those who had never heard it as she'd been serving soup to hungry people in the hallway of the Beje.

As for me, I set my heart every day more firmly on September 1.

And then, all of a sudden, it looked as though we would not have to wait even this long. The Princess Irene Brigade was rumored to be in France, moving toward Belgium. The Brigade was part of the Dutch forces that had escaped to England during the Five-Day War; now it was marching to reclaim its own.

The guards were noticeably tense. Roll call was an agony. The old and the ill who were slow reaching their places were beaten mercilessly. Even the "red light commando" came in for discipline. These young women were ordinarily a favored group of prisoners. Prostitutes, mostly from Amsterdam, they were in prison not for their profession—which was extolled as a patriotic duty—but for infecting German soldiers. Ordinarily, with the male guards anyway, they had a bold, breezy manner; now even they had to form ruler-straight lines and stand hours at frozen attention.

The sound of the firing squad was heard more and more often. One lunchtime when the bell sounded to return to work, Mrs. Floor did not appear at the bench beside me. It always took a while for my eyes to readjust to the dim factory after the bright sun outside: it was only gradually that I saw the hunk of black bread still resting at her place on the bench. There had been no husband to deliver it to.

And so hanging between hope and horror we waited out the days. Rumor was all we lived on. The Brigade was across the Dutch border. The Brigade was destroyed. The Brigade had never landed. Women who had stayed away from the whispered little prayer service around our cot now crowded close, demanding signs and predictions from the Bible.

On the morning of September 1 Mrs. Floor gave birth to a baby girl. The child lived four hours.

Several days later we awoke to the sound of distant explosions. Long before the roll-call whistle the entire barracks was up and milling about in the dark between the cots. Was it bombs? Artillery fire? Surely the Brigade had reached Brabant. This very day they might be in Vught!

The scowls and threats of the guards when they arrived daunted us not at all. Everyone's mind had turned homeward, everyone talked of what she would do first. "The plants will all be dead," said Betsie, "but we'll get some cuttings from Nollie! We'll wash the windows so the sun can come in."

At the Phillips factory Mr. Moorman tried to calm us. "Those aren't bombs," he said, "and certainly not guns. That's demolition work. Germans. They're probably blowing up bridges. It means they expect an attack but not that it's here. It might not come for weeks."

This dampened us a bit, but as the blasts came closer and closer nothing could keep down hope. Now they were so near they hurt our ears.

"Drop your lower jaw!" Mr. Moorman called down the long room. "Keep your mouth open and it will save your eardrums."

We had our midday meal inside with the doors and windows closed. We'd been working again for an hour—or sitting at our benches, no one could work—when the order came to return to dormitories. With sudden urgency women embraced husbands and sweethearts who worked beside them at Phillips.

Betsie was waiting for me outside our barracks. "Corrie! Has the Brigade come? Are we free?"

"No. Not yet. I don't know. Oh, Betsie, why am I so frightened?"

The loudspeaker in the men's camp was sounding the signal for roll call. No order was given here and we drifted about aimlessly, listening we scarcely knew for what. Names were being read through the men's speaker, though it was too far away to make them out.

And suddenly an insane fear gripped the waiting women. A deathlike silence now hung over both sides of the vast camp. The loudspeaker had fallen silent. We exchanged wordless looks, we almost feared to breathe. Then the rifle fire split the air. Around us women began to weep. A second volley. A third. For two hours the executions went on. Someone counted. More than seven hundred male prisoners were killed that day.

There was little sleeping in our barracks that night and no roll call the following morning. About 6:00 A.M. we were ordered to collect our personal things. Betsie and I put our belongings into the pillowcases we had brought from Scheveningen: toothbrushes, needles and thread, a small bottle of Davitamon oil that had come in a Red Cross package, Nollie's blue sweater which was the only thing we had brought with us when we left the quarantine camp ten weeks before. I transferred the Bible in its bag from Betsie's back to my own; she was so thin it made a visible bump between her shoulders.

We were marched to a field where soldiers were passing out blankets from the backs of open trucks. As we filed past, Betsie and I drew two beautiful soft new ones; mine was white with blue stripes, Betsie's white with red stripes—obviously the property of some well-to-do family.

About noon the exodus from camp began. Through the drab streets of barracks we went, past the bunkers, through the maze of barbed-wire compounds and enclosures, and at last onto the rough dirt road through the woods down which we had stumbled that rainy night in June. Betsie hung hard to my arm; she was laboring for breath as she always did when she had to walk any distance.

"March! *Schnell!* Double-time!"

I slipped my arm beneath Betsie's shoulders and half-carried her the final quarter-mile. At last the path ended and we lined up facing the single track, over a thousand women standing toe to heel. Farther along, the men's section was also at the siding; it was impossible to identify individuals among the shaved heads glistening in the autumn sun.

At first I thought our train had not come; then I realized that these freight cars standing on the tracks were for us. Already the men were being prodded aboard, clambering up over the high sides. We could not see the engine, just this row of small, high-wheeled European boxcars stretching out of sight in both directions, machine guns mounted at intervals on the roof. Soldiers were approaching along the track, pausing at each car to haul open the heavy sliding door. In front of us a gaping black interior appeared. Women began to press forward.

Clutching our blankets and pillowcases we were swept along with the others. Betsie's chest was still heaving oddly after the rapid march. I had to boost her over the side of the train.

At first I could make out nothing in the dark car; then in a corner I saw a tall, uneven shape. It was a stack of bread, dozens of flat black loaves piled one on top of another. A long trip then. . . .

The small car was getting crowded. We were shoved against the back wall. Thirty or forty people were all that could fit in. And still the soldiers drove women over the side, cursing, jabbing with their guns. Shrieks rose from the center of the car but still the press increased. It was only when eighty women were packed inside that the door thumped shut and we heard iron bolts driven into place.

Women were sobbing and many fainted, although in the tight-wedged crowd they remained upright. Just when it seemed certain that those in the middle must suffocate or be tampled to death, we worked out a kind of system where, by half-sitting, half-lying with our legs wedged around one another like members of a sledding team, we were able to get down on the floor of the car.

"Do you know what I am thankful for?" Betsie's gentle voice startled me in that squirming madhouse. "I am thankful that Father is in heaven today!"

Father. Yes! Oh Father, how could I have wept for you?

The warm sun beat down on the motionless train, the temperature in the packed car rose, the air grew foul. Beside me someone was tugging at a nail in the ancient wood of the wall. At last it came free; with the point she set to work gouging the hole wider. Others around the sides took up the idea and in a while blessed whiffs of outside air began to circle about us.

It was hours before the train gave a sudden lurch and began to move. Almost at once it stopped again, then again crawled forward. The rest of the day and into the night it was the same, stopping, starting, slamming, jerking. Once when it was my turn at the air-hole I saw in the moonlight trainmen carrying a length of twisted rail. Tracks ahead must be destroyed. I passed the news. Maybe they would not be able to repair them. Maybe we would still be in Holland when liberation came.

Betsie's forehead was hot to my hand. The "red light" girl between whose legs I was wedged squeezed herself into an even tighter crouch so that Betsie could lie almost flat across my lap. I dozed too, from time to time, my head on the shoulder of the friendly girl behind us. Once I dreamed it was storming. I could hear the hailstones on Tante Jans's front windows. I opened my eyes. It really was hailing. I could hear it rattling against the side of the car.

Everyone was awake now and talking. Another storm of hail. And then we heard a burst of machine-gun fire from the roof of the train.

"It's bullets!" someone shouted. "They're attacking the train."

Again we heard that sound like tiny stones striking the wall, and again the machine guns answered. Had the Brigade reached us at last? The firing died away. For an hour the train sat motionless. Then slowly we crawled forward.

At dawn someone called out that we were passing through the border town of Emmerich.

We had arrived in Germany.

13

Ravensbruck

For two more incredible days and two more nights we were carried deeper and deeper into the land of our fears. Occasionally one of the loaves of bread was passed from hand to hand. But not even the most elementary provision had been made for sanitation and the air in the car was such that few could eat.

And gradually, more terrible than the crush of bodies and the filth, the single obsession was: something to drink. Two or three times when the train stopped, the door was slid open a few inches and a pail of water passed in. But we had become animals, incapable of plan or system. Those near the door got it all.

At last, the morning of the fourth day, the train stopped again and the door was opened its full width. Like infants, on hands and knees, we crawled to the opening and lowered ourselves over the side. In front of us was a smiling blue lake. On the far side, among sycamore trees, rose a white church steeple.

The stronger prisoners hauled buckets of water from the lake. We drank through cracked and swollen lips. The train was shorter; the cars carrying the men had disappeared. Only a handful of soldiers—some of them looking no older than fifteen—were there to guard a thousand women. No more were needed. We could scarcely walk, let alone resist.

After a while they got us into straggly columns

and marched us off. For a mile the road followed the shore of the lake, then left it to climb a hill. I wondered if Betsie could make it to the top, but the sight of trees and sky seemed to have revived her and she supported me as much as I her. We passed a number of local people on foot and in horse-drawn wagons. The children especially seemed wonderful to me, pink-cheeked and healthy. They returned my stares with wide-eyed interest; I noticed, however, that the adults did not look at us but turned their heads away as we approached.

From the crest of the hill we saw it, like a vast scar on the green German landscape; a city of low gray barracks surrounded by concrete walls on which guard towers rose at intervals. In the very center, a square smokestack emitted a thin gray vapor into the blue sky.

"Ravensbruck!"

Like a whispered curse the word passed back through the lines. This was the notorious women's extermination camp whose name we had heard even in Haarlem. That squat concrete building, that smoke disappearing in the bright sunlight—no! I would not look at it! As Betsie and I stumbled down the hill, I felt the Bible bumping between my shoulder blades. God's good news. Was it to this world that He had spoken it?

Now we were close enough to see the skull-and-crossbones posted at intervals on the walls to warn of electrified wiring along the top. The massive iron gates swung in; we marched between them. Acres of soot-gray barracks stretched ahead of us. Just inside the wall was a row of waist-high water spigots. We charged them, thrusting hands, arms, legs, even heads, under the streams of water, washing away the stench of the boxcars. A squad of women guards in dark blue uniforms rushed at us, hauling and shouting, swinging their short, hard crops.

At last they drove us back from the faucets and herded us down an avenue between barracks. This camp appeared far grimmer than the one we had left. At least, in marches about Vught, we had caught sight of fields and woods. Here, every vista ended in the same concrete barrier; the camp was set down in a vast man-made valley rising on every side to those towering wire-topped walls.

At last we halted. In front of us a vast canvas tent-roof—no sides—covered an acre or more of straw-strewn ground. Betsie and I found a spot on the edge of this area and sank gratefully down. Instantly we were on our feet again. Lice! The straw was literally alive with them. We stood for a while, clutching blankets and pillowcases well away from the infested ground. But at last we spread our blankets over the squirming straw and sat on them.

Some of the prisoners had brought scissors from Vught: everywhere beneath the huge tent women were cutting one another's hair. A pair was passed to us. Of course we must do the same, long hair was folly in such a place. But as I cut Betsie's chestnut waves, I cried.

Toward evening there was a commotion at one end of the tent. A line of S.S. guards was moving across it, driving women out from under the canvas. We scrambled to our feet and snatched up our blankets as they bore down upon us. Perhaps a hundred yards beyond the tent the chase stopped. We stood about, uncertain what to do. Whether a new group of prisoners had arrived or what the reason was for driving us from the tent, no one knew. Women began spreading their blankets on the hard cinder ground. Slowly it dawned on Betsie and me that we were to spend the night here where we stood. We laid my blanket on the ground, stretched out side by side and pulled hers over us.

"The night is dark and I am far from home . . ." Betsie's sweet soprano was picked up by voices all around us. "Lead Thou me on. . . ."

We were waked up some time in the middle of the night by a clap of thunder and a deluge of rain. The blankets soaked through and water gathered in puddles beneath us. In the morning the field was a vast sodden swamp: hands, clothes, and faces were black from the cinder mud.

We were still wringing water from our blankets when the command came to line up for coffee. It was not coffee but a thin liquid of approximately the same color and we were grateful to get it as we shuffled double-file past the makeshift field kitchen. There was a slice of black bread for each prisoner too, then nothing more until we were given a ladle of turnip soup and a small boiled potato late in the afternoon.

In between we were kept standing at rigid attention on the soggy parade ground where we had spent the night. We were near one edge of the huge camp here, close enough to the outer wall to see the triple row of electric wires running along the top. Two entire days we spent this way, stretching out again the second night right where we stood. It did not rain again but ground and blankets were still damp. Betsie began to cough. I took Nollie's blue sweater from my pillowcase, wrapped it around her and gave her a few drops of the vitamin oil. But by morning she had agonizing intestinal cramps. Again and again throughout that second day she had to ask the impatient woman monitor at the head of our row for permission to go to the ditch that served as sanitary facility.

It was the third night as we were getting ready to lie down again under the sky when the order came to report to the processing center for new arrivals. A ten-minute march brought us to the building. We inched along a corridor into a huge reception room. And there under the harsh ceiling lights we saw a dismal sight. As each woman reached a desk where some officers sat she had to lay her blanket, pillowcase, and whatever else she carried onto a growing pile of these things. A few desks further along she had to strip off every scrap of clothes, throw them onto a second pile, and walk naked past the scrutiny of a dozen S.S. men into the shower room. Coming out of the shower she wore only a thin prison dress and a pair of shoes. Nothing more.

But Betsie needed that sweater! She needed the vitamins! Most of all, we needed our Bible. How could we live in this place without it? But how could I ever take it past so many watchful eyes without the overalls covering it?

We were almost at the first desk. I fished desperately in my pillowcase, drew out the bottle of vitamins and closed my fist around them. Reluctantly we dropped the other things on the heap that was fast becoming a mountain. "Dear God," I prayed, "You have given us this precious Book, You have kept it hidden through checkpoints and inspections, You have used it for so many——"

I felt Betsie stagger against me and looked at her in alarm. Her face was white, her lips pressed tight together. A guard was passing by; I begged him in German to show us the toilets. Without so much as a glance, he jerked his head in the direction of the shower room.

Timidly Betsie and I stepped out of line and walked to the door of the big, dank-smelling room with its row on row of overhead spigots. It was empty, waiting for the next batch of fifty naked and shivering women to be admitted.

"Please," I said to the S.S. man guarding the door, "where are the toilets?"

He did not look at me either. "Use the drainholes!" he snapped, and as we stepped inside he slammed the door behind us. We stood alone in the room where a few minutes later we would return stripped even of the clothes on our backs. Here were the prison things we were to put on, piled just inside the door. From the front and back of each otherwise ordinary dress a large "X" had been cut out and replaced with cloth of another color.

And then we saw something else, stacked in the far corner, a pile of old wooden benches. They were slimy with mildew, crawling with cockroaches, but to me they seemed the furniture of heaven itself.

"The sweater! Take the sweater off!" I hissed, fumbling with the string at my neck. Betsie handed it to me and in an instant I had wrapped it around the Bible and the vitamin bottle and stuffed the precious bundle behind the benches.

And so it was that when we were herded into that room ten minutes later we were not poor, but rich. Rich in this new evidence of the care of Him who was God even of Ravensbruck.

We stood beneath the spigots as long as the flow of icy water lasted, feeling it soften our lice-eaten skin. Then we clustered dripping wet around the heap of prison dresses, holding them up, passing them about, looking for approximate fits. I found a loose long-sleeved dress for Betsie that would cover the blue sweater when she would have a chance to put it on. I squirmed into another dress for myself, then reached behind the benches and shoved the little bundle quickly inside the neck.

It made a bulge you could have seen across the Grote Markt. I flattened it out as best I could, pushing it down, tugging the sweater around my waist, but there was no real concealing it beneath the thin cotton dress. And all the while I had the incredible feeling that it didn't matter, that this was not my business, but God's. That all I had to do was walk straight ahead.

As we trooped back out through the shower room door, the S.S. men ran their hands over every prisoner, front, back, and sides. The woman ahead of me was searched three times. Behind me, Betsie was searched. No hand touched me.

At the exit door to the building was a second ordeal, a line of women guards examining each prisoner again. I slowed down as I reached them but the *Aufseherin* in charge shoved me roughly by the shoulder. "Move along! You're holding up the line!"

And so Betsie and I arrived at Barracks 8 in the small hours of that morning, bringing not only the Bible, but a new knowledge of the power of Him whose story it was. There were three women already asleep in the bed assigned to us. They made room for us as best they could but the mattress sloped and I kept sliding to the floor. At last all five of us lay sideways across the bed and managed to get shoulders and elbows arranged. The blanket was a poor threadbare affair compared with the ones we had given up, but at least the overcrowding produced its own warmth. Betsie had put on the blue sweater beneath her long-sleeved dress and wedged now between me and the others, her shivering gradually subsided and she was asleep. I lay awake a

while longer, watching a searchlight sweep the rear wall
in long regular arcs, hearing the distant calls of soldiers
patrolling the walls. . . .

Morning roll call at Ravensbruck came half an
hour earlier than at Vught. By 4:30 A.M. we had to be
standing outside in the black predawn chill, standing at
parade attention in blocks of one hundred women, ten
wide, ten deep. Sometimes after hours of this we would
gain the shelter of the barracks only to hear the whistle.

"Everybody out! Fall in for roll call!"

Barracks 8 was in the quarantine compound. Next
to us—perhaps as a deliberate warning to newcomers
—were located the punishment barracks. From there, all
day long and often into the night, came the sounds of
hell itself. They were not the sounds of anger, or of
any human emotion, but of a cruelty altogether detached: blows landing in regular rhythm, screams keeping pace. We would stand in our ten-deep ranks with
our hands trembling at our sides, longing to jam
them against our ears, to make the sounds stop.

The instant of dismissal we would mob the door
of Barracks 8, stepping on each other's heels in our
eagerness to get inside, to shrink the world back to
understandable proportions.

It grew harder and harder. Even within these four
walls there was too much misery, too much seemingly
pointless suffering. Every day something else failed to
make sense, something else grew too heavy. "Will You
carry this too, Lord Jesus?"

But as the rest of the world grew stranger, one
thing became increasingly clear. And that was the reason the two of us were here. Why others should suffer
we were not shown. As for us, from morning until
lights-out, whenever we were not in ranks for roll call,
our Bible was the center of an ever-widening circle of
help and hope. Like waifs clustered around a blazing
fire, we gathered about it, holding out our hearts to its
warmth and light. The blacker the night around us
grew, the brighter and truer and more beautiful burned
the word of God. "Who shall separate us from the love
of Christ? Shall tribulation, or distress, or persecution,

or famine, or nakedness, or peril, or sword? . . . Nay, in all these things we are more than conquerors through him that loved us."

I would look about us as Betsie read, watching the light leap from face to face. More than conquerors. . . . It was not a wish. It was a fact. We knew it, we experienced it minute by minute—poor, hated, hungry. We are more than conquerors. Not "we shall be." We are! Life in Ravensbruck took place on two separate levels, mutually impossible. One, the observable, external life, grew every day more horrible. The other, the life we lived with God, grew daily better, truth upon truth, glory upon glory.

Sometimes I would slip the Bible from its little sack with hands that shook, so mysterious had it become to me. It was new; it had just been written. I marveled sometimes that the ink was dry. I had believed the Bible always, but reading it now had nothing to do with belief. It was simply a description of the way things were—of hell and heaven, of how men act and how God acts. I had read a thousand times the story of Jesus' arrest—how soldiers had slapped Him, laughed at Him, flogged Him. Now such happenings had faces and voices.

Fridays—the recurrent humiliation of medical inspection. The hospital corridor in which we waited was unheated, and a fall chill had settled into the walls. Still we were forbidden even to wrap ourselves in our own arms, but had to maintain our erect, hands-at-sides position as we filed slowly past a phalanx of grinning guards. How there could have been any pleasure in the sight of these stick-thin legs and hunger-gloated stomachs I could not imagine. Surely there is no more wretched sight than the human body unloved and uncared for. Nor could I see the necessity for the complete undressing: when we finally reached the examining room a doctor looked down each throat, another—a dentist presumably—at our teeth, a third in between each finger. And that was all. We trooped again down the long, cold corridor and picked up our X-marked dresses at the door.

But it was one of these mornings while we were

waiting, shivering, in the corridor, that yet another page in the Bible leapt into life for me.

He hung naked on the cross.

I had not known—I had not thought. . . . The paintings, the carved crucifixes showed at the least a scrap of cloth. But this, I suddenly knew, was the respect and reverence of the artist. But oh—at the time itself, on that other Friday morning—there had been no reverence. No more than I saw in the faces around us now.

I leaned toward Betsie, ahead of me in line. Her shoulder blades stood out sharp and thin beneath her blue-mottled skin.

"Betsie, they took *His* clothes too."

Ahead of me I heard a little gasp. "Oh, Corrie. And I never thanked Him. . . ."

Every day the sun rose a little later, the bite took longer to leave the air. It will be better, everyone assured everyone else, when we move into permanent barracks. We'll have a blanket apiece. A bed of our own. Each of us painted into the picture her own greatest need.

For me it was a dispensary where Betsie could get medication for her cough. "There'll be a nurse assigned to the barracks." I said it so often that I convinced myself. I was doling out a drop of the Davitamon each morning on her piece of black bread, but how much longer could the small bottle last? "Especially," I would tell her, "if you keep sharing it around every time someone sneezes."

The move to permanent quarters came the second week in October. We were marched, ten abreast, along a wide cinder avenue and then into a narrower street of barracks. Several times the column halted while numbers were read out—names were never used at Ravensbruck. At last Betsie's and mine were called: "Prisoner 66729, Prisoner 66730." We stepped out of line with a dozen or so others and stared at the long gray front of Barracks 28. Half its windows seemed to have been broken and replaced with rags. A door in the center let us into a large room where two hundred or more women bent over knitting needles. On tables between them were piles of woolen socks in army gray.

On either side doors opened into two still larger rooms—by far the largest dormitories we had yet seen. Betsie and I followed a prisoner-guide through the door at the right. Because of the broken windows the vast room was in semi-twilight. Our noses told us, first, that the place was filthy: somewhere plumbing had backed up, the bedding was soiled and rancid. Then as our eyes adjusted to the gloom we saw that there were no individual beds at all, but great square piers stacked three high, and wedged side by side and end to end with only an occasional narrow aisle slicing through.

We followed our guide single file—the aisle was not wide enough for two—fighting back the claustrophobia of these platforms rising everywhere above us. The tremendous room was nearly empty of people; they must have been out on various work crews. At last she pointed to a second tier in the center of a large block. To reach it we had to stand on the bottom level, haul ourselves up, and then crawl across three other straw-covered platforms to reach the one that we would share with—how many? The deck above us was too close to let us sit up. We lay back, struggling against the nausea that swept over us from the reeking straw. We could hear the women who had arrived with us finding their places.

Suddenly I sat up, striking my head on the cross-slats above. Something had pinched my leg.

"Fleas!" I cried. "Betsie, the place is swarming with them!"

We scrambled across the intervening platforms, heads low to avoid another bump, dropped down to the aisle, and edged our way to a patch of light.

"Here! And here another one!" I wailed. "Betsie, how can we live in such a place!"

"Show us. Show us how." It was said so matter of factly it took me a second to realize she was praying. More and more the distinction between prayer and the rest of life seemed to be vanishing for Betsie.

"Corrie!" she said excitedly. "He's given us the answer! Before we asked, as He always does! In the Bible this morning. Where was it? Read that part again!"

I glanced down the long dim aisle to make sure no guard was in sight, then drew the Bible from its pouch. "It was in First Thessalonians," I said. We were on our third complete reading of the New Testament since leaving Scheveningen. In the feeble light I turned the pages. "Here it is: 'Comfort the frightened, help the weak, be patient with everyone. See that none of you repays evil for evil, but always seek to do good to one another and to all. . . .'" It seemed written expressly to Ravensbruck.

"Go on," said Betsie. "That wasn't all."

"Oh yes: '. . . to one another and to all. Rejoice always, pray constantly, give thanks in all circumstances; for this is the will of God in Christ Jesus———'"

"That's it, Corrie! That's His answer. 'Give thanks in all circumstances!' That's what we can do. We can start right now to thank God for every single thing about this new barracks!"

I stared at her, then around me at the dark, foul-aired room.

"Such as?" I said.

"Such as being assigned here together."

I bit my lip. "Oh yes, Lord Jesus!"

"Such as what you're holding in your hands."

I looked down at the Bible. "Yes! Thank You, dear Lord, that there was no inspection when we entered here! Thank You for all the women, here in this room, who will meet You in these pages."

"Yes," said Betsie. "Thank You for the very crowding here. Since we're packed so close, that many more will hear!" She looked at me expectantly. "Corrie!" she prodded.

"Oh, all right. Thank You for the jammed, crammed, stuffed, packed, suffocating crowds."

"Thank You," Betsie went on serenely, "for the fleas and for———"

The fleas! This was too much. "Betsie, there's no way even God can make me grateful for a flea."

" 'Give thanks in *all* circumstances,' " she quoted. "It doesn't say, 'in pleasant circumstances.' Fleas are part of this place where God has put us."

And so we stood between piers of bunks and gave thanks for fleas. But this time I was sure Betsie was wrong.

They started arriving soon after 6:00 o'clock, the women of Barracks 28, tired, sweat-stained, and dirty from the long forced-labor details. The building, we learned from one of our platform mates, had been designed to hold four hundred. There were now fourteen hundred quartered here with more arriving weekly as concentration camps in Poland, France, Belgium, Austria, as well as Holland were evacuated toward the center of Germany.

There were nine of us sharing our particular square, designed for four, and some grumbling as the others discovered they would have to make room for Betsie and me. Eight acrid and overflowing toilets served the entire room; to reach them we had to crawl not only over our own bedmates but over those on the other platforms between us and the closest aisle, always at the risk of adding too much weight to the already sagging slats and crashing down on the people beneath. It happened several times, that first night. From somewhere in the room would come a splintering sound, a shriek, smothered cries.

Even when the slats held, the least movement on the upper platforms sent a shower of dust and straw over the sleepers below—followed by a volley of curses. In Barracks 8 most of us had been Dutch. Here there was not even a common language and among exhausted, ill-fed people quarrels erupted constantly.

There was one raging now as the women sleeping nearest the windows slammed them shut against the cold. At once scores of voices demanded that they be raised again. Brawls were starting all up and down that side of the room; we heard scuffling, slaps, sobs.

In the dark I felt Betsie's hands clasp mine. "Lord Jesus," she said aloud, "send Your peace into this room. There has been too little praying here. The very walls know it. But where You come, Lord, the spirit of strife cannot exist. . . ."

The change was gradual, but distinct. One by one the angry sounds let up.

"I'll make you a deal!" The voice spoke German with a strong Scandinavian accent. "You can sleep in here where it's warmer and I'll take your place by the window!"

"And add your lice to my own!" But there was a chuckle in the answer. "No thanks."

"I'll tell you what!" The third voice had a French burr. "We'll open them halfway. That way we'll be only half-frozen and you'll be only half-smothered."

A ripple of laughter widened around the room at this. I lay back on the sour straw and knew there was one more circumstance for which I could give thanks. Betsie had come to Barracks 28.

Roll call came at 4:40 A.M. here as it had in quarantine. A whistle roused us at 4:00 when, without even shaking the straw from clothes and hair, the stampede began for the ration of bread and coffee in the center room. Lastcomers found none.

The count was made in the *Lagerstrasse,* the wide avenue leading to the hospital. There we joined the occupants of other barracks—some 35,000 at that time—stretching out of sight in the pale glow of the street lamps, feet growing numb on the cold cinder ground.

After roll call, work crews were called out. For weeks Betsie and I were assigned to the Siemens factory. This huge complex of mills and railroad terminals was a mile and a half from the camp. The "Siemens Brigade," several thousand of us, marched out the iron gate beneath the charged wires into a world of trees and grass and horizons. The sun rose as we skirted the little lake; the gold of the late fall fields lifted our hearts.

The work at Siemens, however, was sheer misery. Betsie and I had to push a heavy handcart to a railroad siding where we unloaded large metal plates from a boxcar and wheeled them to a receiving gate at the factory. The grueling workday lasted eleven hours. At least, at noontime we were given a boiled potato and some thin soup; those who worked inside the camp had no midday meal.

Returning to camp we could barely lift our swollen and aching legs. The soldiers patrolling us bellowed and cursed, but we could only shuffle forward inches at a step. I noticed again how the local people turned their eyes another way.

Back at the barracks we formed yet another line —would there never be an end to columns and waits? —to receive our ladle of turnip soup in the center room. Then, as quickly as we could for the press of people, Betsie and I made our way to the rear of the dormitory room where we held our worship "service." Around our own platform area there was not enough light to read the Bible, but back here a small light bulb cast a wan yellow circle on the wall, and here an ever larger group of women gathered.

They were services like no others, these times in Barracks 28. A single meeting night might include a recital of the Magnificat in Latin by a group of Roman Catholics, a whispered hymn by some Lutherans, and a sotto-voce chant by Eastern Orthodox women. With each moment the crowd around us would swell, packing the nearby platforms, hanging over the edges, until the high structures groaned and swayed.

At last either Betsie or I would open the Bible. Because only the Hollanders could understand the Dutch text we would translate aloud in German. And then we would hear the life-giving words passed back along the aisles in French, Polish, Russian, Czech, back into Dutch. They were little previews of heaven, these evenings beneath the light bulb. I would think of Haarlem, each substantial church set behind its wrought-iron fence and its barrier of doctrine. And I would know again that in darkness God's truth shines most clear.

At first Betsie and I called these meetings with great timidity. But as night after night went by and no guard ever came near us, we grew bolder. So many now wanted to join us that we held a second service after evening roll call. There on the *Lugerstrasse* we were under rigid surveillance, guards in their warm wool capes marching constantly up and down. It was the same in the center room of the barracks: half a dozen guards or camp police always present. Yet in the large dormitory room there was almost no supervision at all. We did not understand it.

Another strange thing was happening. The Davitamon bottle was continuing to produce drops. It scarcely seemed possible, so small a bottle, so many doses a day. Now, in addition to Betsie, a dozen others on our pier were taking it.

My instinct was always to hoard it—Betsie was growing so very weak! But the others were ill as well. It was hard to say no to eyes that burned with fever, hands that shook with chill. I tried to save it for the very weakest—but even these soon numbered fifteen, twenty, twenty-five. . . .

And still, every time I tilted the little bottle, a drop appeared at the tip of the glass stopper. It just couldn't be! I held it up to the light, trying to see how much was left, but the dark brown glass was too thick to see through.

"There was a woman in the Bible," Betsie said, "whose oil jar was never empty." She turned to it in the Book of Kings, the story of the poor widow of Zarephath who gave Elijah a room in her home: "The jar of meal wasted not, neither did the cruse of oil fail, according to the word of Jehovah which he spoke by Elijah."

Well—but—wonderful things happened all through the Bible. It was one thing to believe that such things were possible thousands of years ago, another to have it happen now, to us, this very day. And yet it happened this day, and the next, and the next, until an awed little group of spectators stood around watching the drops fall onto the daily rations of bread.

Many nights I lay awake in the shower of straw dust from the mattress above, trying to fathom the marvel of supply lavished upon us. "Maybe," I whispered to Betsie, "only a molecule or two really gets through that little pinhole—and then in the air it expands!"

I heard her soft laughter in the dark. "Don't try too hard to explain it, Corrie. Just accept it as a surprise from a Father who loves you."

And then one day Mien pushed her way to us in the evening food line. "Look what I've got for you!"

Mien was a pretty young Dutch woman we had met in Vught. She was assigned to the hospital and often managed to bring to Barracks 28 some stolen treasure from the staff room—a sheet of newspaper to stuff in a broken window, a slice of bread left untouched on a nurse's plate. Now we peered into the small cloth sack she carried.

"Vitamins!" I cried, and then cast an apprehensive glance at a camp policeman nearby. "Yeast compound!" I whispered.

"Yes!" she hissed back. "There were several huge jars. I emptied each just the same amount."

We gulped the thin turnip water, marveling at our sudden riches. Back at the bunk I took the bottle from the straw. "We'll finish the drops first," I decided.

But that night, no matter how long I held it upside down, or how hard I shook it, not another drop appeared.

On the first of November a coat was issued to each prisoner. Betsie's and mine were both of Russian make, probably once trimmed with fur: threads showed where something had been torn from the collars and cuffs.

Call-ups for the Siemens factory had ceased and we speculated that it had been hit in one of the bombing raids that came within earshot almost nightly now. Betsie and I were put to work leveling some rough ground just inside the camp wall. This too was backbreaking labor. Sometimes as I bent to lift a load my heart cramped strangely; at night spasms of pain gripped my legs.

But the biggest problem was Betsie's strength. One morning after a hard night's rain we arrived to find the ground sodden and heavy. Betsie had never been able to lift much; today her shovels-ful were microscopic and she stumbled frequently as she walked to the low ground where we dumped the loads.

"Schneller!" a guard screamed at her. "Can't you go faster?"

Why must they scream, I wondered as I sank my shovel into the black muck. Why couldn't they speak like ordinary human beings? I straightened slowly, the sweat drying on my back. I was remembering where we had first heard this maniac sound. The Beje. In Tante Jans's rooms. A voice coming from the shell-shaped speaker, a scream lingering in the air even after Betsie had leapt to shut it off. . . .

"Loafer! Lazy swine!"

The guard snatched Betsie's shovel from her hands and ran from group to group of the digging crew, exhibiting the handful of dirt that was all Betsie had been able to lift.

"Look what Madame Baroness is carrying! Surely she will over-exert herself!"

The other guards and even some of the prisoners laughed. Encouraged, the guard threw herself into a parody of Betsie's faltering walk. A male guard was with our detail today and in the presence of a man the women guards were always animated.

As the laughter grew, I felt a murderous anger rise. The guard was young and well fed—was it Betsie's fault that she was old and starving? But to my astonishment, Betsie too was laughing.

"That's me all right," she admitted. "But you'd better let me totter along with my little spoonful, or I'll have to stop altogether."

The guard's plump cheeks went crimson. "I'll decide who's to stop!" And snatching the leather crop from her belt she slashed Betsie across the chest and neck.

Without knowing I was doing it I had seized my shovel and rushed at her.

Betsie stepped in front of me before anyone had seen. "Corrie!" she pleaded, dragging my arm to my side. "Corrie, keep working!" She tugged the shovel from my hand and dug it into the mud. Contemptuously the guard tossed Betsie's shovel toward us. I picked it up, still in a daze. A red stain appeared on Betsie's collar; a welt began to swell on her neck.

Betsie saw where I was looking and laid a bird-thin hand over the whip mark. "Don't look at it, Corrie. Look at Jesus only." She drew away her hand: it was sticky with blood.

In mid-November the rains started in earnest, chill, drenching day-long downpours that left beads of moisture even on the inside walls. The *Lagerstrasse* was never dry now; even when the rain let up, deep puddles stood in the road. We were not allowed to step around them as the ranks were formed: often we stood in water up to our ankles, and at night the barracks reeked with rotting shoe leather.

Betsie's cough began to bring up blood. We went to sick call at the hospital, but the thermometer registered only 102°, not enough to admit her to the wards. Alas for my fantasies of a nurse and a dispensary in each barracks. This large bare room in the hospital was where all the sick in the camp had to assemble, often standing outside in the rain for hours just to get through the door.

I hated the dismal place full of sick and suffering women, but we had to go back, again and again, for Betsie's condition was growing worse. She was not repelled by the room as I was. To her it was simply a setting in which to talk about Jesus—as indeed was everyplace else. Wherever she was, at work, in the food line, in the dormitory, Betsie spoke to those around her about His nearness and His yearning to come into their lives. As her body grew weaker, her faith seemed to grow bolder. And sick call was "such an important place, Corrie! Some of these people are at the threshold of heaven!"

At last one night Betsie's fever registered over the required 104°. There was another long wait until a nurse appeared to lead her and half a dozen others into the hospital proper. I stayed with them as far as the door to the ward, then made my way slowly back to the barracks.

As usual, as I stood in the door of the dormitory, it reminded me most of an anthill. Some women were already asleep after the long workday, but most were stirring about, some waiting for a turn at the toilets, others picking lice off themselves and their neighbors. I twisted and squirmed through the crowded aisles to the rear where the prayer service was just ending. Nights when Betsie and I reported to sick call we left the Bible with Mrs. Wielmaker, a saintly Roman Catholic woman from The Hague who could render the Dutch words in German, French, Latin, or Greek. Women crowded around me, asking after Betsie. How was she? How long would she have to stay?

Lights-out blew and the scramble into the bunks began. I hoisted myself to the middle tier and crawled across those already in place. What a difference since Betsie had come to this room! Where before this had been the moment for scuffles and cursing, tonight the huge dormitory buzzed with "Sorry!" "Excuse me!" And "No harm done!"

I found our section in the dark and squeezed into a spot in the middle. From the doorway a searchlight swept the room, lingering on blocks where anything stirred. Someone's elbow dug into my back, another woman's feet were two inches from my face. How was it possible, packed so close, to be so utterly and miserably alone?

14

The Blue Sweater

In the morning a cold wet mist hung over the *Lager-strasse*. I was grateful that Betsie did not have to stand outside.

All day the blanketing fog hung over Ravensbruck, an eerie day when sound was muffled and the sun never rose. I was on potato detail, one of a crew hauling baskets of potatoes to long trenches to be covered with dirt against the freezing weather ahead. I was glad of the hard physical work that drove some of the damp from my bones and for the occasional bite of raw potato when guards were not watching.

Next day when the white pall still lay over the camp, my loneliness for Betsie became too much to bear. As soon as roll call was dismissed, I did a desperate thing. Mien had told me a way to get into the hospital without passing the guardpost inside the door. The latrine at the rear, she said, had a very large window too warped to close tight. Since no visiting was permitted in the hospital relatives of patients often took this way of getting inside.

In the dense fog it was easy to get to the window unseen. I hoisted myself through it, then clapped my hand to my nose against the stinging odor. A row of lidless, doorless toilets stretched along one wall in the pool of their overflow. I dashed for the door, then stopped, my flesh crawling. Against this opposite wall a dozen naked corpses lay side by side on their backs

Some of the eyes were open and seemed to stare unblinkingly at the ceiling.

I was standing there, lead-footed with horror, when two men pushed through the door carrying a sheet-wrapped bundle between them. They did not even glance at me and I realized they took me for a patient. I ducked round them into the hall and stood for a moment, stomach knotting with the sight I had seen. After a while I started aimlessly off to the left.

The hospital was a maze of halls and doors. Already I was not sure of the way back to the latrine. What if the potato crew left before I got back? And then a corridor looked familiar. I hurried, almost running from door to door. At last, the ward where I had left Betsie! No hospital personnel was in sight: I walked eagerly down the aisles of cots looking from face to face.

"Corrie!"

Betsie was sitting up in a cot near the window. She looked stronger, eyes bright, a touch of color in her sunken cheeks. No nurse or doctor had seen her yet, she said, but the chance to lie still and stay indoors had already made a difference.

Three days afterward, Betsie returned to Barracks 28. She still had received no examination or medicine of any kind and her forehead felt feverish to my touch. But the joy of having her back outweighed my anxiety.

Best of all, as a result of her hospitalization, she was given a permanent assignment to the "knitting brigade," the women we had seen the very first day seated about the tables in the center room. This work was reserved for the weakest prisoners, and now overflowed into the dormitories as well.

Those working in the sleeping rooms received far less supervision than those at the tables, and Betsie found herself with most of the day in which to minister to those around her. She was a lightning knitter who completed her quota of socks long before noon. She kept our Bible with her and spent hours each day reading aloud from it, moving from platform to platform.

One evening I got back to the barracks late from a

wood-gathering foray outside the walls. A light snow lay on the ground and it was hard to find the sticks and twigs with which a small stove was kept going in each room. Betsie was waiting for me, as always, so that we could wait through the food line together. Her eyes were twinkling.

"You're looking extraordinarily pleased with yourself," I told her.

"You know we've never understood why we had so much freedom in the big room," she said. "Well—I've found out."

That afternoon, she said, there'd been confusion in her knitting group about sock sizes and they'd asked the supervisor to come and settle it.

"But she wouldn't. She wouldn't step through the door and neither would the guards. And you know why?"

Betsie could not keep the triumph from her voice: "Because of the fleas! That's what she said, 'That place is crawling with fleas!' "

My mind rushed back to our first hour in this place. I remembered Betsie's bowed head, remembered her thanks to God for creatures I could see no use for.

Though Betsie was now spared heavy outdoor labor, she still had to stand the twice-daily roll call. As December temperatures fell, they became true endurance tests and many did not survive. One dark morning when ice was forming a halo around each street lamp, a feeble-minded girl two rows ahead of us suddenly soiled herself. A guard rushed at her, swinging her thick leather crop while the girl shrieked in pain and terror. It was always more terrible when one of these innocent ones was beaten. Still the *Aufseherin* continued to whip her. It was the guard we had nicknamed "The Snake" because of the shiny dress she wore. I could see it now beneath her long wool cape, glittering in the light of the lamp as she raised her arm. I was grateful when the screaming girl at last lay still on the cinder street.

"Betsie," I whispered when The Snake was far enough away, "what can we do for these people? Afterward I mean. Can't we make a home for them and care for them and love them?"

"Corrie, I pray every day that we will be allowed to do this! To show them that love is greater!"

And it wasn't until I was gathering twigs later in the morning that I realized that I had been thinking of the feeble-minded, and Betsie of their persecutors.

Several days later my entire work crew was ordered to the hospital for medical inspection. I dropped my dress onto the pile just inside the door and joined the file of naked women. Ahead of us, to my surprise, a doctor was using a stethoscope with all the deliberateness of a real examination.

"What is this for?" I whispered to the woman ahead of me.

"Transport inspection," she hissed back, not moving her head. "Munitions work."

Transport! But they couldn't! They mustn't send me away! Dear God, don't let them take me away from Betsie!

But to my terror I passed one station after another —heart, lungs, scalp, throat—and still I was in the line. Many were pulled out along the way, but those who remained looked hardly stronger. Swollen stomachs, hollow chests, spindly legs: how desperate for manpower Germany must be!

I halted before a woman in a soiled white coat. She turned me around to face a chart on the wall, her hand cold on my bare shoulder. "Read the lowest line you can."

"I—I can't seem to read any of them. (Lord forgive me!) Just the top letter. That big E." The top letter was an F.

The woman seemed to see me for the first time. "You can see better than that! Do you want to be rejected?"

At Ravensbruck, munitions transport was considered a privilege; food and living conditions in the factories were said to be far better than here in the camp.

"Oh yes, Doctor! My sister's here at Ravensbruck! She's not well! I can't leave her!"

The doctor sat down at her table and scrawled something on a piece of paper. "Come back tomorrow to be fitted for glasses."

Catching up to the line, I unfolded the small blue slip of paper. Prisoner 66730 was instructed to report for an optical fitting at 6:30 the following morning. Six-thirty was the time the transport convoys were loaded.

And so as the huge vans rumbled down the *Lagerstrasse* the next day, I was standing in a corridor of the hospital waiting my turn at the eye clinic. The young man in charge was perhaps a qualified eye doctor, but his entire equipment consisted of a box of framed glasses, from gold-rimmed bifocals to a plastic-framed child's pair. I found none that fitted and at last was ordered back to my work detail.

But, of course, I had no work assignment, having been marked down for transport. I walked back uncertainly toward Barracks 28. I stepped into the center room. The supervisor looked up over the heads of the knitting crew.

"Number?" she said.

I gave it and she wrote it in a black-covered book. "Pick up your yarn and a pattern sheet," she went on. "You'll have to find a place on one of the beds, there's no room here." And she turned back to the pile of finished socks on the table.

I stood blinking in the center of the room. Then grabbing a skein of the dark gray wool I dashed through the dormitory door. And thus began the closest, most joyous weeks of all the time in Ravensbruck. Side by side, in the sanctuary of God's fleas, Betsie and I ministered the word of God to all in the room. We sat by deathbeds that became doorways of heaven. We watched women who had lost everything grow rich in hope. The knitters of Barracks 28 became the praying heart of the vast diseased body that was Ravensbruck, interceding for all in the camp—guards, under Betsie's prodding, as well as prisoners. We prayed beyond the concrete walls for the healing of Germany, of Europe, of the world—as Mama had once done from the prison of a crippled body.

And as we prayed, God spoke to us about the world after the war. It was extraordinary; in this place where whistles and loudspeakers took the place of decisions, God asked us what we were going to do in the years ahead.

Betsie was always very clear about the answer for her and me. We were to have a house, a large one—much larger than the Beje—to which people who had been damaged by concentration-camp life would come until they felt ready to live again in the normal world.

"It's such a beautiful house, Corrie! The floors are all inlaid wood, with statues set in the walls and a broad staircase sweeping down. And gardens! Gardens all around it where they can plant flowers. It will do them such good, Corrie, to care for flowers!"

I would stare at Betsie in amazement as she talked about these things. She spoke always as though she were describing things that she saw—as if that wide, winding staircase and those bright gardens were the reality, this cramped and filthy barracks the dream.

But it wasn't a dream. It was really, achingly, endlessly true, and it was always during roll calls that the accumulated misery threatened to overwhelm me.

One morning three women from Barracks 28 lingered inside a few minutes to avoid the cold. All the following week the entire barracks was punished by an extra hour at attention. The lights on the *Lagerstrasse* were not even lit when we were driven from our bunks at 3:30 A.M.

It was during this preinspection lineup one morning that I saw what I had till then refused to believe. Headlights appeared at the far end of the long street, wavering over the snow. Trucks with open flat-beds in the rear were approaching, spattering slush as they passed. They pulled up at the front door of the hospital. The door opened and a nurse appeared, supporting an old woman whose legs buckled as she limped down the steps. The nurse lifted her gently onto the back of a truck. They were pouring out of the door now, leaning on the arms of nurses and hospital helpers, the old, the ill. Last of all came orderlies with stretchers between them.

Our eyes took in every detail of the scene; our brains refused. We had known, of course, that when overcrowding reached a certain point, the sickest were taken to the brick building at the foot of the great square smokestack. But, that these women here in front of us—these very ones. It was not possible. Above all I could not put it together with the kindly behavior of the nurses. That one in the truck just ahead, bending solicitously, even tenderly, over her patient. . . . What was passing through her mind just now?

And all the while, it grew colder. One night during evening roll call a platoon somewhere far down the *Lagerstrasse* began a rhythmic stamping. The sound grew as others picked it up. The guards did not stop us and at last the entire street was marching in place, pounding tattered shoes against the frozen ground, driving circulation back into numb feet and legs. From now on this was the sound of roll call, the stamping of thousands of feet on the long dark street.

And as the cold increased, so did the special temptation of concentration-camp life: the temptation to think only of oneself. It took a thousand cunning forms. I quickly discovered that when I maneuvered our way toward the middle of the roll-call formation we had a little protection from the wind.

I knew this was self-centered: when Betsie and I stood in the center, someone else had to stand on the edge. How easy it was to give it other names! I was acting only for Betsie's sake. We were in an important ministry and must keep well. It was colder in Poland than in Holland; these Polish women probably were not feeling the chill the way we were.

Selfishness had a life of its own. As I watched Mien's bag of yeast-compound disappear I began taking it from beneath the straw only after lights-out when others would not see and ask for some. Wasn't Betsie's health more important? (You see, God, she can do so much *for* them! Remember that house, after the war!)

And even if it wasn't right—it wasn't so *very* wrong, was it? Not wrong like sadism and murder and the other monstrous evils we saw in Ravensbruck every day. Oh, this was the great ploy of Satan in that kingdom of his: to display such blatant evil that one could almost believe one's own secret sins didn't matter.

The cancer spread. The second week in December, every occupant of Barracks 28 was issued an extra blanket. The next day a large group of evacuées arrived from Czechoslovakia. One of them assigned to our platform had no blanket at all and Betsie insisted that we give her one of ours. So that evening I "lent" her a blanket. But I didn't "give" it to her. In my heart I held onto the right to that blanket.

Was it coincidence that joy and power imperceptibly drained from my ministry? My prayers took on a mechanical ring. Even Bible reading was dull and lifeless. Betsie tried to take over for me, but her cough made reading aloud impossible.

And so I struggled on with worship and teaching that had ceased to be real. Until one drizzly raw afternoon when just enough light came through the window to read by, I came to Paul's account of his "thorn in the flesh." Three times, he said, he had begged God to take away his weakness, whatever it was. And each time God had said, Rely on Me. At last Paul concluded—the words seemed to leap from the page—that his very weakness was something to give thanks for. Because now Paul knew that none of the wonders and miracles which followed his ministry could be due to his own virtues. It was all Christ's strength, never Paul's.

And there it was.

The truth blazed like sunlight in the shadows of Barracks 28. The real sin I had been committing was not that of inching toward the center of a platoon because I was cold. The real sin lay in thinking that any power to help and transform came from me. Of course it was not *my* wholeness, but Christ's that made the difference.

The short winter day was fading; I could no longer separate the words on the page. And so I closed the

Bible and to that group of women clustering close I told the truth about myself—my self-centeredness, my stinginess, my lack of love. That night real joy returned to my worship.

Each roll call the wind seemed sharper. Whenever she could, Mien smuggled newspapers from the staff room at the hospital, which we placed inside our clothes. Nollie's blue sweater beneath Betsie's dress was black with newsprint.

The cold seemed to be affecting Betsie's legs. Sometimes in the morning she could not move them at all and two of us would have to carry her between us. It was not hard—she weighed no more than a child. But she could no longer stamp her feet as the rest of us did to keep the blood flowing. When we returned to the dormitory I would rub her feet and hands, but my own only picked up the chill from hers.

It was the week before Christmas that Betsie woke up unable to move either legs or arms. I shoved my way through the crowded aisles to the center room. The Snake was on duty.

"Please!" I begged. "Betsie is ill! Oh please, she's got to get to the hospital!"

"Stand at attention. State your number."

"Prisoner 66730 reporting. Please, my sister is sick!"

"All prisoners must report for the count. If she's sick she can register at sick call."

Maryke de Graaf, a Dutch woman on the tier above ours, helped me form a cradle with our arms and carry Betsie outside. The rhythmic stamping had already begun in the *Lagerstrasse*. We carried her to the hospital, then stopped. In the light of the street lamps, the sick-call line stretched to the edge of the building and out of sight around the corner. In the sooty snow alongside, three bodies lay where they had fallen.

Without a word Maryke and I turned and carried our load back to the *Lagerstrasse*. After roll call we got her back into bed. Her speech was slow and blurred, but she was trying to say something.

"A camp, Corrie—a concentration camp. But

we're . . . in charge . . ." I had to bend very close to hear. The camp was in Germany. It was no longer a prison, but a home where people who had been warped by this philosophy of hate and force could come to learn another way. There were no walls, no barbed wire, and the barracks had windowboxes. "It will be so good for them . . . watching things grow. People can learn to love, from flowers. . . ."

I knew by now which people she meant. The German people. I thought of The Snake standing in the barracks door that morning. "State your number. All prisoners must report for the count."

I looked into Betsie's shrunken face. "We are to have this camp in Germany instead, Betsie? Instead of the big house in Holland?"

"Oh no!" she seemed shocked. "You know we have the house first! It's ready and waiting for us . . . such tall, tall windows! The sun is streaming in——"

A coughing fit seized her; when finally she lay still, a stain of blood blackened the straw. She dozed fitfully during the day and night that followed, waking several times with the excitement of some new detail about our work in Holland or Germany.

"The barracks are gray, Corrie, but we'll paint them green! Bright, light green, like springtime."

"We'll be together, Betsie? We're doing all this together? You're sure about that?"

"Always together, Corrie! You and I . . . always together."

When the siren blew next morning, Maryke and I again carried Betsie from the dormitory. The Snake was standing at the street door. As we started through it with our fragile burden she stepped in front of us. "Take her back to the bunks."

"I thought all pris——"

"Take her back!"

Wonderingly, we replaced Betsie on the bed. Sleet rattled against the windows. Was it possible that the atmosphere of Barracks 28 had affected even this cruel guard? As soon as roll call was dismissed I ran back to the dormitory. There, beside our bed, stood The Snake. Beside her two orderlies from the hospital were setting

down a stretcher. The Snake straightened almost guiltily as I approached. "Prisoner is ready for transfer,"
she snapped.

I looked at the woman more closely: Had she
risked fleas and lice to spare Betsie the sick-call line?
She did not stop me as I started after the stretcher.
Our group of knitters was just entering the big room.
As we passed, a Polish friend dropped to her knees
and made the sign of the Cross.

Sleet stung us as we reached the outside. I stepped
close to the stretcher to form a shield for Betsie. We
walked past the waiting line of sick people, through the
door and into a large ward. They placed the stretcher
on the floor and I leaned down to make out Betsie's
words.

". . . must tell people what we have learned here.
We must tell them that there is no pit so deep that He
is not deeper still. They will listen to us, Corrie, because we have been here."

I stared at her wasted form. "But when will all
this happen, Betsie!"

"Now. Right away. Oh, very soon! By the first of
the year, Corrie, we will be out of prison!"

A nurse had caught sight of me. I backed to the
door of the room and watched as they placed Betsie
on a narrow cot close to the window. I ran around to
the outside of the building. At last Betsie caught sight
of me; we exchanged smiles and soundless words until
one of the camp police shouted at me to move along.

About noontime I put down my knitting and went
out to the center room. "Prisoner 66730 reporting.
Request permission to visit the hospital." I stood ram-
rod straight.

The Snake glanced up, then scrawled out a pass.
Outside it was still sleeting. I reached the door of the
ward but the horrible nurse would not let me enter,
even with my pass. So I went again to the window next
to Betsie's cot. I waited until the nurse left the room,
then tapped gently.

Betsie's eyes opened. Slowly she turned her head.
"Are you all right?" I formed with my lips.
She nodded.

"You must get a good rest," I went on.

She moved her lips in reply but I could not follow. She formed the words again. I bent my head to one side, level with hers. The blue lips opened again:

". . . so much work to do. . . ."

The Snake was off duty during the afternoon and evening and though I asked the other guards repeatedly, I did not again get permission to leave. The minute roll call was dismissed the following morning, I headed for the hospital, permission or no.

I reached the window and cupped my eyes to peer in. A nurse was standing directly between me and Betsie. I ducked out of sight, waited a minute, then looked again. A second nurse had joined the first, both now standing where I wanted to see. They stepped to the head and foot of the bed: I gazed curiously at what lay on it. It was a carving in old yellow ivory. There was no clothing on the figure; I could see each ivory rib, and the outline of the teeth through the parchment cheeks.

It took me a moment to realize it was Betsie.

The nurses had each seized two corners of the sheet. They lifted it between them and carried the bundle from the room before my heart had started to beat again in my chest.

Betsie! But—she had too much to do! She could not——

Where were they taking her? Where had they gone! I turned from the window and began running along the side of the building, chest hurting me as I breathed.

Then I remembered the washroom. That window at the rear—that was where . . .

My feet carried me mechanically around to the back of the building. And there, with my hand on the windowsill, I stopped. Suppose she was there? Suppose they had laid Betsie on that floor?

I started walking again. I walked for a long time, still with that pain in my chest. And each time my feet took me back to the washroom window. I would not go in. I would not look. Betsie could not be there.

I walked some more. Strangely enough, although I passed several camp police, no one stopped or questioned me.

"Corrie!"

I turned around to see Mien running after me. "Corrie, I've looked for you everywhere! Oh, Corrie, come!"

She seized my arm and drew me toward the back of the hospital.

When I saw where she was headed I wrenched my arm free. "I know, Mien. I know already."

She didn't seem to hear. She seized me again, led me to the washroom window, and pushed me in ahead of her. In the reeking room stood a nurse. I drew back in alarm, but Mien was behind me.

"This is the sister," Mien said to the nurse.

I turned my head to the side—I would not look at the bodies that lined the far wall. Mien put an arm around my shoulder and drew me across the room till we were standing above that heart-breaking row.

"Corrie! Do you see her!"

I raised my eyes to Betsie's face. Lord Jesus— what have You done! Oh Lord, what are You saying! What are You giving me!

For there lay Betsie, her eyes closed as if in sleep, her face full and young. The care lines, the grief lines, the deep hollows of hunger and disease were simply gone. In front of me was the Betsie of Haarlem, happy and at peace. Stronger! Freer! This was the Betsie of heaven, bursting with joy and health. Even her hair was graciously in place as if an angel had ministered to her.

At last I turned wonderingly to Mien. The nurse went silently to the door and opened it for us herself. "You can leave through the hall," she said softly.

I looked once more at the radiant face of my sister. Then Mien and I left the room together. A pile of clothes was heaped outside in the hallway; on top lay Nollie's blue sweater.

I stooped to pick it up. The sweater was threadbare and stained with newsprint, but it was a tangible link with Betsie. Mien seized my arm. "Don't touch those things! Black lice! They'll all be burned."

And so I left behind the last physical tie. It was just as well. It was better. Now what tied me to Betsie was the hope of heaven.

15

The Three Visions

The beauty of Betsie's face sustained me over the next days, as I went from one to another of the women who had loved her, describing to them her peace and her joy.

Two mornings after her death the count was off at roll call. The other barracks were dismissed, 28 remained in ranks, eyes front. The loudspeaker beeped and a voice came on: a woman was missing; the entire barracks would stand on the *Lagerstrasse* until she was found. Left, right, left, right, endlessly tramping to drive the chill from weary legs. The sun came up, a wan wintry sun that did not warm. I looked down at my feet: my legs and ankles were swelling grotesquely. By noontime there was no feeling in them. Betsie, how happy you are today! No cold, no hunger, nothing between you and the face of Jesus!

The dismissal order came in the afternoon. We learned later that the missing woman had been found dead on one of the upper platforms.

It was the following morning when over the loudspeaker during roll call came the words: "Ten Boom, Cornelia!"

For an instant I stood stupidly where I was. I had been Prisoner 66730 for so long that I almost failed to react to my name. I walked forward.

"Stand to the side!"

What was going to happen? Why had I been singled out? Had someone reported the Bible?

The roll call dragged on. From where I stood I could see almost the entire *Lagerstrasse*, tens of thousands of women stretching out of sight, their breath hanging white in the night air.

The siren blew for dismissal; the guard signaled me to follow her. I splashed through the slush, trying to keep up with the strides of her tall boots. My legs and feet were still painfully swollen from the long count the day before, my shoes were held together with bits of string.

I hobbled behind the guard into the administration barracks at the opposite end of the *Lagerstrasse* from the hospital. Several prisoners were standing in line at a large desk. An officer seated behind it stamped a paper and handed it to the woman in front of him.

"Entlassen!" he said.

Entlassen? Released? Was—was the woman free then? Was this—were we all—

He called a name and another prisoner stepped to the desk. A signature, a stamp:

"Entlassen!"

At last "Ten Boom, Cornelia," was called. I stepped to the desk, steadying myself against it. He wrote, brought down the stamp, and then I was holding it in my hand: a piece of paper with my name and birthdate on it, and across the top in large black letters: CERTIFICATE OF DISCHARGE

Dazed, I followed the others through a door at our left. There at another desk I was handed a railway pass entitling me to transportation through Germany to the Dutch border. Outside this office a guard pointed me down a corridor into still another room. There the prisoners who had been ahead of me were tugging their dresses over their heads and lining up against the rear wall.

"Clothing over here!" a smiling prison trusty told me. *"Entlassen* physical," she explained.

I drew the Bible over my head along with the dress, rolled them together and buried the bundle at the bottom of the clothing pile. I joined the others, the wooden wall rough against my bare back. Strange how the very word "Release" had made the procedures of prison a hundred times more hateful. How often Betsie and I had stood like this. But the thought of freedom had stirred in me and the shame of this inspection was greater than all the others.

At last the doctor arrived, a freckled-faced boy in a military uniform. He glanced along the lineup with undisguised contempt. One by one we had to bend, turn around, spread our fingers. When he reached me his eyes traveled down to my feet and his lips puckered in disgust.

"Edema," he said. "Hospital."

He was gone. With one other woman who had not "passed" I scrambled back into my clothes and followed the trusty from the building. Day had broken, a sullen gray sky spitting snow. We started up the *Lagerstrasse*, past the endless streets of barracks.

"Then—we're not—aren't we to be released?"

"I imagine you will be, as soon as the swelling in your legs goes down," the trusty said. "They only release you if you're in good condition." I saw her look at the other prisoner: the woman's skin and eyes were a dull dark yellow.

Sick call stretched around the side of the hospital, but we walked straight through the door and into a ward at the rear. The room was crammed with double-decker cots. I was assigned a place on an upper bunk next to a woman whose body was covered with erupting pustules. But at least it was near a wall where I could keep my swollen legs elevated. That was what mattered now: to get the swelling down, to pass the inspection.

Whether that ray of freedom shed a new, relentless light on Ravensbruck, or whether this was truly the most savage place yet, I could not tell. The suffering was unimaginable. Around me were survivors of a prison train which had been bombed on its way here. The women were horribly mutilated and in terrible pain, but at each moan two of the nurses jeered and mimicked the sounds.

Even in the other patients I saw that stony indifference to others that was the most fatal disease of the concentration camp. I felt it spread to myself: how could one survive if one kept on feeling! The paralyzed and the unconscious kept falling out of the crowded narrow cots; that first night four women fell from upper bunks and died on the floor. It was better to narrow the mind to one's own need, not to see, not to think.

But there was no way to shut out the sounds. All night women cried out a German word I didn't know. *"Schieber!"* Over and over from rasping throats: *"Schieber!"*

Finally I realized that they were calling for bedpans. It was out of the question for most of the women in this room to make it to that filthy latrine next door. At last, reluctant to lower my legs, I climbed down from my cot and set about the chore. The gratitude of the patients was heart-wrenching. "Who are you? Why are you doing this?"—as though cruelty and callousness were the norm, ordinary decency the marvel.

As a wintry dawn crept through the windows, I realized it was Christmas Day.

I went each morning to the clinic at the front of the hospital where I could hear the tramping of feet on the *Lagerstrasse* outside. Each time the verdict was "Edema of the feet and ankles." Many of those who attended the clinic were, like myself, discharged prisoners. Some had been released months ago: their discharge papers and railway passes were ragged from opening and refolding. And—what if Betsie were still alive? Surely our prison term would have been up together. But Betsie would never, never have passed the physical. What if she were here with me? What if I were to pass the inspection and she . . .

There are no "ifs" in God's kingdom. I could hear her soft voice saying it. His timing is perfect. His will is our hiding place. Lord Jesus, keep me in Your will! Don't let me go mad by poking about outside it.

I kept looking for someone to give the Bible to. How easy it would be, back in Holland, to get another —a hundred others. There were not many Hollanders in the ward who would be able to read the Dutch text, but at last I slipped it around the neck of a grateful young woman from Utrecht.

The sixth night I spent in the ward both bedpans were suddenly and mysteriously missing. In an upper bunk on the center aisle were two Hungarian gypsies whose muttering was part of the babble of the room. I never walked past their cot because one of them had a gangrenous foot which she would thrust in the face of anyone who came near. Now someone screamed out that the gypsies had the bedpans, hidden under their blankets to save them the trip to the toilets. I went to their cot and pleaded with them—though I didn't know whether they understood German or not.

Suddenly in the dark something wet and sticky coiled round my face. The woman had taken the bandage from her foot and flung it at me. I ran sobbing down the corridor and washed and washed beneath the wall spigot in the latrine. I would never step into that aisle again! What did I care about the wretched bedpans! I couldn't bear . . .

But of course I did go back. I had learned much, in the past year, about what I could and could not bear. As the gypsies saw me heading down the aisle toward them, both bedpans clattered onto the floor.

The next morning the doctor on duty at the clinic stamped the medical approval on my discharge form. Events that had dragged so slow now moved with bewildering speed. In a dressing shed near the outer gate of the camp I was outfitted with clothes. Underthings; a woolen skirt; a truly beautiful silk blouse; sturdy, almost-new shoes; a hat; an overcoat. I was handed a form to sign stating that I had never been ill at Ravensbruck, never had an accident, and that the treatment had been good. I signed.

In another building I received a day's bread ration and food coupons for three additional days. I was also given back my watch, my Dutch money, and Mama's ring. And then I was standing with a group of ten or twelve just inside the gate.

The heavy iron doors swung open; at the heels

of a woman guard we marched through. We climbed the little hill: now I could see the lake, frozen from shore to shore. The pines and the distant church steeple sparkled in the winter sun like an old-fashioned Christmas card.

I could not believe it. Perhaps we were only going to the Siemens factory; tonight we would march back to camp. But at the top of the hill we turned left, toward the center of the small town. I could feel my feet swelling in the tight new shoes, but I bit my lip and made myself stride along. I imagined the guard turning around, pointing a scornful finger: "Edema! Send her back to camp!"

At the small train station the guard turned and left us without a backward glance. Apparently we were all traveling as far as Berlin, then each pursuing her separate route home. There was a long wait on cold iron benches.

The feeling of unreality persisted. Only one thing seemed familiar, the hungry hollow in my stomach. I put off getting into my bread allowance as long as I could, but at last reached into my overcoat pocket. The packet was gone. I sprang up from the bench, looking beneath it, retracing my steps through the station. Whether I had dropped it or it had been stolen, the bread was gone, and with it the ration coupons.

At last a train pulled into the station and we crowded eagerly to it but it was for military personnel only. Late in the afternoon we were allowed aboard a mail train, only to be put off two stops farther on to make room for a food shipment. The trip became a blur. We reached the huge, bomb-gutted terminal in Berlin sometime after midnight.

It was New Year's Day, 1945. Betsie had been right: she and I were out of prison. . . .

Snow drifted down from a shattered skylight as I wandered, confused and frightened, through the cavernous station. I knew that I must find the train to Uelzen, but months of being told what to do had left me robbed of initiative. At last someone directed me to a distant platform. Each step now was agony in the stiff new shoes. When I reached the platform at last, the sign said not Uelzen but Olsztyn, a town in Poland in exactly the opposite direction. I had to cross those acres of concrete floors again.

Ahead of me an elderly man, pink-cheeked from working in the roofless station, was raking bomb rubble into a pile. When I asked him for directions he took me by the arm and led me himself to the proper platform. "I was to Holland once," he said, voice wistful with recollection. "When the wife was alive, you know. Right on the sea we stayed."

A train was standing on the track and I climbed aboard. It was hours before anyone else arrived, but I did not dare get off for fear I would not find my way back again. By the time the train started up I was dizzy for lack of food. At the first stop outside Berlin I followed the other passengers into the station café. I showed the woman behind the cashbox my Dutch guilders and told her I had lost my coupons.

"That's an old story! Get out of here before I call the police!"

The trip was endless. Many miles of track could be traveled only at a crawl. Some sections were gone altogether and there were interminable, long detours and many changes of train. Often we did not stop in a station at all, for fear of air raids, but exchanged freight and passengers in the countryside.

And all the while, out my window passed once-beautiful Germany. Fire-blackened woods, the gaunt ribs of a church standing over a ruined village. Bremen especially brought tears to my eyes. In all that wasteland I saw one human being, an old woman poking at a heap of bricks.

In Uelzen there was a long wait between trains. It was late at night, the station was deserted. As I dozed in an empty coffee bar my head dropped forward until it rested on the small table in front of me. A blow on my ear sent me sprawling almost to the floor.

"This is not a bedroom!" the furious station agent shrieked. "You can't use our tables to sleep on!"

Trains came. Trains didn't come. I climbed on and off. And then I was standing in a line at a customs shed and the sign on the little station building said

Nieuwerschans. As I left the building a workman in a blue cap and blue overalls stepped up to me. "Here! You won't get far on those legs! Hang onto my arm." He spoke Dutch.

I clung to him and hobbled across some tracks to where another train was waiting, engine already puffing smoke. I was in Holland.

We jerked forward. Flat, snow-covered fields glided past the window. Home. It was still occupied Holland, German soldiers still stood at intervals along the tracks—but it was home.

The train was going only as far as Groningen, a Dutch city not far from the border. Beyond that rails were torn up and all except government travel banned. With the last of my strength I limped to a hospital near the station.

A nurse in a sparkling white uniform invited me into a little office. When I had told my story, she left the room. In a few minutes she was back with a tray of tea and rusk. "I left the butter off," she said. "You're suffering from malnutrition. You must be careful what you eat."

Tears tumbled into the hot tea as I drank. Here was someone who felt concern for me. There were no available beds in the hospital, she said, but one of the staff was away and I was to have her room. "Right now I have a hot tub running."

I followed her down gleaming corridors in a kind of happy dream. In a large bathroom clouds of steam were rising from a glistening white tub. Nothing in my life ever felt as good as that bath. I lay submerged to my chin, feeling the warm water soothe my scab-crusted skin. "Just five minutes more!" I would beg each time the nurse rapped at the door.

At last I let her hand me a nightgown and lead me to a room where a bed was turned down and waiting. Sheets. White sheets top and bottom. I could not get enough of running my hands over them. The nurse was tucking a second pillow beneath my swollen feet. I struggled to stay awake: to lie here clean and cared for was such joy I did not want to sleep through a minute of it.

I stayed in the hospital at Groningen ten days, feeling my strength return. For most meals I joined the nurses in their own dining room. The first time I saw the long table set with silverware and glasses, I drew back in alarm.

"You're having a party! Let me take a tray to my room!" I did not feel ready yet for laughter and social chatter.

The young woman beside me laughed as she pulled out a chair for me. "It's not a party! It's just supper—and skimpy enough at that."

I sat down blinking at knives, forks, tablecloth —had I once eaten like this, every day in the year? Like a savage watching his first civilized meal I copied the leisurely gestures of the others as they passed bread and cheese and unhurriedly stirred their coffee.

The ache in my heart was to get to Willem and Nollie—but how could it be done with the travel ban? Telephone service, too, was more limited than ever, but at last the girl at the hospital switchboard reached the telephone operator in Hilversum with the news of Betsie's death and my release.

In the middle of the second week, hospital authorities arranged a ride for me on a food truck headed south. We made the illegal trip at night and without headlights: the food had been diverted from a shipment headed for Germany. In the gray early morning the truck pulled up to Willem's big brick nursing home. A tall, broad-shouldered girl answered my knock, and then went dashing down the hallway with the news that I was here.

In a moment my arms were around Tine and two of my nieces. Willem arrived more slowly, limping down the corridor with the help of a cane. We held each other a long time while I told them the details of Betsie's illness and death.

"Almost," said Willem slowly, "almost I could wish to have this same news of Kik. It would be good for him to be with Betsie and Father." They had had no word of this tall blond son since his deportation to Germany. I remembered his hand on my shoulder, guiding me on our bicycles through the blacked-out streets to Pickwick's. Remembered his patient coaching: "You *have* no cards, Tante Corrie! There *are no Jews.*" Kik! Are the young and brave as vulnerable as the old and slow?

I spent two weeks in Hilversum, trying to adjust to what my eyes had told me that first moment. Willem was dying. Only he seemed unaware of it as he hobbled along the halls of his home bringing comfort and counsel to the sick people in his care. They had over fifty patients at the moment, but what I could not get over was the number of young women in help: nurse's aides, kitchen helpers, secretaries. It was several days before I perceived that most of these "girls" were young men in hiding from the forced-labor conscription which had grown more ruthless than ever.

And still something in me could not rest until I got back to Haarlem. Nollie was there, of course. But it was the Beje, too, something in the house itself that called me, beckoned me, told me to come home.

The problem, again, was getting there. Willem had the use of an official car for nursing-home business, but only within a radius of Hilversum. Finally, after many relayed phone calls, he told me the trip had been arranged.

The roads were deserted as we set out; we passed only two other cars all the way to the rendezvous spot with the car from Haarlem. Ahead, pulled off onto the snow at the side of the road, we saw it, a long black limousine with official government plates and curtained rear windows. I kissed Willem goodbye and then stepped quickly, as instructed, into the rear of the limousine. Even in the curtained gloom the ungainly bulk beside me was unmistakable.

"Oom Herman!" I cried.

"My dear Cornelia." His great hand closed around both of mine. "God permits me to see you again."

I had last seen Pickwick sitting between two soldiers on the prison bus in The Hague, his poor bald head bruised and bleeding. Now here he was, waving aside my sympathy as though that had been an incident too trivial to recall.

He seemed as well informed as ever about everything that went on in Haarlem, and as the uniformed driver sped us along the empty roads, he filled me in on all the details I ached to know. All of our Jews were safe except for Mary Itallie, who had been sent to Poland following her arrest in the street. Our group was still operating, although many of the young men were in hiding.

He warned me to expect changes at the Beje. After the police guard had been removed, a series of homeless families had been housed there, although at the moment he believed the living quarters above the shop were empty. Even before the house was unsealed, loyal Toos had returned from Scheveningen and reopened the watch business. Mr. Beukers, the optician next door, had given her space in his shop from which she had taken orders to give to our repairmen in their homes.

As my eyes adjusted to the dim light I made out my friend's face more clearly. There was perhaps an extra knob or two on the misshapen head, teeth were missing—but to that vast, kindly ugliness the beating had made no real difference at all.

Now the limousine was threading the narrow streets of Haarlem. Over the bridge on the Spaarne. Across the Grote Markt in the shadow of St. Bavo's, into the Barteljorisstraat. I was out of the car almost before it stopped, running down the alley, through the side door, and into Nollie's embrace. She and her girls had been there all morning, sweeping, washing windows, airing sheets for my homecoming. Over Nollie's shoulder I saw Toos standing in the rear door to the shop, laughing and sobbing both at once. Laughing because I was home; crying because Father and Betsie, the only two people she had ever allowed herself to love, would never be.

Together we trooped through the house and shop, looking, stroking—"Remember how Betsie would set out these cups?" "Remember how Meta would scold Eusie for leaving his pipe here?" I stood on the landing outside the dining room and ran my hand over the smooth wood of the Frisian clock. I could see Father stopping here, Kapteyn at his heels.

"We mustn't let the clock run down. . . ."

I opened the glass face, moved the hands to agree with my wristwatch, and slowly drew up the weights. I was home. Life, like the clock, started again: mornings repairing watches in the workshop, noons most often bumping on my tireless bicycle out to Bos en Hoven Straat.

And yet . . . in a strange way, I was not home. I was still waiting, still looking for something. I spent days prowling the alleys and canal banks nearby, calling Maher Shalal Hashbaz by name. The elderly vegetable lady three stores down told me that the cat had mewed at her door the night of our arrest and she had taken him in. For months, she said, the small children of the neighborhood had banded together to bring food to "Opa's kitty." They had brought scraps from garbage pails and even tidbits from their own scanty plates smuggled past watchful mothers, and Mr. Hashbaz had remained sleek and fat.

It was mid-December, she said, when he had not appeared one night to her call, nor had she seen him since. And so I searched, but with a sinking heart: in this winter of Holland's hunger, all my searching brought not one single cat or dog to my call.

I missed more than the cat; the Beje needed people to fill its rooms. I remembered Father's words to the Gestapo chief in The Hague: "I will open my door to anyone in need. . . ." No one in the city was in greater need than its feeble-minded. Since the start of the Nazi occupation they had been sequestered by their families in back rooms, their schools and training centers shut down, hidden from a government which had decided they were not fit to live. Soon a group of them was living at the Beje. They still could not go out on the streets, but here at least they had new surroundings and a program of sorts with the time I could take from the shop.

And still my restlessness continued. I was home, I was working and busy—or was I? Often I would come to with a start at my workbench to realize that I had sat for an hour staring into space. The repairmen Toos had found—trained under Father—were excellent. I spent less and less time in the shop; whatever or whoever I was looking for was not there.

Nor upstairs. I loved the gentle people in my care, but the house itself had ceased to be home. For Betsie's sake I bought plants for every windowsill, but I forgot to water them and they died.

Maybe I missed the challenge of the underground. When the national group approached me with a request, I agreed eagerly. They had false release papers for a prisoner in the Haarlem jail. What could be simpler than to carry this document around the corner and through those familiar wooden doors.

But as the doors closed behind me my heart began to race. What if I couldn't get out? What if I was trapped?

"Yes?" A young police lieutenant with bright orange hair stepped from behind the reception desk. "You had an appointment?"

It was Rolf. Why was he being so stiff with me? Was I under arrest? Were they going to put me in a cell? "Rolf!" I said. "Don't you know me?"

He peered at me as though trying to refresh his memory. "Of course!" he said smoothly. "The lady at the watch shop! I heard you were closed down for a while."

I gaped at him. Why, Rolf knew perfectly—and then I recalled where we were. In the central foyer of the police station with half a dozen German soldiers looking on. And I had greeted one of our group by name, practically admitted a special relationship between us, when the cardinal rule of the underground was . . . I ran my tongue over my lips. How could I have been so stupid?

Rolf took the forged papers from my shaking hands and glanced through them. "These must be passed upon by the police chief and the military over-command together," he said. "Can you return with them tomorrow afternoon at four? The chief will be in a meeting until——"

I heard no more. At the words "tomorrow afternoon" I had bolted for the door. I stood thankfully on the sidewalk until my knees stopped knocking. If I

had ever needed proof that I had no boldness or clever-
ness of my own, I had it now. Whatever bravery, or
skill I had ever shown were gifts of God—sheer loans
from Him of the talent needed to do a job. And it was
clear, from the absence of such skills now, that this
was no longer His work for me.

I crept meekly back to the Beje. And it was at
that moment, as I stepped into the alley, that I knew
what it was I was looking for.

It was Betsie.

It was Betsie I had missed every moment of every
day since I ran to the hospital window and found that
she had left Ravensbruck forever. It was Betsie I had
thought to find back here in Haarlem, here in the
watchshop and in the home she loved.

But she was not here. And now for the first time
since her death, I remembered. "We must tell people,
Corrie. We must tell them what we learned. . . ."

That very week I began to speak. If this was
God's new work for me, then He would provide the
courage and the words. Through the streets and suburbs of Haarlem I bumped on my bicycle rims, bringing the message that joy runs deeper than despair.

It was news that people needed to hear that cheer-
less spring of 1945. No Bride of Haarlem tree filled
the air with fragrance; only the stump had been too
big to haul off for firewood. No tulips turned fields into
carpets of color: the bulbs had all been eaten. No
family was without its tragedy. In churches and club
rooms and private homes in those desperate days I
told the truths Betsie and I had learned in Ravensbruck.

And always at these meetings, I spoke of Betsie's
first vision: of a home here in Holland where those
who had been hurt could learn to live again unafraid.
At the close of one of these talks a slender, aristocratic
lady came up to me. I knew her by sight: Mrs. Bierens
de Haan whose home in the suburb of Bloemendaal
was said to be one of the most beautiful in Holland.
I had never seen it, only the trees at the edge of the
huge park in which it was set, and so I was astonished

when this elegantly dressed lady asked me if I were still living in the ancient little house on the Barteljorisstraat.

"How did you—yes, I do. But——"

"My mother often told me about it. She went there frequently to see an aunt of yours who, I believe, was in charitable work?"

In a rush it all came back. Opening the side door to let in a swish of satin and rustle of feathers. A long gown and a plumed hat brushing both sides of the narrow stairs. Then Tante Jans standing in her doorway with a look that froze in the bones the thought of bouncing a ball.

"I am a widow," Mrs. Bierens de Haan was saying, "but I have five sons in the Resistance. Four are still alive and well. The fifth we have not heard from since he was taken to Germany. As you spoke just now something in me kept saying, 'Jan will come back and in gratitude you will open your home for this vision of Betsie ten Boom.'"

It was two weeks later that a small boy delivered a scented envelope to the side door; inside in slanted purple letters was a single line, "Jan is home."

Mrs. Bierens de Haan herself met me at the entrance to her estate. Together we walked up an avenue of ancient oaks meeting above our heads. Rounding the final bend, we saw it, a fifty-six-room mansion in the center of a vast lawn. Two elderly gardeners were poking about the flowerbeds.

"We've let the gardens go," Mrs. Bierens de Haan said. "But I thought we might put them back in shape. Don't you think released prisoners might find therapy in growing things?"

I didn't answer. I was staring up at the gabled roof and the leaded windows. Such tall, tall windows. . . .

"Are there—" my throat was dry. "Are there inlaid wood floors inside, and a broad gallery around a central hall, and—and bas-relief statues set along the walls?"

Mrs. Bierens de Haan looked at me in surprise. "You've been here then! I don't recall——"

"No," I said. "I heard about it from——"

I stopped. How could I explain what I did not understand?

"From someone who's been here," she finished simply, not understanding my perplexity.

"Yes," I said. "From someone who's been here."

The second week in May the Allies retook Holland. The Dutch flag hung from every window and the "Wilhelmus" was played on the liberated radio day and night. The Canadian army rushed to the cities the food they had stockpiled along the borders.

In June the first of many hundreds of people arrived at the beautiful home in Bloemendaal. Silent or endlessly relating their losses, withdrawn or fiercely aggressive, every one was a damaged human being. Not all had been in concentration camps; some had spent two, three, even four years hidden in attic rooms and back closets here in Holland.

One of the first of these was Mrs. Kan, widow of the watch-shop owner up the street. Mr. Kan had died at the underground address; she came to us alone, a stooped, white-haired woman who started at every sound. Others came to Bloemendaal, scarred body and soul by bombing raids or loss of family or any of the endless dislocations of war. In 1947 we began to receive Dutch people who had been prisoners of the Japanese in Indonesia.

Though none of this was by design, it proved to be the best possible setting for those who had been imprisoned in Germany. Among themselves they tended to live and relive their special woes; in Bloemendaal they were reminded that they were not the only ones who had suffered. And for all these people alike, the key to healing turned out to be the same. Each had a hurt he had to forgive: the neighbor who had reported him, the brutal guard, the sadistic soldier.

Strangely enough, it was not the Germans or the Japanese that people had most trouble forgiving; it was their fellow Dutchmen who had sided with the enemy. I saw them frequently in the streets, NSBers with their shaved heads and furtive eyes. These former collaborators were now in pitiful condition, turned out of homes and apartments, unable to find jobs, hooted at in the streets.

At first it seemed to me that we should invite them too to Bloemendaal, to live side by side with those they had injured, to seek a new compassion on both sides. But it turned out to be too soon for people working their way back from such hurt: the two times I tried it, it ended in open fights. And so as soon as homes and schools for the feeble-minded opened again around the country I turned the Beje over to these former NSBers.

This was how it went, those years after the war, experimenting, making mistakes, learning. The doctors, psychiatrists, and nutritionists who came free of charge to any place that cared for war victims, sometimes expressed surprise at our loose-run ways. At morning and evening worship people drifted in and out, table manners were atrocious, one man took a walk into Haarlem every morning at 3:00 A.M. I could not bring myself to sound a whistle or to scold, or to consider gates or curfews.

And, sure enough, in their own time and their own way, people worked out the deep pain within them. It most often started, as Betsie had known it would, in the garden. As flowers bloomed or vegetables ripened, talk was less of the bitter past, more of tomorrow's weather. As their horizons broadened, I would tell them about the people living in the Beje, people who never had a visitor, never a piece of mail. When mention of the NSBers no longer brought on a volley of self-righteous wrath, I knew the person's healing was not far away. And the day he said, "Those people you spoke of—I wonder if they'd care for some homegrown carrots," then I knew the miracle had taken place.

I continued to speak, partly because the home in Bloemendaal ran on contributions, partly because the hunger for Betsie's story seemed to increase with time. I traveled all over Holland, to other parts of Europe, to the United States.

But the place where the hunger was greatest was Germany. Germany was a land in ruins, cities of ashes and rubble, but more terrifying still, minds and hearts of ashes. Just to cross the border was to feel the great weight that hung over that land.

It was at a church service in Munich that I saw him, the former S.S. man who had stood guard at the shower room door in the processing center at Ravensbruck. He was the first of our actual jailers that I had seen since that time. And suddenly it was all there—the roomful of mocking men, the heaps of clothing, Betsie's pain-blanched face.

He came up to me as the church was emptying, beaming and bowing. "How grateful I am for your message, *Fraulein.*" he said. "To think that, as you say, He has washed my sins away!"

His hand was thrust out to shake mine. And I, who had preached so often to the people in Bloemendaal the need to forgive, kept my hand at my side.

Even as the angry, vengeful thoughts boiled through me, I saw the sin of them. Jesus Christ had died for this man; was I going to ask for more? Lord Jesus, I prayed, forgive me and help me to forgive him.

I tried to smile, I struggled to raise my hand. I could not. I felt nothing, not the slightest spark of warmth or charity. And so again I breathed a silent prayer. Jesus, I cannot forgive him. Give me Your forgiveness.

As I took his hand the most incredible thing happened. From my shoulder along my arm and through my hand a current seemed to pass from me to him, while into my heart sprang a love for this stranger that almost overwhelmed me.

And so I discovered that it is not on our forgiveness any more than on our goodness that the world's healing hinges, but on His. When He tells us to love our enemies, He gives, along with the command, the love itself.

It took a lot of love. The most pressing need in postwar Germany was homes; nine million people were said to be without them. They were living in rubble heaps, half-standing buildings, and abandoned army trucks. A church group invited me to speak to a hundred families living in an abandoned factory building.

Sheets and blankets had been hung between the various living quarters to make a pretense of privacy. But there was no insulating the sounds: the wail of a baby, the din of radios, the angry words of a family quarrel. How could I speak to these people of the reality of God and then go back to my quiet room in the church hostel outside the city? No, before I could bring a message to them, I would have to live among them.

And it was during the months that I spent in the factory that a director of a relief organization came to see me. They had heard of my rehabilitation work in Holland, he said, and they wondered—I was opening my mouth to say that I had no professional training in such things, when his next words silenced me.

"We've located a place for the work," he said. "It was a former concentration camp that's just been released by the government."

We drove to Darmstadt to look over the camp. Rolls of rusting barbed wire still surrounded it. I walked slowly up a cinder path between drab gray barracks. I pushed open a creaking door; I stepped between rows of metal cots.

"Windowboxes," I said. "We'll have them at every window. The barbed wire must come down, of course, and then we'll need paint. Green paint. Bright yellow-green, the color of things coming up new in the spring. . . ."

Since Then . . .

Together with a committee of the German Lutheran Church, Corris opened the *camp* in Darmstadt in 1946 as a home and place of renewal. It functioned in this way until 1960 when it was torn down to make room for new construction in a thriving new Germany.

The *home* in Bloemendaal served ex-prisoners and other war victims exclusively until 1950, when it also began to receive people in need of rest and care from the population at large. It is still in operation today, in its own new building, with patients from many parts of Europe. Since 1967 it has been governed by the Dutch Reformed Church.

Willem died of tuberculosis of the spine in December, 1946. His last book, a study of sacrifice in the Old Testament, was written standing because the pain of his illness would not allow him to sit at a desk.

Just before his death Willem opened his eyes to tell Tine: "It is well—it is very well—with *Kik*." It was not until 1953 that the family learned definitely that this twenty-year-old son had died in 1944 at the concentration camp in Bergen-Belsen. Today a "ten Boom Street" in Hilversum honors Kik.

As a result of his wartime experiences, *Peter* van Woerden dedicated his musical gifts to God's service. He has composed many devotional songs, including a musical setting for the Psalms and Proverbs. Today Peter, his wife, and their five children travel all over Europe and the Near East as a family singing group with a message of God's love.

In 1959 Corrie was part of a group which revisited Ravensbruck, now in East Germany, to honor Betsie and the ninety-six thousand other women who died there. There Corrie learned that her own release had been the result of a clerical "error"; one week later all women her age were taken to the gas chambers.

Well into her eighties, Corrie continued her indefatigable travels in obedience to Betsie's certainty that they must "tell people," working in sixty-one countries on both sides of the Iron Curtain. To African students on the shores of Lake Victoria, to farmers in a Cuban sugar field, to prisoners in an English penitentiary, to factory workers in Uzbekistan, she brought the truth they learned in Ravensbruck: Jesus can turn loss into glory.

Her final years were spent in a pleasant home, provided by friends, in Orange County, California. There a series of strokes curtailed first her physical movement, then her writing schedule, finally even her power of speech. But not her ministry. Those who came to cheer the bedridden and speechless old lady reported, marveling, that they were the ones cheered, uplifted, challenged. Only the close companions of those last years knew how eagerly she longed for the "real home" where her family had gone so long ahead. Homecoming fell for Corrie on her ninety-first birthday, April 15, 1983.

ABOUT THE AUTHORS

In the years since the closing chapter of this book, COR-RIE TEN BOOM has traveled ceaselessly, carrying her message of triumphant living all over the world, especially behind the Iron Curtain. The author of devotional books treasured by millions, she is also a colorful, amusing speaker with a hold on young audiences that is but one of her many intriguing personal mysteries. This is the full story behind the faith that has touched and stirred and changed so many lives, everywhere.

The writers with whom Corrie has shared the intimate recollections of THE HIDING PLACE are the American authors, JOHN and ELIZABETH SHERRILL. Both are *Guideposts* magazine editors; their previous books include *The Cross and the Switchblade, They Speak With Other Tongues* and *God's Smuggler.* The Sherrills live in a suburb of New York and have three children, Scott, Donn, and Elizabeth.

Extraordinary true tales of courage
from these remarkable people

ANNE FRANK: *The Diary of a Young Girl*
"One of the most moving personal documents to come out of World War II." —*The Philadelphia Inquirer*
Discovered in the attic in which she spent the last years of her life, Anne Frank's remarkable diary has since become a world classic—a powerful reminder of the horrors of war and an eloquent testament to the human spirit.   ___29698-1 $4.99/$5.99

ALICIA: *My Story* by Alicia Appleman-Jurman
The award-winning memoir of the thirteen-year-old girl who courageously led Jews to safe hideouts through Nazi-controlled Poland. "A compelling voice, lucid prose . . . a luminous testimony to the heroism and humanity of one remarkable person." —*San Francisco Chronicle*
___28218-2 $6.99/$8.99

THE HIDING PLACE by Corrie Ten Boom
Sent to a concentration camp for helping Jews escape, Corrie Ten Boom was sustained through times of profound horror by God's strength. This is an extraordinary tale of one courageous woman who became a militant heroine of the anti-Nazi underground.   ___25669-6 $6.99/$9.99

THE WAR AGAINST THE JEWS: 1933–1945
by Lucy S. Dawidowicz
"A major work of synthesis, providing for the first time a full account of the Holocaust . . . a work of high scholarship and profound moral import." —*The New York Times Book Review*   "If any book can tell what Hitlerism was like, this is it. . . . A book that one reads in tears, in despair, but above all, with gratitude." —Alfred Kazin   ___34532-X $16.95/$23.95

The fascinating true stories behind these extraordinary public figures

IT DOESN'T TAKE A HERO: *The Autobiography*
by General H. Norman Schwarzkopf with Peter Petre
Rarely does a figure appear of such compelling leadership and personal charisma as to capture the imagination of an entire nation. Now, in this candid, outspoken, and eagerly awaited autobiography, General Schwarzkopf reveals the full story of his remarkable life and a career spanning nearly four decades.

_____56338-6 $7.50/$9.99 in Canada

YEAGER: *An Autobiography*
by Chuck Yeager with Leo Janos
From his humble West Virginia roots to his role as the test pilot who first broke the sound barrier, this is the story of the man who rose to lead America into space.
_____25674-2 $7.50/$9.99

MARINE! *The Life of Chesty Puller*
by Burke Davis
This is the explosive true story of the most courageous and controversial commander of them all--the only marine in history to win five Navy crosses. Here is the fabulous tale of a real-life hero.

_____27182-2 $6.99/$8.99